T0320839

*Cognitive Skills You Need for
the 21st Century*

Cognitive Skills
You Need for
the 21st Century

STEPHEN K. REED

OXFORD
UNIVERSITY PRESS

OXFORD
UNIVERSITY PRESS

Oxford University Press is a department of the University of Oxford. It furthers
the University's objective of excellence in research, scholarship, and education
by publishing worldwide. Oxford is a registered trade mark of Oxford University
Press in the UK and certain other countries.

Published in the United States of America by Oxford University Press
198 Madison Avenue, New York, NY 10016, United States of America.

Library of Congress Cataloging-in-Publication Data
Names: Reed, Stephen K., author.
Title: Cognitive skills you need for the 21st century / Stephen K. Reed,
Center for Research in Mathematics and Science Education, Department of
Psychology, San Diego State University, Department of Psychology,
University of California, San Diego.
Other titles: Cognitive skills you need for the twenty-first century
Description: New York, NY : Oxford University Press, [2020] |
Includes bibliographical references and index.
Identifiers: LCCN 2020007987 (print) | LCCN 2020007988 (ebook) |
ISBN 9780197529003 (hardback) | ISBN 9780197529010 (epub) |
ISBN 9780197529034
Subjects: LCSH: Cognitive psychology—Popular works.
Classification: LCC BF201 .R44 2020 (print) | LCC BF201 (ebook) |
DDC 153—dc23
LC record available at https://lccn.loc.gov/2020007987
LC ebook record available at https://lccn.loc.gov/2020007988

1 3 5 7 9 8 6 4 2

Printed by Integrated Books International, United States of America

Contents

PART V. ARTIFICIAL INTELLIGENCE

PART VI. EDUCATION

Preface

There is a bookshelf labeled "Popular Science" in the Geisel Library on the University of California, San Diego, campus that provided inspiration for writing this book. I admire those authors who can explain science to a general audience, and I continue their tradition in this book on cognitive skills. My objective as a professor emeritus of cognitive psychology is to write a book that does not require specific background knowledge to understand it. I therefore define terms when discussing research and include personal anecdotes that I hope inspire readers to think of related experiences in their own life. I also occasionally include problems to encourage reflection.

A quick glance at the contents reveals the scope of the book. The introduction begins with a Future of Jobs report that contrasts trending and declining skills required by the workforce in 2022. Trending skills include analytical thinking and innovation, active learning strategies, creativity, reasoning, and complex problem-solving that I discuss in the remainder of the book. Part I on acquiring knowledge contains chapters on cognitive processes that are critical for learning. Part II on organizing knowledge explains how matrices, networks, and hierarchies offer contrasting methods for visualizing organization. Part III on reasoning discusses visuospatial reasoning, reasoning from imperfect knowledge, and reasoning strategies. Part IV on problem-solving focuses on the knowledge and strategies required to solve different types of problems, including those that involve design and dynamic changes. Part V on artificial intelligence (AI) contains chapters on the data sciences, explainable AI, the information sciences, and general AI. Part VI on education consists of three chapters on educating 21st-century skills at all levels of instruction.

The broad scope of the book makes it useful for people who are experts on some of its themes. It should help them relate their expertise to other domains by embedding their knowledge within a broader context. I initially had some knowledge about the topics in each of the 20 chapters, but writing this book enabled me to fill in gaps and better understand how this knowledge is connected. One of my interests is building bridges between AI and cognitive psychology—the title of my article that appeared in the summer 2019 issue of *AI Magazine*. The four chapters in Part V on AI (data sciences, explainable AI, information sciences, and general AI) should be of particular interest for those of you who share my interests in AI.

Another group of potential readers is students. Some universities have generic courses for freshmen, and others are designing courses to provide direction for freshmen who have not yet selected a major. I hope instructors will consider this book as a resource for these courses because of its breadth of coverage and its universal theme. I also discuss continuing education for people in the work force.

When I became a professor emeritus in 2014, I found that I now had sufficient time to search for the big pictures that organize knowledge. My resulting articles are summarized in my publication "Searching for the Big Pictures" in *Perspectives on Psychological Science*. These articles provide depth of coverage to supplement the brief coverage of these topics in this book.

I continued my academic work during my first year of "retirement" as a visiting scholar at the Center for the Study of Language and Information on the Stanford campus. It has since continued as a visiting scholar in the Department of Psychology at the University of California, San Diego. I thank these institutions for their support. Discussions with friends and family have helped me keep a broad perspective. I dedicate this book to my extended family for their inspiration. I particularly thank my wife Karen for managing our home, our finances, and our purchases so I can continue to pursue my academic interests.

The talented people at Oxford University Press have been instrumental in turning my manuscript into a book. Joan Bossert, Phil Velinov, Alisa Larson, and Sankari Balasubramanian and Prabha Karunakaran at Newgen Knowledge works have been my guides. I am delighted that Oxford University Press is publishing this book. Oxford University Press is the largest university press in the world and the second oldest, so it had to wait until 1586 for its founding. The Delegates of the Press, consisting of 21 academics from different faculties, contribute to its decisions. Oxford academics included such creative authors as Lewis Carroll (*Alice in Wonderland*), J. R. R. Tolkien (*The Lord of the Rings*), and C. S. Lewis (*Chronicles of Narnia*). I wonder if any of them have been a delegate, rejecting manuscripts that lacked imagination.

Stephen Reed
La Jolla, CA
April 2020

Introduction

In 2017 a group of investigators at the Educational Testing Service in Princeton, New Jersey took on a new mission. The Educational Testing Service is the home of such widely used tests as the Graduate Record Exam (GRE) to measure critical skills required for graduate programs and TOEFL to assess English proficiency. Their new mission was to determine which skills are needed for the workplace as a result of the rapid changes occurring as the United States shifted from an industrial to an information-based economy.

They accomplished their mission by analyzing 142,000 online job advertisements that were posted between February and April of that year. The most highly requested skills were oral communication (28%), written communication (23%), collaboration (22%), and problem solving (19%). The skills created by technological advances have received a variety of names but the Princeton group decided to label them "21st-century skills." They defined 21st-century skills as a combination of cognitive (nonroutine problem solving, critical thinking, metacognition), interpersonal (social), and intrapersonal (emotional, self-regulation) skills.

The World Economic Forum's *Future of Jobs Report 2018* took a different approach by asking executives of some of the world's largest employers to report on the latest employment, skills, and human investment trends across their industries. The survey revealed an accelerating demand for new specialist roles related to understanding and using the latest emerging technologies: artificial intelligence (AI) and machine-learning specialists, big data specialists, process automation experts, information security

Cognitive Skills You Need for the 21st Century. Stephen K. Reed, Oxford University Press (2020). © Oxford University Press. DOI: 10.1093/oso/9780197529003.001.0001.

analysts, human–machine interaction designers, and robotics engineers.

There will be increasing importance of skills related to technology and programming according to the employers surveyed for the report. Skills such as creativity, originality, critical thinking, negotiation, and complex problem-solving will increase in value. Leadership, emotional intelligence, and social influence will also see an increase in demand. Table I.1 lists those skills that will be either increasing or declining by the year 2022. The report predicted that by 2020 54% of employees would require significant retraining. About 35% are expected to require additional training up to six months.

Thomas Davenport and Julia Kirby specifically addressed the effects of technology on employment in their book *Only humans Need Apply: Winners and Losers in the Age of Smart Machines*. They argued that the key to increasing productivity and business success is to use technology to help people work better, faster, and smarter. Winners include people who manage problem-solving at a higher cognitive level than machines because they understand the bigger picture, people who make routine decisions and tweak machines for better performance, and people who build the next generation of smart machines.

In their article in *Nature*, Iyad Rahwan, Manuel Cebrian, and Nick Obradovich discuss the tremendous impact of computer algorithms. Figure I.1 displays examples. The authors argue that understanding the effect of AI on our lives is critical for maximizing its benefits and minimizing its potential pitfalls. The effects of both will accelerate in the near future as discussed in a special November 12, 2019, report in *The Wall Street Journal* titled "5G: What's Next."

The world, however, did not have to wait for the arrival of AI for its inhabitants to begin accumulating cognitive skills. Although examples of the impact of technology are scattered throughout this book, many other examples do not involve technology. *Cognitive Skills You Need for the 21st Century* describes how research in

Table I.1 Trends According to the *Future of Jobs 2018 Report*

Today, 2018	Trending, 2022	Declining, 2022
Analytical thinking and innovation	Analytical thinking and innovation	Manual dexterity, endurance and precision
Complex problem-solving	Active learning and learning strategies	Memory, verbal, auditory and spatial abilities
Critical thinking and analysis	Creativity, originality and initiative	Management of financial, material resources
Active learning and learning strategies	Technology design and programming	Technology installation and maintenance
Creativity, originality and initiative	Critical thinking and analysis	Reading, writing, math and active listening
Attention to detail, trustworthiness	Complex problem-solving	Management of personnel
Emotional intelligence	Leadership and social influence	Quality control and safety awareness
Reasoning, problem-solving and ideation	Emotional intelligence	Coordination and time management
Leadership and social influence	Reasoning, problem-solving and ideation	Visual, auditory and speech abilities
Coordination and time management	Systems analysis and evaluation	Technology use, monitoring and control

Source: World Economic Forum, 2018, *Future of jobs 2018 report*. https://www.weforum.org/reports/the-future-of-jobs-report-2018. Reprinted with permission.

DEMOCRACY

NEWS RANKING ALGORITHMS
Does the algorithm create filter bubbles?
Does the algorithm disproportionately censor content?

ALGORITHMIC JUSTICE
Does the algorithm discriminate against a racial group in granting parole?
Does a predictive policing system increase the false conviction rate?

KINETICS

AUTONOMOUS VEHICLES
How aggressive is the car's overtaking?
How does the car distribute risk between passengers & pedestrians?

AUTONOMOUS WEAPONS
Does the weapon respect necessity and proportionality in its use of force?
Does the weapon distinguish between combatants and civilians?

MARKETS

ALGORITHMIC TRADING
Do algorithms manipulate markets?
Does the algorithm's behaviour increase systemic risk of market crash?

ALGORITHMIC PRICING
Do competitors' algorithms collude to fix prices?
Does the algorithm exhibit price discrimination?

SOCIETY

ONLINE DATING
Does the matching algorithm use facial features?
Does the matching algorithm amplify or reduce homophily?

CONVERSATIONAL ROBOTS
Does the robot promote products to children?
Does the algorithm affect collective behaviours?

Figure I.1. Examples of questions that fall into the domain of machine behavior.

Based on I. Rahwan, M. Cebrian, N. Obradovich, J. Bongard, J-F. Bonnefon, C. Breazeal, . . . M. Wellman, 2019, Machine behavior, *Nature, 568,* 477–486. Figure contributed by I. Rahan.

artificial intelligence, education, and psychology are enhancing these skills. The book is divided into six parts on acquiring knowledge, organizing knowledge, reasoning, problem-solving, artificial intelligence, and education.

PART I
ACQUIRING KNOWLEDGE

1

Comprehension

My journey that culminated in writing this book began during my freshman year at the University of Wisconsin. I was a chemistry major, but it became increasingly obvious that chemistry and I were not a match made in heaven. I took an honors introductory course that was so abstract that I had no idea what was happening. And then there were the 11 hours a week I spent in a lab for a miserly two credits. During one of these hours I was heating a flask of water over a Bunsen burner when it erupted like a geyser. The water hit the ceiling and began to drip down on my notes. I decided to change my major before I created more serious damage.

I enjoyed my sophomore year as a psychology major and decided to obtain a PhD to become a college professor. My only reservation was that I considered PhDs to be people who knew a lot about very little. I wanted greater breadth so decided to change my major to the history of science. I could then study all of the sciences within an historical context. I excitedly explained my plan to a friend who asked, "Why would anyone study the history of science when they could do science?" I could not answer his question so immediately dropped my plan to switch majors. I have since wondered how often a single remark can alter the course of one's life. I imagine it happens to many people.

I retired six years ago but did not want to abandon the enjoyment of an academic life so decided to write articles on organizing knowledge in my specialty—cognitive psychology. Cognitive psychology is ideally suited for this task because cognitive psychologists are interested in how people organize knowledge so I could write about how scientists organize knowledge about how people organize knowledge. I am also very interested in artificial intelligence, which

Cognitive Skills You Need for the 21st Century. Stephen K. Reed, Oxford University Press (2020). © Oxford University Press. DOI: 10.1093/oso/9780197529003.001.0001.

is also kept very busy these days in creating and organizing knowledge. Let's begin with the topic of reading, a task that provides much of our knowledge.

The Select-Organize-Integrate Framework

Acquiring knowledge requires comprehension as we try to understand and make sense of the world. Comprehension occurs in multiple ways such as exploring, listening, and reading. This chapter is about reading and begins with an extensive research program conducted by Richard Mayor and his colleagues at the University of California, Santa Barbara. Their mission was to study how college students understand explanatory text on topics such as science.

Box 1.1 shows part of a passage on tire pumps followed by questions. Retention questions ask students to recall material from the lesson. Transfer questions ask students to use the information in a creative way to solve problems. The findings of Mayer's research typically showed that although students performed adequately on the retention test, they performed poorly on the transfer test.

Mayer proposed three cognitive processes that are required to make sense of explanatory material. The first requires *selecting* information from the passage. Strategies for acquiring knowledge are often not explicitly taught in the classroom so it may be helpful for teachers and students to discuss techniques for selecting important parts of the text. A second process is *organizing* the selected information into a coherent body of knowledge. Understanding how a pump works requires understanding how its different components work together. Pushing down the handle causes the piston to move down, which causes the inlet valve the close. A final step in making sense of a text is *integrating* the knowledge derived from a text with previous knowledge stored in long-term memory. It should help students understand how a tire pump works if they already understand the functioning of similar tools such as a syringe. In addition,

---

Box 1.1 Part of a Passage on Tire Pumps

Bicycle Tire Pumps

When the handle is pulled up, the piston moves up, the inlet valve opens, the outlet valve closes, and air enters the lower part of the cylinder. When the handle is pushed down, the piston moves down, the inlet valve closes, the outlet valve opens, and air moves out through the hose.

Retention Question

Please describe how a bicycle pump works.

Transfer Question

Suppose you push down and pull up the handle of a pump several times, but no air comes out. What could have gone wrong?

Based on Mayer (1996). Learning strategies for making sense out of expository text: the SOI model for guiding three cognitive processes in knowledge construction. *Educational Psychology Review, 4*, 357–371.

---

explaining the material in their own words often helps them to integrate knowledge in the text with their previous knowledge. Mayer refers to these three processes of selecting, organizing, and integrating as the SOI model of constructing knowledge. Let's now look at each of these processes in more detail.

Selecting Information

It is useful to consider the selection of information within the broader context of how readers manage their goals during text comprehension.

Jean-Francois Rouet, M. Anne Britt, and Amanda Dirik constructed a model of purposeful reading that has five assumptions.

The first is that people read to the extent that they see it as relevant for achieving their purposes. Sometimes we read for entertainment; other times we read to accomplish a specific goal. The second assumption is that processing resources such as memory are limited, placing constraints on our achievements. The third assumption is that we evaluate what we know when deciding whether to read, what to read, and how to read it. The fourth assumption is that readers determine the benefits of reading with respect to the efforts required to achieve their goals. The last assumption is that these goals determine specific actions such as skimming, skipping, reading for comprehension, pausing, and rereading.

A recent review of students' study strategies by cognitive psychologists at Washington University in St. Louis recommended several improvements. One tactic that most of us have used when selecting information is to mark material in the text that we believe is important. A limitation of the strategy is marking noncritical information. The authors therefore recommended skimming through the text to acquire an understanding of its structure before selecting critical information.

I have used this strategy for many years by bracketing information that I find useful. I recently did an informal survey at a campus bookstore by browsing through used textbooks to see what students had marked. I was amazed to discover that the vast majority of used textbooks had no markings. Many were in mint condition; a wonderful opportunity for students, but it did not help my survey. I did find some texts that had highlighted or underlined sentences. A bookstore manager told me that some students prefer to purchase used books marked by a previous student because information is already highlighted. I only recently improved my own selection strategy by circling important words. I wished I had adopted this strategy earlier because key concepts now leap off the page. I did not find any used textbooks with circled words.

Organizing Information

A second process in comprehension is organizing information into a coherent body of knowledge. Material that is hard to organize is difficult both to comprehend and to recall. You can demonstrate this effect by reading the passage in Box 1.2 and then recalling as many ideas as you can.

The paragraph describes a very familiar procedure, but the ideas are presented so abstractly that the procedure is difficult to recognize. People who read the passage in an experiment by John

---

Box 1.2 An (Un)familiar Task

The procedure is actually quite simple. First you arrange things into different groups. Of course, one pile may be sufficient depending on how much there is to do. If you have to go somewhere else due to lack of facilities, that is the next step; otherwise you are pretty well set. It is important not to overdo things. That is, it is better to do too few things at once than too many. In the short run this may not seem important, but complications can easily arise. A mistake can be expensive as well. At first the whole procedure will seem complicated. Soon, however, it will become just another facet of life. It is difficult to foresee any end to the necessity for this task in the immediate future, but then one never can tell. After the procedure is completed, one arranges the materials into different groups again. Then they can be put into their appropriate places. Eventually they will be used once more, and the whole cycle will then have to be repeated. However, that is part of life.

Source: J. D. Bransford & M. K. Johnson, 1973, Considerations of some problems of comprehension. In W. G. Chase (Ed.), *Visual information processing* (pp. 383–438). Orlando, FL: Academic Press, p. 400.

Bransford and Marcia Johnson recalled only 2.8 ideas. A different group of participants, who were informed *after* reading the passage that it referred to washing clothes, didn't do any better; they recalled only 2.7 ideas. But a third group who was told *before* they read the passage that it described washing clothes recalled 5.8 ideas. Statements such as "It is important not to overdo things" and "A mistake can be expensive" can now be linked. My interpretation is that light clothes should be washed separately from dark clothes to avoid costly errors. The results demonstrate that knowledge about a familiar task isn't sufficient for comprehension if people don't recognize the task. Providing the appropriate context before the passage increased both comprehension and recall by enabling readers to organize ideas in the text.

You may be surprised by the finding that identifying the topic after the passage did not serve as an effective retrieval cue. We have had many experiences in which a retrieval cue aids recall. People are even able to provide their own cue on some of these occasions; for instance, knowing the beginning letter of a word when in a "tip of the tongue" dilemma typically helps us recall the word. An effective retrieval cue, however, requires information in memory to retrieve. If there is nothing there, a cue will be ineffective.

Bransford and Johnson hypothesized that if people initially understand a text and are then encouraged to think of the ideas in a new perspective, they might recall additional ideas. A study by Richard Anderson and James Pichert supports this hypothesis. Participants read six paragraphs about a house from a perspective of either a burglar or a homebuyer. After a short delay, they were asked to write down as much of the exact story as they could remember. Some students then received a new perspective that helped them recall additional details. Someone with the new homebuyer's perspective might now remember that the house was recently painted, and someone with the new burglar's perspective might now recall that the back door of the house was left unlocked. Notice that these findings differ from the previous findings in demonstrating the effectiveness of a retrieval cue. Because the story was easy to comprehend, comprehension wasn't a problem; the problem was being able to recall an overwhelming amount of detail. Organizing ideas was my biggest challenge in writing this book. I had to skim through long, technical articles to uncover a few key ideas that I could clearly explain in one or two paragraphs. After bracketing major sentences, I selected a few promising ones and numbered them in my planned presentation order. The numbers did not always follow the presentation order in the article. I also duplicated numbers. If I later found a concrete example that illustrated a generic point in number 3, I also assigned it number 3. It reduces writing to following numbers.

Integrating Information

Comprehension is much easier if we can integrate the material with knowledge stored in long-term memory. The passage on washing clothes is an excellent example. People who were told the topic before they read the passage were able to interpret the abstract ideas because they could use their knowledge of washing clothes to organize the text.

Perhaps the best method to encourage students to integrate ideas in the text with their knowledge in long-term memory is to ask them to explain the ideas in their own words. Although generating self-explanations often improves learning it is not always effective. Bethany Rittle-Johnson and Abbey Loehr at Vanderbilt University recently reviewed a large number of studies to determine when self-explanations are effective. They found four constraints that are summarized in Table 1.1. The first is that asking students to explain material is particularly effective for topics that have general principles. Many of the success stories have focused on learning mathematics and science. These include asking preschool children about mimicry; elementary school children about mathematical

Table 1.1 Four Constraints on When Prompted Self-Explanation
Aids Learning

Constraint on:	Description
1. Target outcomes and domains	Promotes comprehension and transfer in domains that are consistently guided by general principles or heuristics.
2. What is being explained	Best if to-be-explained content is known to be correct or incorrect rather than learners' own potentially incorrect ideas.
3. Explanation prompts	Prompts direct attention to particular information, so can reduce attention to other important information.
4. Effectiveness relative to alternative instructional techniques	Alternative instructional techniques such as instructional explanations, solving unfamiliar problems and retrieval practice can sometimes be equally or more effective.

B. F. Rittle-Johnson and A. M. Loehr (2017). Eliciting explanations: Constraints on when self-explanation aids learning. *Psychonomic Bulletin & Review, 24*, 1501–1510.

equivalence; a range of students about biology; high school students about geometry, algebra, and probability; and undergraduates about scientific argumentation, proofs, programming, and chemistry. In contrast, self-explanations did not help students learn a topic that has exceptions to general rules such as English grammar.

You may have already anticipated another variable that influences the effectiveness of self-explanations. What if students' explanations are based on their existing incorrect theories? These explanations direct attention to incorrect information, away from information in the text. Explaining incorrect information, however, can be very effective if students know it is incorrect such as asking them to find an error in a solution to a math problem. Another factor in evaluating instruction requires determining whether explanation prompts ignore important parts of the text that now go unnoticed because the prompts shift attention away from this material.

The final constraint in Table 1.1 requires comparing self-explanations to other instructional interventions. Imagine an experiment in which one group only read the material while another group self-explained the material after they read it. The second group would have an unfair advantage because they had more study time. It is necessary to control for study time to evaluate the effectiveness of instruction. The first group should have the same amount of study time by either giving them a different instructional intervention or by allowing them to use their own methods for learning the material.

A group of investigators from Simon Fraser University in Canada analyzed the impact of 20 variables on the effectiveness of self-explanations. They found that self-explanations were effective for a variety of outcome measures such as the ability to make inferences, recall information, solve problems, and transfer to new tasks. The investigators also found that self-explanations benefit students at all levels of education from elementary school to high school to undergraduate studies to professional programs. These findings suggest that generating explanations encourages students to retrieve relevant information from long-term memory and to elaborate it with the new information. People, however, do not always add the new information to memory, as discussed in the next section.

Adding Information

I want to add a fourth aspect to comprehension that follows selecting, organizing, and integrating. Integrating information involves using knowledge in long-term memory to aid comprehension. Adding information involves incorporating the new information into long-term memory rather than dismissing it as irrelevant or wrong. The decision whether to add information is important in an era of misinformation.

The spread of measles was a major concern as I was writing this chapter, so I checked the website of the Centers for Disease Control and Prevention. It informed me that from January 1 to May 10, 2019, 839 cases of measles had been confirmed in the United States. This is the greatest number of cases reported here since 1994. The majority of people who got measles were unvaccinated. The website also reported that measles can spread when it reaches a community where groups of people are unvaccinated.

Vaccinating children to prevent the spread of infectious diseases is one of four case studies reviewed in an article by Kara Weisman and Ellen Markman at Stanford University. The study attempted to change the attitudes of those adults who believed a vaccination against measles was dangerous because it increased the risk of autism. Psychologists at the University of Illinois and UCLA used materials from the Centers for Disease Control website to compare an autism correction perspective with a disease risk perspective. Adults assigned to the autism correction condition read information summarizing recent research showing that vaccinations do not increase the risk of autism in children. Adults assigned to the disease risk condition read information summarizing the risks suffered by children who get measles. Only the participants in the disease risk condition changed their beliefs about vaccinations. Focusing on the dangers of a communicable disease had a positive impact on people's attitudes whereas attempting to dispel misconceptions about vaccinations was ineffective.

The other three studies reviewed by Weisman and Markman were (a) washing hands to prevent the spread of viral epidemics, (b) completing a full course of antibiotics to reduce antibiotic resistance, and (c) eating a variety of healthy foods to improve unhealthy diets. Based on these and other research studies, the authors recommended five guidelines for designing explanations to motivate change to healthy behavior:

1. Identify a specific target for behavior change that is clearly linked to a desired outcome such as washing hands to prevent the spread of viral epidemics.
2. Identify the conceptual prerequisites necessary for understanding how and why engaging in this behavior would bring about the desired outcome.
3. Assess the theories currently held by the targeted audience.
4. Design educational materials to address misconceptions and gaps in people's current theories.
5. Provide just enough information to instill confidence in the causal framework of the correct theory such as why washing hands is helpful.

The intention of the last guideline is that providing too many details can distract from the causal principles.

Recent research by psychologists at Brown University and University College, London, studied how adults evaluate everyday explanations. The participants rated the quality of explanations that followed eight different questions including

- Why has the price of higher education skyrocketed in the United States, and who is profiting from it?
- Why don't opponents of illegal immigration go after the employers who hire illegal immigrants?
- How has Switzerland managed to stay in a neutral position during times of conflict like World War II?

Each question was followed by one of three different possible explanations that differed along multiple attributes.

In addition to rating the overall quality, participants rated 20 attributes of the explanations. The attributes that correlated most strongly with overall perceived quality were the perceived truth of the explanation, its coherence, the extent to which most people would agree with the general principles, the quality of the articulation, and the ease of visualizing the principles. Perhaps surprisingly, people preferred more complex explanations that had more causal mechanisms to explain the effect. The authors proposed that the preference for complexity is due to a desire to identify enough causes to make the effect seem inevitable.

2

Action

I have reviewed how reading is a primary source for acquiring knowledge, but some theorists have argued that the end goal of acquisition is action. We acquire knowledge to use it, and using it typically requires performing actions. Larry Barselou at Emory University published a very influential article in 1999 that argued perception and action are central components of cognition. They had previously been considered as peripheral components in which perception is the input, action is the output, and cognition occurs as the intermediary thought processes that link them. Elevating the status of perception and action in cognitive theories is referred to as "embodied cognition."

Arthur Glenberg is a major contributor to theories of embodied cognition. In one of his studies, Glenberg and his co-investigators tested the implications of the theory for helping young readers. As children read sentences, they moved toys to simulate the meaning of sentences they read. For example, in a story about activities on a farm, the child might read, "The farmer drove the tractor to the barn." Then she would put the toy farmer into a toy tractor and move the tractor to the barn. This activity requires the child to use her perceptual system to link words such as "tractor" to the toy tractor and to enact the syntax of the sentence—the who does what to whom—using her own actions. After children are successful in this physical manipulation, they are taught to imagine manipulating the toys as a step toward independent reading. Both physical and imagined manipulation produced large gains in reading comprehension.

Cognitive Skills You Need for the 21st Century. Stephen K. Reed, Oxford University Press (2020). © Oxford University Press. DOI: 10.1093/oso/9780197529003.001.0001.

An iPad app called EMBRACE (Enhanced Moved By Reading to Accelerate Comprehension of English) is the latest application of this intervention. The app is designed to help English-language learners improve their comprehension of written English. Each chapter begins with a short vocabulary list, and the computer selects words on the list based on the child's previous performance. When the child taps a word in the list, the word is pronounced in both the child's native language and in English while highlighting the corresponding image on the screen. For physical manipulation, the child moves images on the iPad screen. The computer demonstrates the manipulation if the child makes a mistake.

Figure 2.1 shows a narrative containing the sentence, "Then, he brought the baby down to the kitchen for breakfast and put her into the highchair." To complete the manipulation, the child first moves

Figure 2.1. A screen shot from the narrative text "The Lopez Family Mystery."
Contributed by Arthur Glenberg.

the father (a policeman) from the bathroom to the baby's crib. The iPad combines the father and baby, and the child moves the combined image to the highchair. The iPad then changes the illustration so that the baby appears in the highchair. If children move the wrong image or move the image to the wrong place, a warning noise occurs, and the image is snapped back to its original location.

These projects on improving reading provide a helpful introduction to this chapter because they include the physical, virtual, and mental manipulation of objects. Object manipulation requires both an action and an object, which typically have the same representation. We usually perform physical actions on physical objects, virtual actions on virtual objects, and mental actions on mental objects.

There are exceptions, however, in which the representation of the action differs from the representation of the object. These exceptions, such as in augmented reality, motivated my creation of the taxonomy in Table 2.1 that combines physical, virtual, and mental actions with physical, virtual, and mental objects. I discuss these combinations in the following sections on the physical, virtual, and mental manipulation of objects.

Table 2.1 Combinations of Physical, Virtual, and Mental Actions and Objects

| | Objects | | |
Actions	Physical	Virtual	Mental
Physical	Montessori manipulatives	Wii sports games	Gestures
Virtual	Robotic surgery	Virtual experiments	Teaching the blind
Mental	Brain–computer robotic interfaces	Brain–computer cursor interfaces	Sports simulations

From Reed (2018). Combining physical, virtual, and mental actions and objects. *Educational Psychology Review, 30*, 1091–1113.

Physical Actions

I suspect that most readers have some knowledge about the emphasis on physical manipulatives in Montessori schools. In her book *Montessori: The Science Behind the Genius*, Angeline Lillard discusses Montessori's work and subsequent research that has supported many of Montessori's ideas about learning and development. Maria Montessori, the first female physician in Italy, designed learning materials in the early 20th century that a teacher would evaluate in a Rome classroom. After consulting with the teacher, Montessori would redesign the materials to make them more effective.

A journal article on what makes mathematics manipulatives effective contained four recommendations based on the work of Montessori and subsequent research findings. The first recommendation is to use manipulatives consistently over a long period of time. The authors refer to the Montessori golden bead materials that represent the base-10 number system by individual beads that can be assembled into 10 connected beads that form a 10 by 10 square of 100 square beads that comprise a cube of 1,000 beads. The materials are used throughout the early elementary years to help children develop an understanding of the base-10 system. Their second recommendation is to begin with concrete representations and move to more abstract representations. Figure 2.2 shows the replacement of the concrete beads with more abstract numerical tiles that can be used without the physical representation of the quantities. The third recommendation is to avoid manipulatives that resemble everyday objects or have distracting irrelevant features. Because the beads are all the same color and size, children are not distracted by irrelevant attributes. The fourth recommendation is to explicitly explain the relation between a manipulative and a mathematical concept. It is unreasonable to expect children to make the connection between concrete materials and abstract concepts without explicit guidance.

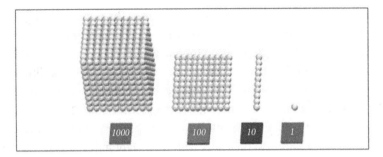

Figure 2.2. Numerical tiles help children connect an abstract representation to the more concrete beads.

From E. V. Laski, J. R. Jor'dan, C. Daoust, & A. K. Murrray, 2015, What makes mathematics manipulatives effective? Lessons from cognitive science and Montessori education, *SAGE Open,* April–June, 1–8.

The next combination in Table 2.1 pairs physical actions with virtual objects. Physical actions on virtual objects became very popular when Nintendo launched the video game console Wii in 2006. The tracking of the Wii remote in three-dimensional space enabled players to use physical actions to control a virtual game on a screen. One of the sports—bowling—works by mimicking the action of bowling by moving the arm and twisting the wrist to put spin on the ball. The screen shows the trajectory of the ball, which hopefully knocks over pins.

Gestures offer a third combination—a physical action on a mental object. Although gestures contain many components of the actions they mimic, they also eliminate components. The force needed to lift an object is missing in a gesture that lifts nothing. However, gestures offer a potential advantage for transfer to other objects because an action such as lifting is not linked to a particular object.

Support for this claim comes from a study that compared third-grade children on a mathematical-equivalence task of the form $2 + 9 + 4 = \underline{\quad} + 4$. The problems were written on a white magnetic board with numerical magnets (2, 9, 4) superimposed over the numbers on the left side of the equation. The instructor taught students in the *action* condition to physically move the first two number tiles to the right side of the equation to learn that 11 should be entered in the blank. Students in the *concrete gesture* condition mimicked placing the first two numbers in the blank without physically moving the tiles. Students in the *abstract gesture* condition pointed to the first two numbers with their left hand while simultaneously pointing to the blank with their right index finger. After the instruction all students completed a paper-and-pencil test consisting of both instructed problems and transfer problems that required a modification of the trained procedure. The three groups did not differ on the trained problems but, as hypothesized, the gesture conditions were more effective for transfer. Moving mental numbers did not link specific numbers to mathematical operations, which would reduce transfer to other specific numbers.

Virtual Actions

After diagramming the nine cells of the taxonomy, I was uncertain whether I could find examples to fill all of the cells. My search led me to articles that I normally wouldn't read. Two of them described training on robotic surgery. One was by a group of authors associated with the Department of Urology at the University College London Hospital. Another was by a group of authors associated with the Department of Surgery at the Medical College of Wisconsin. I classify robotic surgery as performing virtual actions on physical objects because the surgeon sits at a console to operate on the body.

The robotic da Vinci System was designed to improve upon conventional laparoscopy surgery in which the surgeon operates while standing, using hand-held, long-shafted instruments. The da Vinci System consists of a console that the surgeon uses to control four interactive robotic arms. Three of the arms hold instruments such as scalpels and scissors. The instruments exceed the natural range of motion of the human hand while motion scaling and tremor reduction further refine the surgeon's hand movements. Performing surgical movements on the computer console require training unique actions that differ from those used in either open or laparoscopic surgery.

Surgery requires performing very skilled actions but training in a virtual environment (using point and click) can be equivalent to training in a physical environment (using grab and heft) for learning concepts that do not require skilled actions. Lara Triona and David Klahr at Carnegie Mellon University trained fourth- and fifth-grade students to design experiments to measure how far springs stretched for various combinations of springs and weights. The springs could be long or short, wide or narrow, and thin or thick. Good experimental design requires testing only one variable at a time. The results showed that children who trained with virtual materials were as capable of designing good experiments as children who trained with physical materials. The virtual group also did as well as the physical group on a transfer task to evaluate the effect of steepness, length, surface, and type of ball on the time it would take a physical ball to roll down a physical ramp.

A subsequent study at Carnegie Mellon compared the effectiveness of constructing and evaluating toy cars in either a virtual or a real environment. Computer-based virtual design was again as effective as physical design and avoided some of the problems with assembling real cars that occasionally did not travel straight or had too tight wheels. The authors proposed that there are many advantages of computer-based laboratories including portability, safety, cost-efficiency, and flexible, dynamic data displays.

Virtual actions on mental objects occur when someone uses a virtual environment to create mental representations. An example is using a video game to teach navigation skills to the blind. Unlike sighted individuals, the blind must rely on nonvisual information to learn mental maps of the environment. An audio-based environment simulator of a virtual building prepared the learners to subsequently navigate an actual building. Exploration of the virtual building occurred through simple keystrokes while audio information described the location within the building. After training, the learners were evaluated on navigating a series of predetermined paths in the targeted physical building. They were highly successful, including finding shortcuts within the building and the shortest path to exit the building from different starting points.

Mental Actions

Mental actions on physical objects occur whenever someone uses thoughts to manipulate objects in the environment. Performing mental actions on physical objects seemed potentially problematic when I searched for examples. Using the power of thought to bend forks is one example but when I searched Google Scholar for "evidence for telekinesis" not much appeared. A more promising case is the use of brain potentials to control robotic actions on physical objects. This requires the intervention of a robot to carry out the action between the thought and the object. Invasive sensors use surgical implants of electrodes; noninvasive sensors record brain signals from the scalp. Both approaches are based on the principle of cortical preparation that occurs before a cognitive, motor, or emotional response. Cortical preparation can be measured as a voltage shift in electroencephalographic activity that can be used to control a physical device. Figure 2.3 illustrates this procedure.

A recent study by an international team led by Rossella Spataro at the University of Palermo (Italy) used the apparatus in Figure 2.3 to benefit amyotrophic lateral sclerosis (ALS) patients. Four ALS patients and four healthy controls learned to use technology to control a robot to reach and grasp a glass of water. The brain–computer interface consisted of two high-level commands (grasp and give), four directional commands (forward, backward, left, right) and two

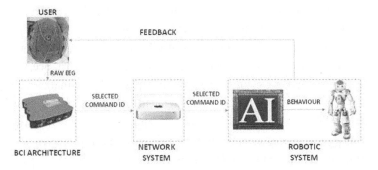

Figure 2.3. Apparatus in which electroencephalography recordings from the scalp are interpreted and used to control a robot.

From R. Spataro, A. Chella, B. Allison, M. Giardina, R. Sorbello, S. Tramonte, ... V. La Bella, 2017, Reaching and grasping a glass of water by locked-in ALS patients through a BCI-controlled humanoid robot, *Frontiers in Human Neuroscience, 11*, 1–10.

turn commands. A few minutes of training was sufficient for enabling all four healthy participants and three of the four ALS patients to control the robot's actions at a high level of accuracy.

The mental actions that control robots can also manipulate objects on a computer screen such as the cursor. A challenge is that moving the cursor occurs along two dimensions, and a single-modality electroencephalographic signal can only exert control along a single dimension. A group of developers at the University of Electronic Science and Technology of China found that imagining more than one signal creates more natural two-dimensional diagonal movements. Horizontal movement occurs by imagining movement of either the left or right hand. Vertical movement occurs by imagining the number 1 or 2. Imagining the four combinations LEFT 1, LEFT 2, RIGHT 1, and RIGHT 2 results in greater efficiency by controlling diagonal movements of the cursor.

Mental actions on mental objects occur during visual simulations that can be used for training in a many domains. In their extensive review of the role of imagery in sports, Jennifer Cumming and Sarah Williams discuss the variables that influence the effects of imagery training on performance. Two commonly discussed attributes are vividness and controllability. Vividness refers to the clarity and sensory richness of the image. Controllability refers to the transformation and maintenance of a generated image. For instance, the ability to change viewing angle can be important in domains such as sports and dance. Research at Bielefeld University in Germany controlled for imagery ability across training conditions to study the performances of novices on an artificial putting green. The training compared (a) mental imagery practice with (b) physical practice using a standard putter and ball, (c) combined mental and physical practice, and (d) a no-practice control. Although the groups did not show significant differences in putting accuracy, the combined group displayed more consistent putting (less variance) than the mental and no-practice groups. Reducing variance is a necessary step toward improving accuracy.

Virtual and Augmented Reality

It occurred to me while writing this chapter that the taxonomy should provide a useful framework for organizing advances in virtual and augmented reality. In 1984, Jaron Lanier and his friends founded the first virtual reality startup, VPL Research, Inc. In his 2017 book *Dawn of the New Everything*, Lanier provides 51 definitions of virtual reality. My favorite is "the substitution of the interface between a person and the physical environment with an interface to a simulated environment" (p. 47). Other "definitions" are consequences or elaborations of this one such as

- An ever-growing set of gadgets that work together and match up with human sensory or motor organs.
- The investigation of the sensorimotor loop that connects people with their world and the ways through which it can be tweaked through engineering.

- Instrumentation to make your world change into a place where it is easier to learn.
- Training simulators for anything, not just flight.
- A way to try out proposed changes to the real world before you commit.
- The medium that can put you in someone else's shoes; hopefully a path to increased empathy.

A 2009 article in *Science* magazine by Chris Dede, a professor in the Graduate School of Education at Harvard, discussed advantages of learning in virtual environments. One advantage of virtual immersion is that it supports multiple perspectives through interacting with objects from both the inside and outside. I found technology extremely helpful in virtually exploring a two-story, five-bedroom home in Burlingame, California, that my wife and I eventually co-purchased with our son and his wife. I was able to virtually navigate through the home in the online listing and then virtually navigate through the neighborhood using Google maps. A second advantage of immersive interfaces is that students can learn skills by exploring virtual environments. Dede's River City project enables learners to figure out why people are getting sick by exploring a historically accurate 19th-century city. A third advantage is to support transfer from simulated to real-world environments. The project on training the blind to navigate through a building by beginning with a virtual floor plan provides an excellent example.

An article in a June 2019 issue of *The Chronicle of Higher Education* provides numerous examples of how virtual reality is impacting the classroom. At Hamilton College, students can practice conducting a virtual orchestra by wearing a headset through which the sound of the orchestra changes as they turn their head. Other tech tools use augmented reality combine the virtual and the physical to enable users to see and interact with the world around them. At Case Western Reserve University, members of the audience wearing augmented glasses can watch live dancers interact with virtual imagery such as tornadoes. Advances in technology, however, also bring new challenges. According to Jeremy Bailenson, the founding director of the Virtual Human Interaction Lab at Stanford, the characteristics that make the new technologies attractive also make them more complicated for use in teaching. He predicts that this problem will be diminished as experts in the learning sciences study the effectiveness of this technology.

Augmented reality is also impacting the business world. Companies such as Apple, Google, and Facebook are rapidly developing augmented reality that overlays instructions and holographic images on the real world. Augmented reality supports tasks such as guiding workers through machine repairs and helping contractors visualize architectural plans at building sites. According to Forrester Research Inc., the number of "smart glasses" used by businesses in the United States will climb from the current level of less than 1 million to 14.4 million by 2025. Research on combining physical, virtual, and mental actions and objects should be helpful in designing these activities.

3

Categorization

Can you to think of an area of knowledge in which categorization is irrelevant? Whenever someone decides whether a smudged form is the letter E or F, a statistics problem requires a t-test or chi-square, a brown-skinned person is Asian or Hispanic, a patient has schizophrenia or a bipolar disorder, he or she must categorize.

Categories consist of objects or events that we group together because we believe they are related. As I was writing this chapter, I visited the campus bookstore and discovered tables of books that had been conveniently classified. Some labels were very traditional such as "History," "Biography, and "Poetry." Other labels were more creative such an as "Welcome to the Post-Apocalypse" and "Books for Young Feminists." The label on the last table was "Most Stolen Books." I wondered how the bookstore had obtained these books.

The ability to categorize enables us to interact with our environment without becoming overwhelmed by its complexity. Bruner, Goodnow, and Austin listed five benefits of forming categories in their influential book *A Study of Thinking*.

1. Categorizing objects reduces the complexity of the environment. Scientists have estimated that there are more than 7 million discriminable colors, but most of us initially learned only seven colors in the color spectrum (with the help of the acronym RoyGBiv). When we classify discriminably different objects as being equivalent, we respond to them in terms of their class membership rather than as unique items.

2. Categorizing is the means by which objects of the world are identified. We believe we have recognized a pattern when we

Cognitive Skills You Need for the 21st Century. Stephen K. Reed, Oxford University Press (2020). © Oxford University Press. DOI: 10.1093/oso/9780197529003.001.0001.

can classify it into a familiar category such as a cat, a table, or the letter B.

3. The third achievement is categories reduce the need for constant learning. We do not have to be taught about a novel object if we can classify it; we use our knowledge of items in the category to respond to the novel object.

4. Categorizing allows us to select an appropriate action. We set our coffee cup on a table, but not on a cat or the letter B.

5. Categorizing enables us to order and relate classes of objects and events. The category table, for example, has lamp table as a subordinate class and furniture as a superordinate class. The three categories form a hierarchy in which furniture contains table as a member and table contains lamp table as a member.

Perceptual Categories

Imagine a color spectrum existing as a line with red on the left and violet on the right. Now imagine drawing lines to separate red from orange, orange from yellow, yellow from green, green from blue, blue from indigo, and indigo from violet. Finally, draw an arrow within each category to indicate the ideal red, ideal orange, etc. My guess is that your ideal colors are near the center of the category. Psychologists refer to these central members as category prototypes.

The usefulness of prototypes is illustrated by the research of Patricia Kuhl at the University of Washington on how infants learn to discriminate among different vowel sounds. Infants are born with the ability to discriminate among basic sounds (phonemes) in many different languages but soon learn the prototypic speech sounds in their own language. Kuhl found that infants as young as six months have formed prototypes to represent these phonemes (Figure 3.1). Forming prototypes of phonemes such as the long-*e*

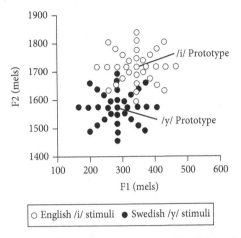

Figure 3.1. Two vowel prototypes, American English and Swedish, each with 32 variations.

From P. K. Kuhl & P. Iverson, 1995, Linguistic experience and the "perceptual magnet effect." In W. Strange (Ed.), *Speech perception and linguistic experience: Issues in cross-language research* (pp. 121–154). Baltimore, MD: York Press.

sound in "speed" reduces discrimination among the pronunciations of different people because the pronunciations begin to sound more like the category prototype. A consequence is that infants become worse at discriminating sounds within a phonemic category as they grow older. Kuhl uses the metaphor of a "perceptual magnet" to describe the effect. The prototypic long-*e* sound draws similar long-*e* sounds closer to it, thus making these variations sound more like the prototype. Notice, however, that this should make it easier to recognize the phonemes by making variations of a phoneme sound more alike.

A consequence is that infants are worse at discriminating among variations of a familiar sound in their own language than among variations of an unfamiliar sound in a different language. Swedish infants were better than American infants at discriminating between a prototypic long-*e* sound and other long-*e* sounds, even though this was an unfamiliar sound to them. The reason is that the American infants had formed a prototypic long-*e* sound and were therefore victims of the magnet effect, whereas the Swedish infants had not formed a prototypic long-*e* sound because this sound did not occur in their language. The opposite result occurred for a vowel that occurred in Swedish, but not in English. American infants were now better in discriminating variations of this vowel from the category prototype.

Hierarchical Categories

As babies grow older, they learn to categorize objects such as apples, socks, and chairs. Eleanor Rosch at the University of California, Berkeley deserves credit for advancing our understanding of how people organize these categories. She labeled very general categories such as tools, clothing, and furniture "superordinate categories." Superordinate categories consist of basic categories, which can be further divided into subordinate categories. Examples of the three levels are musical instruments drum—kettle drum, fruit grapes—Concorde grapes, tools—hammer—ball peen hammer, clothing—shirt—dress shirt, furniture—lamp—desk lamp, and vehicles—car—sports car.

Rosch proposed that it is easier to classify objects at the basic level than at the superordinate or subordinate level. She evaluated this claim by asking people to classify pictures of objects at one of the three hierarchical levels. Before being shown a picture of a sports car, people in the superordinate group received the question "Is this a vehicle?"; people in the basic group received a question "Is this a car?"; and people in the subordinate group received the question "Is this a sports car?" The findings supported her hypothesis. The fastest verification times occurred at the basic level. Rosch proposed that people in all three groups initially recognized the object at the basic level. Answering at the superordinate level subsequently requires making the inference that a car is a vehicle.

Answering at the subordinate level subsequently requires perceptually discriminating a sports car from other types of cars.

Rosch also investigated the effect of hierarchical categories as hints for recognizing objects. The consequences were revealed in an object detection experiment in which observers had to indicate whether a briefly exposed object was on the left or right side of the screen. The object was hidden among lines and curves to make detection very difficult. Each exposure was preceded either by no hint, a superordinate hint (such as a musical instrument), a basic hint (a piano), or a subordinate hint (a grand piano). Do you believe that all of these hints would be effective? Which would be the most effective?

The findings revealed that there was no difference in accuracy between the no-hint and superordinate-hint conditions, demonstrating that superordinate hints are ineffective. A hint that the object was a musical instrument, a fruit, a tool, clothing, furniture, or a vehicle was too general to enable observers to form an image of a generic object. One could, of course, form an image of a particular musical instrument, such as a drum, but this would be counterproductive if one guessed the wrong instrument. A hint at the basic level, such as a piano, did increase accuracy and was as accurate as a hint at the subordinate level. In both cases, people can create a prototypical image to guide their recognition of the object.

Shared Attributes

Although basic categories are particularly helpful some basic categories are better examples than others. We can agree that cars, trucks, and buses are good examples of vehicles but what about wheelbarrows and elevators? Chairs, sofas, and tables are typical examples of furniture but what about rugs, stoves, and clocks? Eleanor Rosch and Carolyn Mervis found that people generally agree on the typicality of category members. For instance, participants ranked car and truck as good (typical) examples of a vehicle and wheelbarrow and elevator as poor (atypical) examples. But how do people make these judgments?

Rosch and Mervis hypothesized that typicality is determined by the extent to which a category member shares attributes with other category members and does not share attributes with the members of other categories. They measured typicality by asking participants to rank order 20 members of each of six superordinate categories (furniture, vehicle, fruit, weapon, vegetable, clothing) based on how well that member fit their "idea or image" of the category name. Participants also listed the attributes of the category members. Rosch and Mervis then calculated a family resemblance score for each category member by determining how often its attributes were also listed for other members of the category. For example, if a steering wheel is one of the attributes listed for car, its family resemblance score would be influenced by how many of the other vehicles also had a steering wheel.

The attributes of the most typical vehicle—car—also occurred in many other vehicles. In contrast, the attributes of the least typical vehicle—elevator—did not occur in many other vehicles. An elevator operates by pushing buttons, works on a pulley system, and only travels vertically. The high correlations between typicality and family resemblance scores for each of the six categories supported the hypotheses that typicality is determined by the extent to which attributes are shared by other category members.

Social Categories

Categories also apply to people. In a 2012 interview for *New York Magazine*, Toni Morrison admitted that "I felt profoundly American, flag waving . . . but you are never out there as someone from Ohio, or even a writer. Because all that is clouded by the box you are put in as a Black Writer." Toni Morrison won both the Pulitzer Prize for Fiction and the Nobel Prize in Literature.

Nancy Cantor and Walter Mischel at Stanford University argued that the structure of semantic categories, such as hierarchical organization and typicality, is also relevant for how we classify people. An example of a superordinate category might be people who have a strong commitment to a particular belief or cause. This category can be subdivided into categories such as social activists, which can be further partitioned according to their particular causes. Cantor and Mischel's work parallels that of Rosch and her colleagues by examining such issues as the number of shared attributes at different levels in the hierarchy.

As we saw at the beginning of this chapter, categorization allows us to create a manageable view of the world, but it also has disadvantages that can be particularly troublesome when the category members are people. Cantor and Genero found that exaggerating within-group similarity by creating stereotypes might not only result in erroneous assumptions about others but also make it more difficult for people to remember impressions that disconfirm their stereotypes. In the process of organizing the world into social categories, people may perceive members of the same social category as remarkably similar and different from members of other social categories.

A social category that has attracted recent interest is generational differences. My colleague in the Psychology Department at San Diego State, Jean Twenge, has been one of the most successful authors in documenting these differences. Her latest book is titled *iGen: Why Today's Super-Connected Kids Are Growing Up Less Rebellious, More Tolerant, Less Happy—and Completely Unprepared for Adulthood*. Twenge reports that this generation, born in 1995 and later, grew up with cell phones and do not remember a time before the Internet. The oldest members were early adolescents when the iPhone was introduced in 2007 and high school students when the iPad arrived in 2010.

Naming categories is important, and Twenge writes that the label *iGen* is broad, concise, and relatively neutral. She argues that the competing label, *Generation Z*, works only if the previous generation is labeled *Generation X* and that name has been largely replaced by the label *Millennials*. As columnist Ben Zimmer writes in the *Wall Street Journal*, the label *Generation Z* also raises the issue of labeling future generations when an age cohort hits the end of the alphabet. Most important, a generational label is helpful if it captures the essence of the generation, and Twenge documents in her book how easy access to technology has shaped the *iGen* generation.

Action Categories

We learned at the beginning of this chapter that one of the benefits of categories is that they enable us to select an appropriate action. Categorizing an object as a chair indicates that a person can sit on it and it should support her weight. Actions such as sitting can be combined to form events. Sitting occurs within a context such as studying, eating, conversing, or watching television.

Gabriel Radvansky has conducted research at the University of Notre Dame that shows how events influence our memory. He defines "event boundaries" as transitions from one event to another, such as occur when we change location or begin a new activity. In some of his studies people move through either virtual or real spaces, picking up an object on a table, moving to the next table, setting the object down, and then picking up another object on that table. In one condition the tables were in the same room, and in another condition the tables were in different rooms. The results showed that people responded more slowly and made more errors identifying the object they were currently carrying when the tables were in different rooms. So now you have an excuse if you enter a room and don't remember why. Simply tell others that crossing an event boundary disrupted your memory.

Jeffrey Zacks at Washington University in St. Louis has been a leader in constructing event models of how people perceive, remember, think about, and respond to events. A recent article by Richmond and Zacks provides a thorough summary of work on this topic. Some of this research investigates how low-level actions become organized into event-level actions. As illustrated in Figure 3.2, low-level actions are described in terms of joints, muscle torques, and contact relations. High-level actions are described as holding, getting, and pouring milk. High-level actions result in smoother changes in behavior and are more learnable. They also allow us to predict behavior by extrapolation from previous actions.

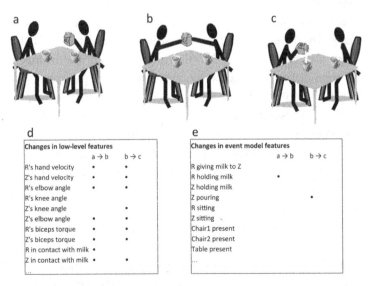

Figure 3.2. Changes in low-level and in event-level actions.

From L. L Richmond & J. M. Zacks, 2017, Constructing experience: Event models from perception to action. *Trends in Cognitive Sciences, 21,* 962–980.

Smooth changes in behavior, however, do not always occur as recognized by those of us who have participated in physical therapy. In a test of progress in improving my walking, my physical therapist designed a course that required me to walk at top speed while avoiding people and objects. She followed behind me with her watch and recorded my time to complete two laps. She then measured my ability to walk with distractions by asking me to repeat the same course while naming male names that begin with letters from A to Z and then repeat the naming task for female names. I was not allowed to skip a letter but could make up a name, and I made up some weird names. My walking rate decreased by 20% while performing the naming task. My therapist told me this is typical. Even a well-practiced skill such as walking can be disrupted by multitasking.

Although a task can be summarized by high-level actions such as walking, these actions can also be represented at a more detailed level as shown in Figure 3.2. Robin Vallacher and Daniel Wegner's research on action identification theory reveals how actions can be changed by directing attention to these lower-level details. A novice tennis player, for example, may devise a strategy to win the match but soon discover that a focus on basic actions (e.g., prepare the racket, follow through with the stroke) is necessary to improve performance. However, if an action is easy for a person, directing attention to lower-level details can be disruptive.

My brother worked for a large corporation in Columbus, Ohio, and years ago invited me to attend the Memorial Open golf tournament, which is to Columbus what the Kentucky Derby is to Lexington. His company had rented a home overlooking the 17th hole, and everyone was having such a great time that no one was watching the tournament. I decided I should go outside and at least take a quick look. A few minutes later a ball landed on the green, followed by the appearance of the world's best player—Tiger Woods. He missed his first, second, and third puts. I learned many years later that, at the height of Tiger's career, he decided that he could improve his shots even though it meant performing at a much lower level while relearning his strokes. I thought what incredible motivation it would take for someone who is the best in the world to attempt to become even better at the cost of losing tournaments during the relearning phase.

4

Abstraction

Abstraction is a double-edged sword. We have all struggled with reading text that was so abstract that it was difficult to understand. We encountered its bad side in the washing clothes passage in Chapter 1 of this book. It therefore might be reasonable to conclude that abstraction should be avoided at all costs. However, one of mankind's most important skills is the ability to think at an abstract level. When I began writing this book on cognitive skills, I selected abstraction as one of the first topics that I wanted to analyze.

The power of abstract thinking is illustrated by the observations of a young engineer who in 1947 graduated at the top of his class at MIT with degrees in electrical engineering and mathematics. He was assigned to an important project that required a weekly meeting with his supervisor whom he describes as follows:

> Each question was precisely the best one based on the information he had uncovered so far. His logic was faultless—he never asked a question that was irrelevant or erroneous. His questions came in rapid-fire order, revealing a mind that was lightning-fast and error-free. In about an hour he led each of us to understand what we had done, what we had encountered, and where to search for the problem's cause. It was like looking into a very accurate mirror with all unnecessary images eliminated, only the important details left.

His supervisor was John von Neumann, and the project was to build one of the world's first computers.

Cognitive Skills You Need for the 21st Century. Stephen K. Reed, Oxford University Press (2020). © Oxford University Press. DOI: 10.1093/oso/9780197529003.001.0001.

I took this quote from George Dyson's book *Turing's Cathedral: The Origins of the Digital Universe*. Dyson grew up in the shadows of the Institute for Advanced Study at Princeton, where his famous father, Freeman Dyson, resided. *Turing's Cathedral* documents Turing's contributions to computing, but my ideal representative of abstract thinking is von Neumann. The following paragraphs summarize a few parts of von Neumann's accomplishments, which are scattered throughout Dyson's book.

John von Neumann, born in Budapest in 1903, received an appointment in the Mathematics Department at Princeton University in 1931 followed two years later by a professorship at the Institute for Advanced Study. His remarkable mathematical abilities had already been demonstrated in his 1928 article on the axiomatization of set theory. Axioms reduce a subject to a minimal set of initial assumptions and provide the foundation for the rest of mathematics. A previous attempt by Bertrand Russell and Alfred North Whitehead (*Principia Mathematica* published between 1910 and 1913) still left fundamental questions unanswered. A surprising aspect of von Neumann's approach was its conciseness; his axioms occupied approximately one page of print. Von Neumann's interest in brevity served him well in developing the first computers.

Another landmark publication with Oskar Morgenstern, *Theory of Games and Economic Behavior*, appeared in 1944. The premise of the book was that a reliable economy could be constructed out of unreliable parts. Military strategists were the first to adopt the principles of game theory, followed by economists. As stated later by the Nobel Prize–winning economist Paul Samuelson, von Neumann "darted briefly into our domain and it has never been the same since."

A third major contribution, indicated by the opening quote, was constructing the architectures of the first computers. The functional elements of a computer consisting of a hierarchical memory, a control system, a central arithmetic unit, and input/output channels are still known as the von Neumann architecture.

If von Neumann's life shows us the power of abstraction, his death at age 53 from cancer reminds us of its fragility. In a poignant interview a 21-year-old Marina von Neumann recalled a visit to her father's hospital room shortly before his death. As described to Dyson her father "clearly realizes that the illness had gone to his brain and that he could no longer think, and he asked me to test him on really simple arithmetic problems, like seven plus four, and I did this for a few minutes, and then I couldn't take it anymore; I left the room," she remembers, overcome by "the mental anguish of recognizing that that by which he defined himself had slipped away."

Definitions of Abstraction

You can likely think of multiple uses of the word *abstract*. If you went to a museum of modern art, you saw abstract paintings that did not copy familiar objects. Some did not look like any objects such as Jackson Pollock's drip paintings. Others, such as Picasso's paintings, modified real objects. His famous 1937 painting "Guernica" distorted a horse, a bull, and people to depict the horrors of bombing a Basque town during the Spanish civil war. Stand in front of the large canvas in the Museo Reina Sofia if you are ever in Madrid, Spain. It is a moving experience.

Cognitive psychologists are more interested in Picasso's than Pollock's approach. They study how people abstract from reality. Three definitions of *abstraction* in the *APA Dictionary of Psychology* influenced my organization of this topic:

1. An abstract entity exists only in the mind, separated from embodiment.
2. Abstraction focuses on only some attributes of stimuli.
3. An abstract idea applies to many particular instances of a category.

Table 4.1   A Taxonomy of Abstraction

Level of Analysis	Concrete Representation	Abstract Representation
Instance	Modal (sensory)	Amodal (linguistic)
Attribute	Equivalent	Distinctive
Category	Example or episode	Prototype, rule, or schema

From Reed (2016). A taxonomic analysis of abstraction. *Perspectives on Psychological Science, 11*, 817–837.

These three characteristics shown in Table 4.1 contrast concrete and abstract representations at the three levels of analysis. Existing only in the mind applies to the members (instances) of categories, focusing only on some attributes applies to the attributes of those instances, and representing categories applies to groups of instances.

I realize that my overview may be too abstract to understand at this point, but I hope the explanations that follow will make it clear. We will begin with instances and then turn to attributes and, finally, categories.

Instances of Categories

Concrete instances can be represented by sensory images. In Glenberg's stories from Chapter 2 of this book, beginning readers could visualize statements such as "The farmer drove the tractor into the barn" because it is easy to form images for the words *farmer, drove, tractor*, and *barn*. Both physical and imagined manipulation produced large gains in reading comprehension.

We now know that visual imagery is an important component of cognition, but imagery for many years was considered off limits for psychological research. In 1926 John Watson wrote a very influential book called *Behaviorism*. It advocated a focus on behavior by sweeping away mental constructs that could not be directly observed. That included visual imagery.

It wasn't until the late 1960s that imagery began again to establish a foothold in psychology through the research efforts of Alan Paivio at the University of Western Ontario. Paivio argued there were two major ways a person could elaborate on material. One type emphasizes verbal associations. A word such as *poetry* can result in many associations that could help you distinguish it from other words. You might think of different styles of poetry, particular poems, or experiences in an English class. The other type of elaboration is creation of a visual image to represent a word. If I asked you to remember the word *juggler*, you might form an image of a person juggling three balls. If I asked you to remember the word *truth*, however, you would probably have difficulty forming an image. The first word refers to a concrete object; the second, to an abstract concept.

If visual images and verbal associations are the two major forms of elaboration, is one more effective than the other? To answer this question, we have to know how easy it is to form an image and a verbal association of a word. The imagery potential of words is usually measured by asking people to rate on a scale how easy it is to form an image for a given word. As we might expect, concrete words are rated high on imagery, and abstract words are rated low. The association value of a word is usually measured by asking people to give as many associations as they can over a one-minute interval. Paivio and his colleagues found that the imagery potential of a word is a more reliable predictor of learning than its association potential. High-imagery words such as *dress, letter,* and *hotel* are easier to learn than low-imagery words such as *effort, quality,* and *necessity*, but high-association words are not necessarily easier to learn than low-association words.

One might interpret these results as indicating that visual images are more effective than verbal associations. However, Paivio did not choose this interpretation. The reason images are effective, according to Paivio, is that an image provides a second kind of memory code to support verbal memory. Paivio's theory is called a dual coding theory because it proposes that concrete words enable two memory codes, either of which can result in recall. A person who has stored both the word *dress* and an image of a dress can use ether the word or the image for recall. A person who has stored the word *quality* has to rely only on the word because there is no image to provide backup help.

Attributes of Instances

Instances of categories are composed of attributes. A dress is made from cloth and is typically worn by females. I distinguish between equivalent attributes and distinctive attributes in Table 4.1. Equivalent attributes are of equal importance, but abstraction creates distinctive attributes by focusing on those that are the most important. Attributes are also referred to as "features," and Eleanor Gibson, a developmental psychologist at Cornell University, popularized the term "distinctive features" in her 1969 book *Principles of Perceptual Learning and Development.*

Gibson's proposed that perceptual learning occurs through the discovery of features that distinguish one pattern from another. For instance, the features of letters consist of different lines and curves. Examples of lines include a horizontal line, a vertical line, and diagonal lines. Examples of curves include a closed circle (the letter O), a circle broken at the top (the letter U), or a circle broken at the side (the letter C). Most letters consist of more than one feature, such as the closed circle and diagonal line in the letter Q. Children learn to identify an object by being able to identify how its features differ from other objects. Learning to discriminate between the letters E and F depends on discovering that a low horizontal line is present in the letter E but not in the letter F. The low horizontal line is a distinctive feature because it is the only feature that differs between the two letters.

Perceptual learning can be facilitated by a learning procedure that highlights distinctive features. An effective method for emphasizing a distinctive feature is to initially make it a different color from the rest of the pattern and then gradually change it back to the original color. Byron Egeland at the University of Minnesota used this procedure to teach prekindergarten children how to distinguish between the confusable letter pairs R–P, Y–V, G–C, Q–O, M–N, and K–X. During the training session, the distinctive feature was gradually changed from red to black to match the rest of the letter. Another group of children viewed only black letters. They received feedback about which of their choices were correct, but they were not told about the distinctive features. Both groups were given a test immediately after the training session and a week later. The group trained on distinctive features made fewer errors on both tests, even though the features were not highlighted during the tests.

Distinctive features also occur for other visual patterns such as faces. Caricaturists take advantage of these distinctive features by making them even more distinct. Experimental findings indicate that we may also form caricatures when we remember faces. Undergraduates in this experiment viewed slides of constructed faces as illustrated by the two faces on the right in Figure 4.1. They later were shown test faces and asked to indicate if each test face was exactly the same as one shown in the first series of slides. The test faces included some faces that were shown, some faces that were not shown, and some faces that were caricatures of the shown faces. The caricatures appear on the left side of Figure 4.1 and were created by making a distinctive feature even more distinct. The high forehead in the top face is made even higher, and the long chin of the bottom face is made even longer. The interesting finding is that the caricatures were better recognized than the shown faces. This finding is consistent with the experimenters' explanation that people encode a face into memory in a manner that makes it even more distinct than the original face.

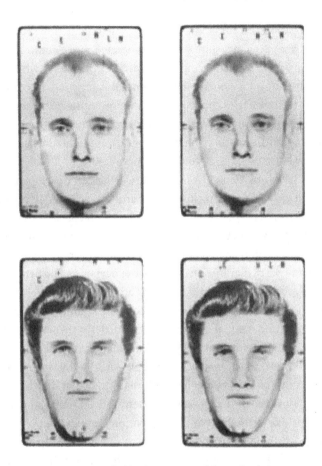

Figure 4.1. Caricatures (left) of constructed faces (right).
From R. Mauro & M. Kubovy, 1992, Caricature and face recognition, *Memory & Cognition, 20,* 433–440.

Categories of Instances

A concrete way to represent a category is to remember many examples (exemplars) of the category. You might represent the category "shoes" by examples you have encountered in stores, worn by others, and in your closet. You also remember action sequences such as shopping at a shoe store. A concrete representation in this case consists of remembering many specific episodes in which you went shopping for shoes. Abstractions of categories, in contrast, consist of summaries that go beyond representing a category as a collection of examples. We saw in the previous chapter that perceptual categories, such as phonemes, can be represented by category prototypes that refer to a typical category member.

The British psychologist Sir Frederick Bartlett developed a general theory of organizing knowledge around "schema" in his 1932 book *Remembering: A Study in Experimental and Social Psychology.* He defined a schema as an active organization of past experiences in which the mind abstracts a general cognitive structure to represent many particular instances of those experiences. Bartlett's book explains schema theory and shows its application to experimental results that he had collected on memory for figures, pictures, and stories. A fundamental assumption of Bartlett's theory is that all new information interacts with old information represented in the schema. This is illustrated by how people who did not share the cultural history of Indians recalled an Indian story that they had read called "The War of the Ghosts." Bartlett noticed that many of the errors people made in recall had been integrated with their prior knowledge about stories.

Although Bartlett emphasized that schemas are organized, he was not always very specific about what is the organization. We now think of a schema as providing a skeleton structure that can be filled out with the detailed properties of a particular instance. We have schemas for solving different kinds of problems, recognizing faces, going shopping for groceries, and forming social stereotypes. For now, let's examine the organization of a particular type of schematic structure—our knowledge about a sequence of events.

Two professors at Yale—a computer scientist named Roger Schank and a social psychologist named Robert Abelson—used the term *script* to refer to what we know about the sequence of events that make up routine activities. For example, a restaurant script would specify what we know about going to a restaurant. At a very general level, a restaurant script consists of standard roles, props or objects, conditions, and results. The conditions for going to a restaurant are that a customer is hungry and is able to pay for the meal. The props are tables and chairs, a menu, food, a bill, and money or a credit card. Supporting actors include waiters or waitresses and sometimes other personnel such as bartenders or busboys. The results are that the customer has less money but is no longer hungry, whereas the owner has more money and less food. Between the times that a customer enters and leaves, there is a fairly standard sequence of events that includes selecting a table, looking at the menu, ordering the food, eating, and paying the bill.

Now imagine that you went to a nice restaurant for dinner, and the next day a friend asks you about your experience. You reply that you selected a table, looked at the menu, ordered food, ate, and paid the bill. Your friend is now either frowning or yawning. But that shouldn't imply that scripts are unimportant. They provide shared knowledge that enables the listener to understand the unique aspects of your experience that you would typically include in your reply.

Gordon Bower at Stanford University performed one of the first investigations of how people's knowledge of such routine activities helps them understand and remember information in a text. The typical events in a script provide a framework for comprehension but are themselves uninteresting because we already know about them. What is usually interesting is the occurrence of an event that is related to the script but unexpected. For example, a customer could need help translating a menu because it is in French, or the waiter might spill water on the customer. Schank and Abelson refer to such events as obstacles because they interrupt the major goals of the script, such as ordering and eating.

Bower and his colleagues tested the hypothesis that readers would focus on these obstacles by asking them to read six script-based stories about making coffee, attending a lecture, getting up in the morning, attending a movie, visiting a doctor, and dining at a restaurant. After reading all six stories and then completing an intervening task for 10 minutes, the readers attempted to recall the stories in writing. The results supported the prediction. The interruptions either prevented or delayed the main character from accomplishing a goal, and this aspect of the story was well remembered.

When a goal is included in a story, people use the goal to organize the actions. A character's attempt to achieve a goal results in the establishment of causal relations among statements in a text. Work by Tom Trabasso and his students at the University of Chicago showed that it is these causal relations that underlie what a reader judges to be important. Causal relations also determine which information people recall from a story and include in its summary.

Remember the testimony at the beginning of this chapter about John von Neumann's supervision of a project to build one of the first computers: "In about an hour he led each of us to understand what we had done, what we had encountered, and where to search for the problem's cause. It was like looking into a very accurate mirror with all unnecessary images eliminated, only the important details left." The testimony reflects the importance of finding causal relations to achieve goals. And if anyone knows where we can obtain a mirror that eliminates the clutter, please share that information.

PART II
ORGANIZING KNOWLEDGE

5

Matrices

The initial four chapters on acquiring knowledge reviewed how people learn how to comprehend, act, categorize, and abstract. Robert Glushko, Paul Maglio, Teenie Matlock, and Lawrence Barsalou refer to this type of acquisition as "cultural categorization." Cultural categories exist for objects, events, mental states, and other components of experience. Kuhl's research on phonological categories and Rosch's research on semantic categories are examples of cultural categorization. Social and linguistic interactions between children and their caregivers play the major role in transmitting cultural categories.

Glushko and his coauthors contrast cultural categorization with institutional categorization. Institutions such as business, industry, law, and science devote considerable time and resources to develop classification systems that serve their goals. Box 5.1 shows a small part of two institutional systems: (a) the Dewey Decimal Classification System for classifying books and (b) the United Nations Standard Products and Services Code for classifying products and services.

The 10 main groups in the Dewey decimal system are 000–099, general works; 100–199, philosophy and psychology; 200–299, religion; 300–399, social sciences; 400–499, language; 500–599, natural sciences and mathematics; 600–699, technology; 700–799, the arts; 800–899, literature and rhetoric; and 900–999, history, biography, and geography. The system is a hierarchy in which a larger category such as "science" is partitioned into smaller categories such as "physics" and "chemistry," which are partitioned into even smaller categories such as "heat" and "electricity" within "physics".

Cognitive Skills You Need for the 21st Century. Stephen K. Reed, Oxford University Press (2020). © Oxford University Press. DOI: 10.1093/oso/9780197529003.001.0001.

Box 5.1 Partial Listings from the Dewey Decimal System and the Standard Products and Services Code

Dewey Decimal Classification System	Standard Products and Services Code
532 Fluid mechanics	10101901 Butterflies
533 Gas mechanics	10101902 Beetles
534 Sound and related vibrations	10101903 Bees
535 Light	10101904 Silkworms
536 Heat	10102000 Wild animals
537 Electricity	10102001 Elephants
538 Magnetism	10102002 Live foxes
539 Modern physics	10110000 Domestic pet products
540 Chemistry and allied sciences	10111300 Domestic pet treatments

Based on Glushko, Maglio, Matlock, and Barsalou (2008). Categorization in the wild. *Trends in Cognitive Sciences, 12*, 129–135.

The classification system on products is also hierarchical although I am puzzled why the adjective *live* appears before *foxes*.

The three chapters in this section describe systematic attempts to organize knowledge by using diagrams to create matrices, networks, and hierarchies. Recall that the benefits of forming categories listed in *A Study of Thinking* include the capability to order and relate classes of objects and events. All these diagrammatic structures enable us to depict relations among categories. At the end of this section in Chapter 7, I include an analysis of how these three diagrammatic structures differ from each other. This research provides useful guidelines for selecting a structure.

My own attempts to organize knowledge have often relied on matrices. A matrix organizes categories along two dimensions. One dimension of the matrix in Table 2.1 is "actions" and the other dimension is "objects." The categories along both dimensions are "physical," "virtual," and "mental." One dimension of the matrix in the table is "level of analysis" consisting of "instance," "attribute," and "category." The other dimension is "representation" consisting of "concrete" and "abstract." Each cell in a matrix combines a category in one dimension with a category in the other dimension. My nomination for the most effective use of a matrix to organize scientific knowledge goes to a Russian chemistry teacher for constructing the periodic table of elements.

Periodic Table of Elements

As told in Hugh Aldersey-Williams's book *Periodic Tales,* the initial version of the periodic elements first appeared in a Russian chemistry book published in 1869. The chemistry teacher, Dmitrii Mendeleev, had struggled to make sense of the elements for his students by rearranging cards that contained the name of one of the 63 discovered elements. The resulting table, based on atomic weights, was initially met with some skepticism, but the discovery of a new element (gallium) with an atomic weight that corresponded to a predicted gap in the table began to convince critics. The discovery of more elements that filled more gaps provided further evidence for Mendeleev's organization. The author of *Periodic Tales* describes the powerful impact of Mendeleev's insights on his own thinking:

> The elements, I understood, were the universal and fundamental ingredient of all matter. There was nothing that was not made out of elements. But the table into which the Russian chemist Dmitrii Mendeleev had sorted them was even more than the sum of these remarkable parts. It made sense of the riotous *variety* of the

elements, placing them sequentially in rows by atomic number (that is to say, the number of protons in in the nuclei of their atoms) in such a way that their chemical relatedness suddenly leapt out (their relatedness is periodic, as revealed in the alignment of columns). Mendelev's table seemed to have a life of its own. For me, it stood as one of the great and unquestionable systems of the world. It explained so much, it seemed so natural, that it must always have been there; it couldn't possibly be the recent invention of modern science.

Figure 5.1 shows the Periodic Table of Elements, which can be downloaded from the Los Alamos National Laboratory website. The website informs us that the periodic table is the most important chemistry reference. It ranges all the known elements from left to right and from top to bottom in order of increasing atomic number. This order usually reflects increasing atomic mass.

The atomic symbols, such as H for hydrogen, consist of one or two letters that are used internationally. The atomic number for hydrogen is 1 and specifies the number of protons in a hydrogen atom. The number of protons determines chemical behavior, as does the configuration of the electrons. The electron distribution enables chemists and physicists to predict properties of the elements such as stability, boiling point, and conductivity.

The complete title of Aldersey-Williams's book is *Periodic Tales: A Cultural History of the Elements From Arsenic to Zinc*. His book informs us that imperial power has always depended on possession of elements. The elements were bronze for the Roman Empire, gold for the Spanish Empire, and iron and coal for the British Empire. The balance of current superpowers is maintained by a nuclear arsenal based on uranium and plutonium. The elements have also influenced popular culture in which elements such as chromium have been replaced by newer elements such as titanium for use in fashionable clothing and equipment. Some

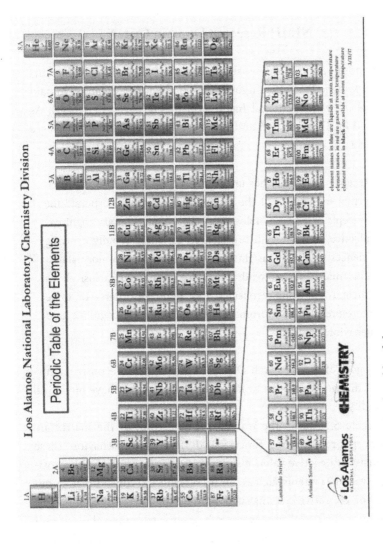

Figure 5.1. The periodic table of elements.
From the Los Alamos National Laboratory Website.

names have been completely detached from the elements. Neither platinum blonds nor platinum credit cards are made of platinum.

NIMH Research Domain Criteria

My nomination of the most important matrix for organizing current knowledge is the ongoing development of Research Domain Criteria by the National Institute of Mental Health (NIMH). As stated by Thomas Insel and Bruce Cuthbert in their 2015 *Science* article:

> Recently psychiatry has undergone a tectonic shift as the intellectual foundation of the discipline begins to incorporate the concepts of modern biology, especially contemporary cognitive, affective, and social neurosciences. As these rapidly evolving sciences yield new insights into the neural basis of normal and abnormal behavior, syndromes once considered exclusively as "mental" are being reconsidered as "brain" disorders—or, to be more precise, as syndromes of disrupted neural, cognitive, and behavioral systems.

The goal of the Research Domain Criteria is to deconstruct current diagnostic groups to identify subgroups that have biological validity.

Table 5.1 shows the framework. The rows of the matrix are concepts representing functional dimensions of behavior. These consist of negative valence systems such as fear and anxiety, positive valence systems such as reward seeking and consummatory behavior, cognitive systems such as attention and working memory, systems for social processes such as understanding the self and the mental states of others, and arousal/regulatory systems such as arousal and circadian rhythms.

Table 5.1 NIMH Research Domain Criteria Framework

	Genes	Molecules	Cells	Circuits	Physiology	Behavior	Reports	Paradigms
Negative valence								
Positive valence								
Cognitive systems								
Social processes								
Arousal/regulatory								

Based on Insel and Cuthbert (2015). Brain disorders? Precisely. *Science, 348*, 499–500.

The columns of the matrix in Table 5.1 are units of analysis. These consist of genes, molecules, cells, circuits defined by brain areas, physiology such as heart rate, behavior, self-reports obtained from interviews, and paradigms based on experimental design. The goal of the project is to fill in the cells of the matrix with research that identifies causal relations between the biological and psychological constructs. We will return to the NIMH research initiative in Chapters 15 and 16 of this volume to see how computer science can help establish connections between the rows and columns in Table 5.1.

Design Tasks

Matrices can also support design. John Carroll, John Thomas, and Ashok Malhotra at the IBM Watson Research Center studied the spontaneous use of matrix diagrams for two variations of a design task. One version required designing a business office for seven employees. Each employee was to be assigned to a corridor a certain number of offices down from a central hallway containing a reception area at one end and accounting at the other end. Compatible employees should occupy the same corridor, and those with higher prestige should be nearer to the central hallway. Examples of constraints are that Employee A uses the accounting records less than C, B and C are compatible, and C has more prestige than B. A goal of the problem is to minimize the number of corridors.

A temporal version of the task had equivalent constraints that were placed on a manufacturing process consisting of seven stages. The columns of a matrix can now be used to represent work shifts rather than corridors. The horizontal dimension represents time and the vertical dimension represents priority. Participants were instructed to assign stages to the same work shift if the stages used the same resources. Some stages had to be assigned to earlier work shifts than others, and some stages had priority over others.

Examples of constraints are that stage A occurs before stage C, stages B and C use the same resources, and stage C has greater priority than stage B.

Participants given the office design not only satisfied more of the constraints but completed their design faster. All 17 used a sketch of the business office to formulate their design, but only 2 of the 18 participants in the manufacturing task used a sketch. When both groups were instructed in a second experiment to use a matrix for their design, there were no differences between the two groups. The differences in the first experiment therefore appear to have been caused by the helpful effects of using a matrix, which was more obvious for designing an office than for designing a manufacturing process.

The matrices in Tables 2.1, 4.1, and 5.1 illustrate how combining categories along two dimensions can result in helpful taxonomies. Matrices are so often used to organize knowledge that we may take them for granted without recognizing the considerable thought underlying their creation. The next chapter is about a less familiar, but increasingly important graph structure based on networks.

6

Networks

Six centuries ago, the Torre del Mangia of the Plazzo Publico in Siena, Italy, towered over the Piazza del Campo that served as a market and meeting place. The setting inspired the name of Niall Ferguson's book *The Square and the Tower: Networks and Power, From the Freemasons to Facebook*. Ferguson explains, "Nowhere in the world will you see so eloquently juxtaposed two forms of human organization depicted in this book: around you, a public space purpose-built for all kinds of more or less informal human interaction; above you, an imposing tower intended to symbolize and project secular power."

Ferguson's central thesis is that most historians, including him, have underestimated the influence of networks on history because of emphasis on the power of hierarchies. Hierarchies (the tower) are vertically structured organizations with centralized top–down command, control, and communication. Networks (the square) provide connections free from the central control of the hierarchy. A person in a network does not have designated power over other members but may nonetheless have considerable influence on those members. Ferguson's book shows how major changes, dating back at least to the Age of Discovery and the Reformation, can be understood as the disruption of hierarchies by networks.

My own introduction to the disruption of organizational hierarchies came from reading Jerry Hirshberg's 1998 book *The Creative Priority*. Hirschberg was the founder and president of Nissan Design International, following 16 years of experience as a design executive at General Motors. He believed the structure at General Motors was too hierarchical, limiting the ability

Cognitive Skills You Need for the 21st Century. Stephen K. Reed, Oxford University Press (2020). © Oxford University Press. DOI: 10.1093/oso/9780197529003.001.0001.

of different groups (engineers, designers, advertisers) to interact with each other. His objective at Nissan was to create a more open space in which members of all groups could easily interact during the initial phases of a design. Such spaces are now more common. As noted by Ferguson, Facebook's headquarters in Menlo Park, the new Apple Park in Cupertino, and Google's new headquarters in Mountain View all reflect a horizontal architecture that more closely resembles a town square than a tower.

Characteristics of Networks

You belong to numerous (family, social, professional) networks but may not have reflected on their characteristics. We need to begin by considering their structure if we are to understand the influence of networks on organizing knowledge. Figure 6.1 will be our guide in learning about these characteristics before applying them to various topics in this chapter. Networks consist of "nodes" (the circles in Figure 6.1) joined by lines that are technically called "edges." I avoid the word *edges* because an object on the edge is in danger of falling. Psychologists are sensitive to the emotional baggage of words and therefore refer to *links* rather than *edges*. An advantage of *links* is that it can be used as a verb. Stating that two nodes are linked together makes sense but stating that two nodes are edged together is awkward. "Edged together" implies that they touch, which leaves no room for a link.

Another technical term that I dislike is *degree*, which refers to the number of links attached to a node. I dislike it because I associate the word *degree* with temperature (as in 45°) or the measure of an angle (as in 45°). I will therefore avoid scary words such as *edge* and confusing words such as *degree* when discussing the characteristics of networks.

The purpose of networks is to show how nodes are linked together, and Figure 6.1 provides several examples. We can see

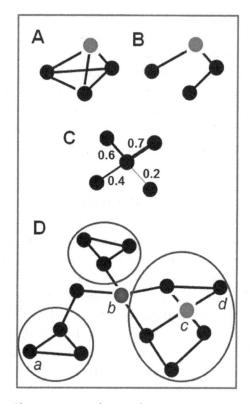

Figure 6.1. Characteristics of networks.

From F. G. Hillary & J. H. Grafman, 2017, Injured brains and adaptive networks: The benefits and costs of hyperconnectivity, *Trends in Cognitive Sciences, 21*, 385–401.

that network A is highly interconnected, in contrast to network B. The density of these connections is referred to as "clusters," which are revealed by the many triangles in network A and the absence of triangles in network B. Two other key network concepts are the weight of a link and the length of a path. The weights shown in network C reveal the strength of a relationship between two nodes. The higher the weight, the stronger the link. "Path length" refers to the number of links between nodes. The shortest path between nodes *a* and *d* in network D is five links. Node *b* in that network is referred to as a "hub" because it frequently appears on the shortest path connecting two nodes. It is easy to spot the hub cities on airline maps that display connections between cities.

Networks provide one approach to representing complexity as discussed by the computer scientist Melanie Mitchell in her very readable book *Complexity: A Guided Tour*. She informs us that an important publication that attracted attention to networks was an article by Duncan Watts and Steven Strogatz in the late 1990s titled "Collective Dynamics of Small World Networks." Watts and Strogatz applied their concept of small world networks to communities of movie actors, electrical power grids, and the connections between neurons in the brain of a worm.

A small-world experience occurred for me when I met with my department chairman, Alan Nash, after joining Florida Atlantic University. I grew up in a small Wisconsin town of 5,000 people, and Alan asked me where I lived in Wisconsin. After replying "Hartford," Alan said "That's where I am from. Where did you live in Hartford?" I replied, "The corner of Center and Prospect," and Alan responded, "I used to be your paper boy."

Another small-world event occurred for me at a San Diego neighborhood block party shortly after Hurricane Edouard, the strongest hurricane in the 1996 Atlantic hurricane season. One of the families, who had moved from France, had a son named Edward. I thought the name "Edouard" might be the French variation of Edward, so I teased him by asking how it felt to have a hurricane named after him. I wish I could have seen the expression on my face when he smiled and replied that the hurricane was named after him. I confirmed his explanation with his parents. His mother worked at the National Weather Service in San Diego where assignments included submitting names for hurricanes. She submitted family names, and the Weather Service selected "Edouard."

Now let's see how characteristics such as path length, number of links per node, and strength of links apply to other networks.

Semantic Networks

A primary use of networks in cognitive psychology is to model semantic relationships as depicted by the spreading activation model in Figure 6.2.

Although the strength of a relation between two nodes in network C (Figure 6.1) is represented by numbers, it can also be represented by distances. The length of each link in Figure 6.2 represents the degree of semantic relatedness between two concepts. For instance, the concept "red" is closely related to other colors and less closely related to red objects. Alan Collins and Elizabeth Loftus proposed

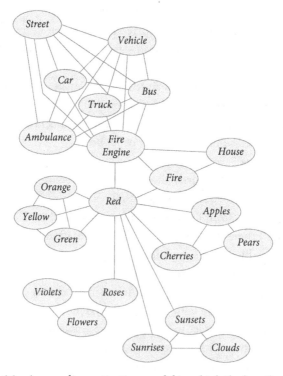

Figure 6.2. A spreading activation model in which the length of each line (link) represents the degree of association between two concepts.
From A. M. Collins & E. F. Loftus, 1975, A spreading activation theory of semantic processing, *Psychological Review, 82,* 407–428.

that activation spreads from a node along the paths of the network but decreases as it travels outward. Reading the word *red* should therefore strongly activate closely related concepts such as "orange" and "fire" but cause less activation of concepts such as "sunsets" and "roses" because activation has to travel further. A good metaphor for spreading activation is throwing a rock into a pond. The waves travel outward in all directions but take more time and become weaker the further they travel.

Although the spreading activation model provides a convenient metaphor, its success depends on how well it can account for experimental results. One such result occurs during a lexical decision task that requires people to quickly judge whether a string of letters forms a word. Some of the letters do (BUTTER), and some do not (NART). If two successive words are semantically related, people are faster in verifying that the second letter string is a word than if the two words are unrelated. For example, people more quickly verified that the string BUTTER is a word when it was preceded by BREAD than when it was preceded by NURSE.

The spreading activation model accounts for these results by proposing that the presentation of a word activates related words. BUTTER will be primed by BREAD but not be by NURSE. Activation of a word makes it easier to identify, resulting in faster response times. Now let's apply this idea to Figure 6.2. Hearing or seeing the word GREEN should activate the words YELLOW, ORANGE, and RED through spreading activation. If one of these words occurs next, it will be recognized more quickly. We will see in Chapter 15 of this volume how organizing semantic knowledge into networks forms a foundation for explainable artificial intelligence.

Event Networks

John Anderson at Carnegie Mellon University made an additional prediction based on the spreading activation model. He tested the assumption that the activation coming from a node is divided among the links to that node; the more links, the less activation that travels along each link. Applying this assumption to the network in Figure 6.2 would mean that activation from the node *red* would move slowly along each of its many links but activation from the word *violets* would move rapidly along its two links.

Now imagine that you learned three facts about someone named Marty: (a) Marty broke the bottle, (b) Marty didn't delay the trip, and (c) Marty cooked spaghetti. Later you had to quickly respond "yes" (Marty cooked spaghetti) or "no" (Marty played tennis) to a test sentence depending on whether you previously learned the fact. Anderson successfully predicted that learning more facts about a person would increase the time to verify any one of those facts because it would increase the number of links to that person. Some critics argued, however, that this assumption would imply that experts, who know many facts, would be slow to retrieve those facts. We all know experts who know a lot and can quickly retrieve that information. How can we resolve this dilemma?

Imagine now that you had learned that (a) Marty broke the bottle, (b) Marty didn't delay the trip, and (c) Marty christened the ship. Do you see how these three facts can be integrated around a common theme? The theme is that the ship launching was on schedule because the bottle broke during the christening. Lynne Reder and John Anderson proposed that, in this case, the three facts are integrated around a subnode, allowing for the quick verification of any of the facts. Subnodes create clusters of knowledge, such as illustrated by network D in Figure 6.1, that facilitate retrieval. They correspond to the scripts and schema discussed in Chapter 4 of this book on abstraction and enable experts to quickly access their extensive knowledge because of its organization.

Brain Networks

The depiction of different networks in Figure 6.1 served as an introduction to an article on adaptive networks following brain injury.

The authors, Frank Hillary and Jordan Grafman, report that brain imaging techniques have demonstrated that information transfer times depend not only on the direct path between nodes but also on the availability of alternative, detour paths. Figure 6.3 shows a schematic diagram of this finding. The connector hub in the figure

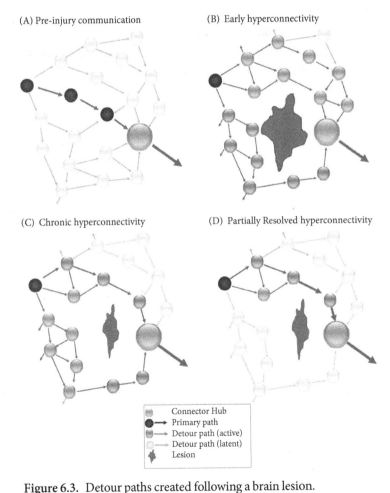

(A) Pre-injury communication

(B) Early hyperconnectivity

(C) Chronic hyperconnectivity

(D) Partially Resolved hyperconnectivity

Connector Hub
Primary path
Detour path (active)
Detour path (latent)
Lesion

Figure 6.3. Detour paths created following a brain lesion.

From F. G. Hillary & J. H. Grafman, 2017, Injured brains and adaptive networks: The benefits and costs of hyperconnectivity, *Trends in Cognitive Sciences, 21,* 385–401.

refers to a particular area of the brain such as the frontal cortex or thalamus.

One consequence of brain injury can be hyperconnectivity caused by an increase in the number and strength of connections. The lesion in Figure 6.3B disrupts the primary pathway to the hub, resulting in the establishment of detour pathways. A problem with increasing connectivity is that there are constraints on the size of the brain, the energy it uses, and the time required to travel long distances. The solution requires reducing the number of pathways to reduce the cost associated with hyperconnectivity. Figures 6.3C and D show this reduction in hyperconnectivity.

7

Hierarchies

Niall Ferguson described the characteristics of hierarchies in his book *The Square and the Tower* by beginning with the observation that a hierarchy is just a special kind of network. The characteristics of networks discussed in the previous chapter are therefore still relevant, but we need to add some constraints. The key to constructing a hierarchy is to start with the top node and always add nodes below it without connecting them laterally. The result is that there is no cycles in which a path leads back to the beginning node. There is only one path connecting any pair of nodes, which makes clear the chain of command and communication in organizations—the focus of Ferguson's scholarly analysis of the relation between networks and power.

A pictorial history of hierarchies is the topic of Manuel Lima's beautifully illustrated *The Book of Trees: Visualizing Branches of Knowledge*. Lima informs us that information visualization is a remarkable, ever-changing field of study that is built on a long succession of efforts. Trees of life, of virtues, of substitutions, of science, and of genealogy have depicted the organization of knowledge over many centuries. He argues that even though their characteristics such as hierarchy and centralization can at times prove problematic when dealing with the many challenges of a modern networked society, trees continue to embody a fundamental principle that reflects the way people look at the world.

The initial chapters in his book show the earliest forms of diagrammatic tree charts that are based on the node–link diagrams depicted in the previous chapter. His second group of chapters discusses more modern and recently popular space-filling

Cognitive Skills You Need for the 21st Century. Stephen K. Reed, Oxford University Press (2020). © Oxford University Press. DOI: 10.1093/oso/9780197529003.001.0001.

techniques based on embedded rectangles. One of these is the Map of the Market created by Martin Wattenberg in 1998 for *SmartMoney* magazine. Each rectangle represents a publicly traded company in which the area shows market capitalization and the color shows change in stock price. The rectangles are grouped into larger rectangles with labels such as "Health Care," "Financial," and "Energy" to enable users to quickly find the performance of a given industry. The Map of the Market became a standard for visualizing financial data, inspiring many subsequent products.

Although space-filling hierarchies are very appealing, cognitive psychologists have used the more traditional tree structures to model knowledge organization. The following sections discuss semantic hierarchies and intuitive ontologies. The chapter concludes with a section on people's ability to select the most appropriate diagram for representing knowledge. This requires understanding how matrices, networks, and hierarchies differ from each other in their representation of information.

Semantic Hierarchies

The semantic network model, discussed in the previous chapter, illustrated how links can represent semantic relations. Restrictions can be placed on the links so they form a hierarchy as occurs in the hierarchical network model proposed by Alan Collins and Ross Quillian (Figure 7.1). By following the links, we know that an ostrich and a canary are examples of birds and that a bird and a fish are examples of animals. We also know that a canary, an ostrich, a shark, and a salmon are animals because the links connect them with the superordinate category animal.

The links also reveal how features are stored at different levels in the hierarchy. Features true of all animals—such as eating and breathing—are stored at the highest level. Features that apply to basic-level categories—such as birds have wings, can fly, and

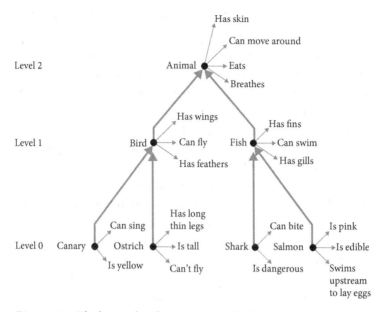

Figure 7.1. The hierarchical network model of semantic memory.
From A. M. Collins & M. R. Quillian, 1969, Retrieval time from semantic memory,
Journal of Verbal Learning and Verbal Behavior, 8, 240–248.

have feathers—are stored at an intermediate level. Features stored at the lowest level are true for a particular member but not for all members of the category. It is at this level that we know a canary is yellow and can sing.

One advantage of a hierarchical network is that it provides an economical way to store information because the information does not have to be repeated at each of the three levels. It isn't necessary to specify that eating and breathing are features of birds, fish, canaries, ostriches, sharks, and salmon because the network tells us that all are examples of animals, which eat and breathe. This economy of storage comes at a cost, however; retrieval of the fact that a canary eats requires two inferences: first, that a canary is a bird and, second, that a bird is an animal. It is necessary to go to the appropriate level in the hierarchy to retrieve the features stored at that level.

Collins and Quillian used the hierarchical network model in Figure 7.1 to make predictions about response times by assuming that it takes time to move from one level in the hierarchy to another and that additional time is required to retrieve the features stored at that level. They tested the model by asking people to rapidly respond true or false to sentences such as "An elm is a plant" or "A spruce has branches." The first statement asks whether one category is a member of another. The second statement asks about the features of a category member.

The average reaction times to six kinds of true sentences are shown in Figure 7.2. The three lower points about categorical relations support the prediction that it takes time to move between levels in the hierarchy. To verify statements such as "A canary is a canary" requires no change in level; "A canary is a bird" requires a one-level change; and "A canary is an animal" requires a two-level change. The upper three points show that it takes longer to respond to statements about features. Furthermore, as predicted, the level in the network where the features are stored influences response times.

Although these successful predictions are impressive, the hierarchical network model cannot account for other findings without additional assumptions. Although the data in Figure 7.2 are based on the average response times for many statements, it is possible to find some statements in which verification time is not a function of levels in the hierarchy. For example, it takes longer to verify that a chimpanzee is a primate than that a chimpanzee is an animal. The model should predict the opposite because primate is at a lower level in the hierarchy than animal. The second finding is that the network model does not account for the typicality effect—the fact that more typical members of categories are easier to classify than less typical ones. It is easier to verify that a canary is a bird than that an ostrich is a bird. However, because both are one level from "bird," as is illustrated in Figure 7.1, the model does not predict differences in response time.

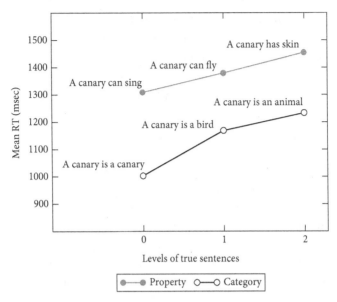

Figure 7.2. Reaction time (RT) to verify statements about properties (features) and category membership.

From A. M. Collins & M. R. Quillian, 1969, Retrieval time from semantic memory, *Journal of Verbal Learning and Verbal Behavior, 8,* 240–248.

It is for this reason that Alan Collins and Elizabeth Loftus developed the spreading activation model discussed in the previous chapter. The model has greater flexibility as illustrated by the assumption that more typical category members have shorter links and are therefore verified more quickly. Spreading activation is now one of the major theoretical constructs in cognitive psychology. Hierarchies nonetheless remain an important tool for people in organizing knowledge as shown in the next section.

Intuitive Ontologies

This section on diagramming knowledge began in Chapter 5 by contrasting cultural categorization with institutional categorization.

The spreading activation model in Figure 6.2 and the hierarchical network model in Figure 7.1 are examples of psychologists' attempts to represent people's shared cultural knowledge about colors, vehicles, birds, and fish. The Dewey Decimal system in Box 5.1 and the Periodic Table of Elements in Figure 5.1 are examples of institutional categories compiled by experts. There is a huge time gap between the cultural categories learned by preschoolers and the institutional categories organized by experts. This gap is filled by the millions of students who acquire academic knowledge.

Michilene Chi constructs ontologies to model students' reasoning on their journey to expertise. Ontologies are theories of knowledge based on hierarchical concepts. An intuitive ontology proposed by Chi to describe novice knowledge distinguishes between three ontological trees depicting *entities*, *processes*, and *mental states* (Figure 7.3). *Entities* in her ontology consist of *objects* and *substances*. *Processes* occur over time and can be *sequential* or *emergent*. *Mental states* are abstract, in one's mind. Parts of Figure 7.3 should look familiar because they depict familiar categories. Other parts, such as the distinction between sequential and emergent processes, are learned in school and will be discussed in subsequent chapters.

Chi uses her ontological framework to analyze how knowledge organization can influence resistance to conceptual change. One type of error is a "hierarchical" error that can occur within the same branch of the hierarchy. Categories within a branch—such as chairs, furniture, artifacts, and objects in Figure 7.3—enable new categories to inherit properties of the more general categories higher in the hierarchy. However, the inheritance of properties is imperfect and can result either in failing to inherit, or incorrectly inheriting, a property of a higher category. Failing to inherit a property is demonstrated by how beliefs about matter can differ from beliefs about a particular instance of matter as discussed by Andrew Shtulman and Joshua Valcarcel. This can result in contradictions such as "All matter has heat" but "Ice does not have heat."

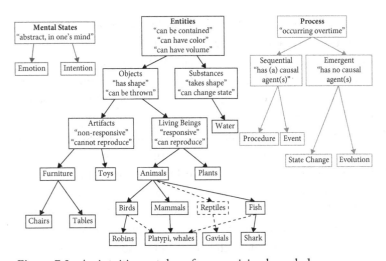

Figure 7.3. An intuitive ontology for organizing knowledge.
From M. T. H. Chi, 2013, Two kinds and four subtypes of misconceived knowledge, ways to change it and the learning outcomes. In S. Vosniadou (Ed.), *International handbook of research on conceptual change* (2nd ed., pp. 49–70). New York: Routledge.

Another example of inheriting a general property, as illustrated in Figure 7.3, involves identifying those situations in which both inanimate *artifacts* and animate *living beings* should inherit the properties of *objects*. While many studies of early knowledge development investigated learning the differences between animate and inanimate objects, some studies investigated situations in which both animate and inanimate objects should be treated as equivalent. Principles of physics such as force, mass, and acceleration apply to both animate (a child) and inanimate (a rock) objects. Gail Heyman found that seven-year-old children were more proficient than five-year-old children in appropriately transferring physics principles between these two kinds of objects.

Chi refers to categories that occupy different branches within an ontology as "laterally" different. She argues that misconceptions assigned to an inappropriate lateral category are more difficult to modify than a hierarchical error within the same branch. An example of a lateral error involves the distinction between *entities* (objects or substances that have volume) and *processes* (that occur over time). Chi discovered that students mistakenly think of force, heat, electricity, and light as *substances*, such as closing a door to keep the heat from escaping. Instead, she argued that heat should be thought of as the speed of molecules, which is a *process*. Ayush Gupta, David Hammer, and Edward Redish's view differs from Chi's ontology perspective. They argue for a more flexible perspective in which entities in the world may have multiple ontological classifications that are sensitive to context and can vary from moment to moment. Both novices and experts may therefore use either matter-based or process-based explanations to reason about the physical phenomena such as heat, light, and electronic current. I can appreciate the process explanation of heat based on the motion of gas particles but think of heat as an object when my wife and I pay our heating bills based on the amount and cost of gas.

Sean Carroll describes how different perspectives influence how we view reality by referring to the air in a room. We can think of air as a continuous fluid that has various properties such as temperature, density, humidity and velocity. But, at a microscopic level, it is composed of individual atoms and molecules. He explains:

> The different stories or theories use utterly different vocabularies; they are different ontologies, despite describing the same underlying reality. In one we talk about the density, pressure, and viscosity of a fluid; in the other we talk about the position and velocity of all the individual molecules. Each story comes with an elaborate set of ingredients—objects, properties, processes, relations—and those ingredients can be wildly different from one story to another, even if they are all "true."

These different perspectives present a challenge for experts who create formal ontologies to organize knowledge. Ontologies such as the Ontology Web Language play a critical role in retrieving knowledge to answer the questions we pose to computers. We will look at several of these ontologies in Chapter 16 when I discuss computer tools that are used in the Information Sciences.

Choosing a Diagram

The effective use of diagrams requires selecting the most appropriate one. This requires understanding how the diagrams differ from each other in their representation of information. In their article "To Matrix, Network, or Hierarchy: That Is the question," Laura Novick and Sean Hurley hypothesized 10 properties that could be used to distinguish between a matrix, a network, and a hierarchy to evaluate whether people use these properties when choosing a diagram.

One distinguishing property is the diagram's global structure. In a matrix, all the values of one variable share all the values of the other variable. In Table 5.1 each functional dimension in the matrix combines with each unit of analysis. In a network there is no predefined formal structure. The network in Figure 6.2 does not have a unique starting or ending node. In a hierarchy, the structure is organized into levels, beginning with a node that branches out into subsequent levels in which the identities of the nodes at a lower level depend on the identities of the nodes at the preceding level. The characteristics of a canary in Figure 7.1 depend on the characteristics of a bird, which depend on the characteristics of an animal.

Another distinguishing property concerns the pathways within a diagram. In the matrix shown Table 5.1, there are no links so it doesn't make sense to talk about moving along pathways. In the network shown in Figure 6.2 there can be multiple paths between nodes. For instance, one can go from "vehicle" to "fire engine" either directly or through any one of five intermediary nodes. In the hierarchy shown in Figure 7.1, there is only a single path from one node to another as illustrated by the path from "canary" to "bird" to "animal." So one property that should influence the choice of a diagram is whether specifying relations among concepts requires no paths, one path, or multiple paths.

Novick and Hurley tested their proposed properties by asking 23 college students (math educators and computer science majors) at Vanderbilt University to select the type of diagram that would be most efficient for organizing information in each of 18 short medical scenarios. Here is an example:

> In the psychiatric ward of a certain hospital, each patient sees only one doctor, who is responsible for diagnosis and treatment. A researcher is interested in determining whether patients would receive different diagnoses from different doctors. Therefore, she selected a group of newly-admitted patients and asked all of the staff psychiatrists to submit a diagnosis for each patient in the group. The department chair would like a diagram showing each doctor's diagnosis for each patient.

The results revealed that the students displayed a high level of performance in selecting the best representation, such as a matrix in the just cited example. They were required to verbally justify each selection and their justifications mentioned 9 of the 10 distinguishing properties identified by Novick and Hurley. These findings are obviously very encouraging, but we need to keep in mind that the participants were majoring in mathematics education and computer science at Vanderbilt. The results nonetheless provide a high bar that can serve as a goal when providing instruction on the selection of an appropriate diagram for organizing knowledge.

PART III
REASONING

8

Visuospatial Reasoning

I began my book *Thinking Visually* with the opening paragraph:

> Language is a marvelous tool for communication, but is greatly
> overrated as a tool for thought. Because we are constantly exposed
> to language, we believe that thinking verbally dominates our
> lives. Thinking visually, if it occurs at all, is hiding in the shadows.

My purpose in writing the book was not to deny the importance of
language but rather to document for a general audience the importance of visualization in comprehension, memory, and thought.

The importance of visual thinking was also documented by Roger
Shepard in his chapter on the imagination of the scientist. As a consequence of his own research on visual reasoning, Shepard became
interested in what scientists said about the mental processes that
resulted in their major achievements. Many of us have heard about
Albert Einstein's thought "experiments" in which he imagined him-
self traveling in a train or alongside a beam of light. Shepard reports
many other cases of how visual thinking aided the contributions of
James Clark Maxwell, Michael Faraday, Hermann van Helmholtz,
Sir Francis Galton, Jacques Hadamard, James Watt, Nicola Tesla,
Sir John Herschel, Omar Snyder, Friedrich Kekule, James Watson,
Richard Feynman, Stephen Hawking, and Mitchell Feigenbaum.
Shepard reports that many of these scientists had a childhood interest in physically manipulating objects, and some had delayed
language development. You can apply your own visual thinking to
the questions in Box 8.1.

Cognitive Skills You Need for the 21st Century. Stephen K. Reed, Oxford University Press (2020). © Oxford
University Press. DOI: 10.1093/oso/9780197529003.001.0001.

Box 8.1   Visual Reasoning Questions

---

1. Form a visual image of the Star of David. Does it contain (a) a triangle, (b) a diamond, and/or (c) a parallelogram (four-sided figure with parallel opposite sides)?
2. A monk leaves at dawn to hike up a mountain. The next day he leaves at dawn to hike down the mountain. Will he ever be at the same location at the same time as on the previous day?
3. You go on a round trip in which you drive to your destination at 60 mph. You encounter rush-hour traffic on your return trip that reduces your average speed to 30 mph. What was your average speed for the entire trip?

The questions in Box 8.1 are difficult, but that is the point. The answer to the first question is that the Star of David does contain a triangle, a diamond, and a parallelogram. You likely perceive the Star of David as two overlapping triangles so you could use your prior knowledge to answer the first question. It is typically difficult, however, to use a visual image to discover embedded figures that you had not previously noticed.

The answer to the second question is that the monk will be at the same location at the same time when hiking down the mountain. This answer may seem unlikely but try to simultaneously imagine the monk hiking up the mountain and down the mountain at the same time. At some point the "two" monks will meet and therefore be at the same location at the same time.

The third question defies mental simulation because it would require simulating particular speeds. A computer animation may nonetheless help people understand the problem and improve their estimates of the correct answers. That was our team's purpose in designing the Animation Tutor to assist people in visual reasoning.

Animation Tutor

The Animation Tutor provides animation and manipulation software to help students understand and solve mathematical problems. My book *Thinking Visually* contains an Animation Tutor DVD consisting of modules on Dimensional Thinking, Chemical Kinetics, Personal Finance, Population Growth, Average Speed, Catch Up, Task Completion, and Leaky Tanks.

Let's return to the question about average speed in which a car travels 60 mph in one direction and 30 mph in the other direction. What is the average speed for the entire trip? This is a typical problem on the Animation Tutor, as illustrated in Figure 8.1. The upper car simulates the problem, and the bottom car simulates the student's estimate of average speed. If the estimate is correct, the two cars complete the trip at the same time. Students typically estimate the arithmetic average—45 mph—and their car returns too quickly.

An answer of 45 mph would be correct if the driver spent the same amount of time traveling at 60 mph and at 30 mph. However, it took twice as much time to return at 30 mph. The correct answer is 40 mph and is found by weighting the two speeds by the relative amount of time spent traveling at those speeds. The equation in this case is:

Average Speed $= 1/3 \times 60$ mph $+ 2/3 \times 30$ mph $= 40$ mph

The Average Speed module explains the principle of a weighted average and provides animation-based feedback to help students

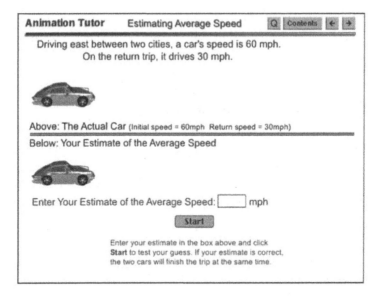

Figure 8.1. A screenshot from the Animation Tutor: Average speed module.

Created by S. K. Reed, J. Sale, & S. Phares.

improve their estimates. The Animation Tutor modules also enable students to evaluate the correctness of their solutions when they replace estimates by calculated answers.

Now think about a problem from the Catch Up module:

A man is standing on a bridge, 300 feet from the left side and 500 feet from the right side. A train is approaching the left side. If the man runs at a speed of 10 mph towards the train, he will reach the left end of the bridge just as the train does. If the man runs at a speed of 10 mph away from the train, he will reach the right end of the bridge just as the train overtakes him. What is the speed of the train?

The bridge problem can be solved algebraically by constructing two equations to solve for the two unknowns: the location and speed of the train. However, spatial reasoning enables the problem to be solved without having to do the algebra. You may want to try this approach before reading further.

The key is to imagine the man running at 10 mph away from the train, rather than toward the train. Where will the man be when the train reaches the left end of the bridge? Figure 8.2 shows the end of the animation. You now know the location of both the man and the train. The train has to cover four times the distance of the man to reach the right end of the bridge at the same time. The problem now becomes a simple proportional reasoning problem.

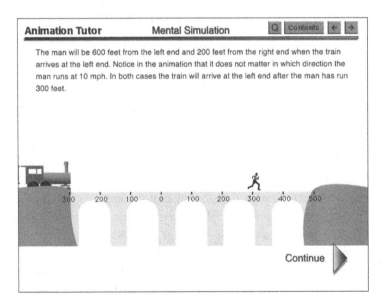

Figure 8.2. A screen shot from the Animation Tutor: Catch up module.

Created by S. K. Reed, B. Hoffman, & S. Phares.

Cognitive Architectures

Computers are needed to execute instructional software but they have indirectly influenced the construction of theoretical frameworks to organize cognitive processes. Allen Newell, the U. A. and Helen Whitaker Professor of Computer Science at Carnegie Mellon University when he died in 1992, proposed in his 1990 book *Unified Theories of Cognition* that cognitive architectures provided the necessary structure. Newell expressed his motivation for constructing unified theories in a 1973 paper titled "You Can't Play 20 Questions With Nature and Win." Typical psychological theories were constructed around dichotomies such as whether we process information in parallel or sequentially. Newell argued that even if a long list of dichotomies could be resolved, psychology would still lack in an integrated theory of cognition. He and his students had been working on an artificial intelligence system called Soar, and his book *Unified Theories of Cognition* explored how Soar could be expanded to serve as a cognitive architecture for organizing the findings of cognitive psychologists.

A cognitive architecture shows the interrelationships among the major components that support cognition such as perception, attention, memory, and action. Perception converts sensory stimuli into representations that can be stored in working memory or directly converted into actions by the motor component. Attention limits the amount of available perceptual information. Working memory provides a temporary storage space where perceptual information can be integrated with information from Long-term declarative and long-term procedural memory. Declarative memory is the store for facts and concepts. Procedural memory contains knowledge about actions. The motor component uses the body to execute the actions. I will discuss this cognitive architecture in Chapter 17 on general artificial intelligence.

A limitation of the initial design of Soar is that computers, being computers, prefer procedures rather than pixels. I was therefore excited to discover in 2011 that Scott Lathrop, Samuel Wintermute, and John Laird added a spatial/visual system to Soar to create Soar/ SVS. The primary new component was a visual buffer composed of pixels that can be set to a color or to a value indicating emptiness. The word *pixel*, an abbreviation for picture element, is the smallest visual unit on a screen. It determines screen resolution; for instance, a screen resolution of 1024 × 768 means there are 1,024 pixels displayed in each row and 768 pixels displayed in each column.

Motion occurs in Soar/SVS by shifting the location of the pixels that depict objects. Part of my excitement about the visual buffer resulted from my own experience in moving pixels on a computer screen. The Animation Tutor screenshots in Figures 8.1 and 8.2 move pixels and evolved from a simple computer program that I wrote in 1985 using Basic to run on my Apple II computer. I did not know how to create objects so I depicted each of the two cars in Figure 8.1 by a single pixel. Rather than watch cars go across the screen, participants in my research watched a race between two pixels that looked like two small dots. The pixels provided the necessary feedback on the accuracy of the estimates but I was concerned that students would soon become bored by watching the two pixels. Skilled programmers in the Animation Tutor project subsequently replaced the individual pixels by groups of pixels depicting cars, trucks, planes, and people.

SOAR/SVS moves pixels to provide information such as whether one object intersects another object. If the pixels representing a moving car overlap with the pixels representing the wall of a house, the driver is in trouble. Overlapping pixels is also a bad sign in video games. The first, and last, video game I ever played was called PAC-MAN. I had to navigate my character through a maze while being chased by another character. I was eaten when our pixels overlapped as it caught me, which usually occurred after 30 seconds. Then I had to watch one of my young sons avoid being caught for several minutes, followed by a several-minute turn by my other young son, before I played again for another 30 seconds.

You can understand now why it was the last video game I ever played. I have observed others playing more recent video games in which an overlap of pixels can result in an explosion. Video games have become more humane. I would rather die suddenly in an explosion than die slowly while being eaten.

Using Soar/SVS to Model Human Visuospatial Reasoning

My primary interest in Soar/SVS was to model human visuospatial reasoning. I did this by identifying the most relevant components of its cognitive architecture (visual buffer, spatial scene, predicate extraction, predicate projection, visual generation, procedural memory) for each of 16 tasks studied by psychologists, science educators, and computer scientists. I present three of those tasks here to illustrate how different aspects of Soar/SVS apply to each. A common denominator is that all involve visual simulations and therefore require the visual buffer.

The first task you can try for yourself. Form a visual image of the pattern in Figure 8.3 and then look away. Then see if you can use your visual image to reinterpret it as a new animal. Deborah Chambers and Daniel Reisberg performed this experiment at Reed College. None of the 15 participants could use their visual image

Figure 8.3.   An ambiguous figure.

From D. Chambers & D. Reisberg, 1985, Can mental images be ambiguous? *Journal of Experimental Psychology: Human Perception and Performance, 11,* 317–328.

to reinterpret the figure but all 15 could reinterpret the figure when reshown a drawing of the figure. Chambers and Reisberg hypothesized in a later study that people encoded and maintained only the more important attributes such as those on the face of the encoded animal. The slight indentation in the back of the duck's head is a subtle noncritical feature for the duck but is an important functional feature (the mouth) for the rabbit. People who perceived the figure as a duck should therefore have a detailed description of the left facial side of the duck and those who perceived the pattern as a rabbit should have a detailed description of the right facial side of the rabbit. The results from a recognition-memory test confirmed this hypothesis.

Reinterpreting visual images is difficult because of the loss of critical detail that is needed to form a new interpretation. The predicate extraction function of Soar/SVS is needed to account for this finding. Predicate extraction includes properties of objects such as size, symmetry, shape, and color. Only some of the features that determine the shape of the pattern were stored in the image. Participants therefore needed to take another look at the pattern to reinterpret it.

The second task requires designing useful and novel products by combing parts. Mentally combining parts utilizes the visual generation process in the Soar/SVS architecture. Examples of such tasks are discussed by Ron Finke in his book *Creative Imagery: Discoveries and Inventions in Visualization*. The parts in Finke's research consisted of three-dimensional forms such as a sphere, half sphere, cube, cone, cylinder, rectangular block, wire, tube, bracket, flat square, hook, wheels, ring, and handle. After either the experimenter or the participant selected three parts, the participants were instructed to close their eyes and imagine combining the parts to make a practical object or device. They had to use all three parts but could vary their size, position, and orientation. Participants were quite successful in executing this assignment and were more creative when the experimenter selected the parts. An important function of the visual buffer in this case is that it supports analogue operations such as shrinking, moving, and rotating.

The third task illustrates the use of visual simulation to derive rules for making predictions in a chain of events consisting of horizontally connected gears. Daniel Schwartz and John Black asked students at Columbia University, "If you turn the gear on the far left clockwise, which direction would the gear on the far right turn?" Students initially answered the question for different numbers of gears by mentally simulating the rotations in the visual buffer. After a few simulations they discovered a general rule: the last gear in the chain will rotate in the same direction as the first gear if the number of gears is odd and will rotate in the opposite direction if the number of gears is even. The procedural memory component of Soar/SVS can store the rule so subsequent questions can be answered simply by counting the number of gears.

Geographical Reasoning

In his chapter on cognitive geography, Daniel Montello defines the topic as the study of cognition about space, place, and the environment. It includes cognitive processes such as perception, thinking, learning, memory, attention, imagination, language, reasoning, and problem-solving. Cognitive geography considers both geographic knowledge that is directly acquired through interacting with the world and symbolic knowledge incorporated into materials such as maps. Its applications include improving spatial orientation, geographic education, map design, urban planning, and landscape design.

Barbara Tversky at Stanford and Columbia has done a lot of research on imagery in spatial reasoning, including how imagery can lead to distortions. She cites a study that asked the question, "Which city is further west—San Diego, California or Reno,

Nevada?" Research at the University of California, San Diego, revealed that even people who live in San Diego tended to answer this question incorrectly. To account for this and related geographical misconceptions, the investigators proposed that spatial information is stored hierarchically.

We have seen examples of how hierarchies support reasoning but occasionally they can trick us. There is a strong tendency to distort judged locations to conform with the location of regions higher in the hierarchy. Many people incorrectly infer that because California is west of Nevada, San Diego must be west of Reno. I confess that I would have made the same incorrect inference after being a resident of San Diego for over 30 years. The correct answer depends on knowledge of how the coastline of California curves southeastward.

Another type of geographical bias discussed by Tversky is that people tend to judge geographical areas as more aligned than they actually are. She discovered that one type of distortion occurs because people align North America and Europe along the same horizontal axis and North America and South America along the same vertical axis. I was surprised during a cruise from San Diego to Acapulco when we were told to make a time zone adjustment. I was even more surprised when the next day I had to make a second adjustment. I thought we were sailing " south" but Acapulco is more aligned with Dallas than with San Diego. The western coast of Central America and South America continues to curve eastward so most of South America is east of North America. I blame my error on faulty labels. If North and South America had more accurately labeled Northwest and Southeast America, I would not have made this mistake.

9

Imperfect Knowledge

Organizing knowledge would be much easier if knowledge were perfect. Computer scientist Adam Pease and I believe that both computers and people find it difficult to organize knowledge because it is imperfect. Box 9.1 lists seven types of imperfect knowledge, and we analyzed four of these (ambiguous, contradictory, misclassified, uncertain) in our article "Reasoning From Imperfect Knowledge." My goal in this chapter is to provide an introduction to the four kinds of imperfect knowledge described in our article and, as a bonus, throw in fragmented knowledge. I will discuss conditional and inert knowledge in Chapter 11 in the context of solving problems.

Ambiguous Knowledge

Words are responsible for a major proportion of ambiguous knowledge because they often have more than one meaning as we saw for the word *degree* in reference to networks. It is easy to compose sentences such as "A woman with 3 degrees sat in a 65-degree room studying a 4-degree node in which the links were separated by 90 degrees." However, context typically comes to our rescue. A context such as "weather" or "geometry" guides us toward a correct interpretation.

A classic study by David Swinney and Harold Hakes demonstrated that word ambiguity without a context slows comprehension. Participants in their study listened to sentences such as "Rumor had it that, for years, the government building had been

Cognitive Skills You Need for the 21st Century. Stephen K. Reed, Oxford University Press (2020). © Oxford University Press. DOI: 10.1093/oso/9780197529003.001.0001.

Box 9.1 Challenges for Reasoning From Imperfect Knowledge

Ambiguous knowledge. The challenge is to recognize and resolve the ambiguity. Resolving the ambiguity can be difficult but context usually provides a hint.

Conditional knowledge. The challenge is to identify conditions that distinguish between correct and incorrect applications of knowledge. These conditions support the appropriate transfer of information.

Contradictory knowledge. The challenge is to discover a contradiction when it is not immediately obvious. It can be difficult to find contradictions in a large knowledge base.

Fragmented knowledge. The challenge is to integrate related knowledge stored in long-term memory. One consequence of fragmented knowledge is that observations about the world are not connected to their causes.

Inert knowledge. The challenge is to activate relevant knowledge when it is needed. Inert knowledge is knowledge stored in long-term memory that is relevant for interpreting a situation but goes unnoticed.

Misclassified knowledge. The challenge is to identify and reclassify it. Misclassified knowledge is difficult to correct when it is partially effective in producing plausible explanations.

Uncertain knowledge. The challenge is to incorporate probabilities into reasoning. Probabilities determine our ability to predict the outcome of events.

Based on Reed and Pease (2017). Reasoning from imperfect knowledge. *Cognitive Systems Research, 41,* 56–72.

plagued with problems. The man was not surprised when he found several bugs in the corner of his room."

The ambiguous word *bugs* slowed comprehension relative to a control condition in which it was replaced by the unambiguous word *insects*. However, comprehension was not delayed when the sentence was elaborated with the phrase "he found roaches, spiders, and other bugs in the corner of his room." In this case the context made it clear that bugs referred to insects rather than to an electronic device used by spies.

This finding is likely unsurprising to you but there is a surprising interpretation based on subsequent research. Cognitive psychologists are clever at inventing experimental paradigms to study the mind, and one of these is the lexical decision task described in Chapter 6. The spreading activation model proposed by Collins and Loftus assumes that activation spreads from a word to prime words with similar meanings. We would therefore expect that interpreting *bug* as an insect would prime the word *ant* but not the word *spy*. Surprisingly, both *ant* and *spy* were recognized more quickly even with the constraining context referring to roaches and spiders. The context therefore did not suppress an initial incorrect interpretation but rather enabled listeners to more quickly select the correct interpretation following the activation of both meanings.

An advantage of activating multiple meanings occurs when the clarifying context comes after the ambiguous word. See whether you can find the ambiguous word in the following partial sentence: "Since Ken really liked the boxer, he took a bus to the nearest . . . " The ambiguous word is *boxer*, and we don't yet have enough information to know whether Ken is interested in a fighter or a dog. It is helpful to keep both interpretations of the word active in working memory until we have more information. People who have a large working memory capacity therefore have an advantage over people who have a smaller working memory capacity.

Contradictory Knowledge

One of the tasks of a computer while assessing a knowledge base is to check for contradictions. My computer scientist co-author designed the following task to illustrate how a computer does deductive reasoning to answer the question posed in Box 9.2. Computers and (some) people can apply rules of logic to answer the question.

The first six lines of Figure 6 in our article on reasoning from imperfect knowledge translated the six statements in Box 9.2 into formal logic. The next six lines applied rules of logic to derive conclusions. Line 13 in our derivation concluded that Heather will be fired. Line 14 concluded that Heather will not be fired. Computers can identify contradictions in a knowledge base, but people must then decide how to change them to make the statements logically consistent.

People also need to determine whether a computer's logically valid deductions actually make sense. I had to laugh when I saw the

---

Box 9.2 Will Heather Be Fired?

1. Either Heather attended the meeting, or Heather was not invited.
2. If the boss wanted Heather at the meeting, then she was invited.
3. The boss likes Heather.
4. Heather did not attend the meeting.
5. If the boss did not want Heather there, and the boss did not invite her there, then she is going to be fired.
6. The boss doesn't fire anyone he likes.

Based on Reed and Pease (2017). Reasoning from imperfect knowledge. *Cognitive Systems Research, 41*, 56–72.

following statements on a shirt worn by a Silicon Valley gas-station attendant:

I am nobody.
Nobody is perfect.
I am perfect.

The conclusion is logically valid but semantically suspect. Why? Multiple meanings of a word again raise havoc. The word *nobody* in the first statement refers to a person without influence. The same word in the second statement tells us that human beings, including the one mentioned in the first statement, are not perfect. Mixing the different meanings of *nobody* invalidates the conclusion. Humans have a large knowledge base that allows them to avoid errors a computer might make when it follows rules that do not make sense. The caveat is that because humans are not perfect, they may not always identify these errors.

Fragmented Knowledge

Fragmented knowledge is not well connected to other knowledge stored in long-term memory. Andy diSessa's knowledge-as-pieces theory provides an excellent example of how fragmented knowledge limits understanding the principles of physics. The pieces consist of small knowledge structures, typically consisting of only a few parts. Examples include balance, equilibrium, force, resistance, and work.

Let's look again at network D in Figure 6.1. The three clusters could represent pieces of knowledge about force, resistance, and work. Node *b* in the network connects them, but eliminate it and the concepts become fragmented, rather than integrated. Imagine that you are pushing a stroller toward the beach and you encounter greater resistance when the pavement turns to sand. You retaliate by increasing your force on the stroller. If node *b* were missing in your network, you might not even realize that you are now working harder.

The knowledge-as-pieces theory contrasts with those theories that propose knowledge involves a more coordinated use of concepts. Examples of the latter approach include Susan Carey's theory of conceptual development, Michilene Chi's theory of intuitive categories, and Stella Vosniadou's framework theory of conceptual change. diSessa, Sherin, and Levin refer to these theories as integrated systems consisting of strong internal constraints that differ from the fragmentation and independence of small clusters.

Vosniadou's framework theory provides an integration of the fragmentation and integration perspectives. She and Irini Skopeliti propose that children possess a relatively coherent conceptual system that they use to explain and predict everyday phenomena. However, problems arise when they learn science and must replace their ideas about intuitive physics. These problems may include the creation of fragmentary knowledge. Fragmentation occurs when learners create scientific explanations without concern for internal consistency and coherence.

For instance, many children initially classify the earth as a physical object that is distinct from other solar objects like the sun, the moon, and the stars. The later reclassification of the earth as a solar object changes it to a spherical planet rotating in space rather than a flat, stable physical object with the sky and solar objects above it. Instruction for conceptual change must support not only the acquisition of new explanations and theories, according to Vosniadou and Skopeliti, but hypothesis testing skills that will prepare students for meaningful, lifelong learning.

Misclassified Knowledge

Misclassified knowledge was a problem for the intuitive ontologies described in Chapter 7. People sometimes classify knowledge into the wrong category. Even institutions are not immune from misclassifications.

Misclassifications are revealed in institutional ontologies when an organization reclassifies its knowledge. In 2006, for the first time in its history, the International Astronomical Union defined the characteristics of a "planet" in our solar system and consequently demoted Pluto from "planet" to "dwarf planet." The society defined a "planet" as a celestial body that (a) is in orbit around the Sun, (b) has sufficient mass for its self-gravity to overcome rigid body forces so that it assumes a hydrostatic equilibrium (nearly round) shape, and (c) has cleared the neighborhood around its orbit. A "dwarf planet" has the first two attributes but not the third. The classification of Pluto as a dwarf planet creates ontological problems because "dwarf planet" would typically be a subclass of "planet" and therefore inherit its attributes, including a cleared neighborhood around its orbit.

There is a precedent in cognitive psychology, however, for a subclass not inheriting all of the attributes of its superordinate class. An attribute of a category example can override the attributes of its category in the hierarchical network model proposed by Collins and Quillian in Figure 7.1. For instance, the attribute "cannot fly" is stored at the example level for ostriches, overriding the attribute "fly" stored at the bird level. Organizing knowledge can benefit from such flexibility when necessary.

Uncertain Knowledge

There are many occasions in life when we anticipate a future event. We hope for the best, but life is uncertain. If we are fortunate, the event exceeds our expectations. Such an event occurred for me when I was working as a 20-year-old student at a hotel in the Bavarian Alps. The owners' son invited me to accompany him on a trip to Salzburg, Austria. We did not spend much time there but did learn that its residents were excited about a movie being filmed near the town. I eagerly waited for the movie to open and was mesmerized when the opening shot revealed a meadow surrounded by beautiful mountains. There appeared to a person standing in the meadow, which was confirmed as the camera slowly zoomed in on a spinning Julie Andrews. It was the most spectacular opening of a movie that I have ever seen, and the rest of the movie was delightful.

In their clearly written book *A Mind at Play: How Claude Shannon Invented the Information Age*, Jimmy Soni and Rob Goodman inform us that the information in Shannon's formulation is related to uncertainty. A coin that always lands heads or always lands tails would not provide any information. The maximum uncertainty, and maximum amount of information, occurs when a coin has a 0.5 probability of landing heads. Now imagine a coin in which both sides are heads. We would quickly get bored watching coin flips because we would know the outcome, which is the reason why I dislike sports dynasties.

A recent example of a sports dynasty is the New England Patriots football team. The Patriots have won six Super Bowl championships (XXXVI, XXXVIII, XXXIX, XLIX, LI, and LIII). They also played in and lost Super Bowls XX, XXXI, XLII, XLVI, and LII. I was not the only one disappointed that the Patriots again qualified for the 2019 Super Bowl. The *Wall Street Journal* sportswriter Jason Gay wrote in a prelude to the Super Bowl:

> It's gotten old, hasn't it? Wasn't it old five years ago? The Patriots, doormats in their early decades, have risen to become football's never-ending nightmare, it's destroyer of dreams, it's eradicator of souls – and that's putting it gently.

The only exception that I make for my dislike of sports dynasties is when the dynasty is one of my own teams. I arrived at UCLA in 1966, just in time to see Lew Alcindor (who later changed his name to Kareem Abdul Jabbar) come off the bench. It will seem odd in an era of one-and-done stars who leave for the NBA after their freshman year, but freshman were not allowed to play when one of the most highly prized recruits in the history of college basketball arrived at UCLA. But now he could play, and I was there to witness it by attending most of the home games.

I was doubly blessed that season because my Green Bay Packers arrived at the Los Angeles Memorial Coliseum in January for the AFL–NFL World Championship Game, later renamed Super Bowl I. The Coliseum was one-third empty so I had no trouble purchasing a $10 ticket. The Vince Lombardi coached Packers defeated the Kansas City Chiefs 35–10 in Super Bowl I, and the New England Patriots defeated the Los Angeles Rams 13–3 in Super Bowl LIII. After the game, the Patriots received the Lombardi Trophy, a reminder that a long, long time ago a team not named the Patriots had won a Super Bowl.

The only drawback in watching UCLA basketball games was that they lacked suspense. John Wooden coached UCLA to 10 national titles in 12 years from 1964 to 1975. I knew that UCLA was going to win when I attended one of their games. There was less predictability in the 2019 NCAA basketball finals. An article in the March 25th issue of *Sports Illustrated* informed us that Duke, Gonzaga, Kentucky, North Carolina, and Virginia were the clear favorites to reach the Final Four. Only Virginia made the trip. In contrast, three of the four predicted women's teams (Baylor, Connecticut, Notre Dame) survived. Women are apparently more predictable than men.

High predictability makes life routine but is typically quite helpful. We expect cars to stop at a red light, continue at a green light, and speed up at a yellow light. Cars continuing through a red light with a probability of 0.5 would be informative but the information would not be pretty.

10

Reasoning Strategies

There are some big names in this chapter. Two have won Nobel prizes. Daniel Kahneman at Princeton University won the 2002 Nobel Prize in Economics for the large body of research that he had conducted with Amos Tversky. He describes their research in his 2011 book *Thinking Fast and Slow*. Richard Thaler at the University of Chicago won the 2017 Nobel Prize in Economics for his research on behavioral economics. His 2008 book *Nudge: Improving Decisions About Health, Wealth, and Happiness* with Cass Sunstein describes their philosophy. Another big name is author Michael Lewis who wrote best sellers such *The Big Short* (2010) before writing *The Undoing Project: A Friendship That Changed Our Minds* (2016) about Kahneman and Tversky's collaboration. Some of his books have been made into movies.

Kahneman describes two types of reasoning in *Thinking Fast and Slow*, which he labels System I and System II. I have collected characteristics of these two types and display them in Table 10.1. This chapter contrasts each of these characteristics.

Associations Versus Rules

Steven Sloman at Brown University made a distinction between reasoning that is based on associations and reasoning that is based on rules (Table 10.2). Associative reasoning uses associations such as

Cognitive Skills You Need for the 21st Century. Stephen K. Reed, Oxford University Press (2020). © Oxford University Press. DOI: 10.1093/oso/9780197529003.001.0001.

Table 10.1 Characteristics of Two Types of Reasoning

System I	System II
Associations	Rules
Intuitive	Analytic
Fast	Slow
Biases	Competencies
Nudges	Boosts
Novices	Experts

Table 10.2 Associative Versus Rule-Based Reasoning

Characteristics	Associative System	Rule-Based System
Principle of operation	Similarity	Symbol manipulation
Source of knowledge	Personal experience	Language and culture
Relations	Associations	Causal and logical
Nature of processing	Reproductive	Productive
	Automatic	Strategic
Functions	Intuition	Deliberation
	Creativity	Formal analysis
	Visual recognition	Verification
	Associative memory	Strategic memory

Based on Sloman (2002). Two systems of reasoning. In T. Gilovich, D. Griffin, & D. Kahneman (Eds.), *Heuristics and biases: The psychology of intuitive judgment* (pp. 379–396). Cambridge, UK: Cambridge University Press.

the ones represented in the semantic networks of Chapter 6. Many are learned through personal experiences rather than through cultural institutions such as schools. In contrast, causal and logical rules support strategic reasoning. The correct application of a rule is often determined by the relations among symbols rather than by the meaning of the symbols. For example, you can apply rules to solve for x in the equation $11 + x = 14$ without knowing the meaning of x.

Intuitive Versus Analytic

The distinction between intuitive and analytical thinking is apparent in Table 10.2. Gordon Pennycock, Jonathan Fugelsang, and Derek Koehler at the University of Waterloo use the questions in Table 10.3 to clarify this distinction. Try answering these questions before reading further to classify your own thinking.

The correct answer to the first question on base-rate neglect is that it is more likely that Jack is a lawyer because most of the people tested were lawyers (the base rate). Kahneman and Tversky nonetheless found that participants typically answered Jack is an engineer because of the similarity between Jack's description and their

Table 10.3 Sample Questions to Evaluate Analytical Thinking

Name	Example Items
Base-rate neglect	In a study, 1,000 people were tested. Among the participants there were 5 engineers and 995 lawyers. Jack is a randomly chosen participant of this study. Jack is 36 years old. He is not married and is somewhat introverted. He likes to spend his free time reading science fiction and writing computer programs. What is most likely? (a) Jack is a lawyer, or (b) Jack is an engineer.
Belief bias syllogism	All mammals can walk. Whales are mammals. Therefore, whales can walk. Is this logically valid?
Cognitive reflection test	A bat and a ball cost $1.10 in total. The bat costs $1.00 more than the ball. How much does the ball cost? ___ cents If it takes 5 machines 5 minutes to make 5 widgets, how long would it take 100 machines to make 100 widgets? _____ minutes. In a lake, there is a patch of lily pads. Every day, the patch doubles in size. If it takes 48 days for the patch to cover the entire lake, how long would it take for the patch to cover half of the lake? _____ days.

Based on Pennycook, Fugelsang, and Koehler (2015). Everyday consequences of analytic thinking. *Current Directions in Psychological Science, 24*, 425–432.

stereotype of engineers. The intuitive answer to the second question is that it is not logically valid because whales cannot walk. However, the statements follow the rules of logic and are therefore logically valid.

The last three questions are from the Cognitive Reflection Test designed by Shane Frederick. The intuitive answer to the bat-and-ball question is $0.10 but the bat would then cost $1.10 for a total of $1.20. The intuitive answer to the machine question is 100 minutes. The correct answer is five minutes because increasing the number of machines increases the number of widgets by the same proportion during an equal time period. The intuitive answer to the lake question is 24 days. The correct answer is 47 days because on the 48th day the patch doubles in size to fill the entire lake.

Pennycock, Fugelsang, and Koehler report that the emphasis on studying intuitive thinking has caused less effort devoted to studying analytic thinking. As a result, research on the real-world consequences of analytic thought is still in its infancy. They lobby for more research to identify the causes of analytic thinking and investigate those aspects of our everyday lives in which analytic thinking is most consequential.

Fast Versus Slow

Daniel Kahneman's book *Thinking Fast and Slow* describes two forms of reasoning that he refers to as System I and System II. System I is fast and intuitive while System II is slow and analytical. His book focuses on the biases of System I. His goal is to help us improve our ability to identify errors of judgments so we can make better judgments.

Kahneman and Tversky's research challenged two ideas that Kahneman informs us were widely accepted when they began their work in the 1970s. The first is that people are usually rational and their thinking is normally sound. The second is that emotions such as fear and affection cause departures from rationality. Their research findings revealed a different picture in which cognition causes errors when people rely too much on System I. The bat-and-ball question in Table 10.3 can serve as an example. If you made a mistake on this question, you have lots of company. Shane Frederick and Daniel Kahneman studied this question and found that more than 50% of the students at such elite universities as Harvard, MIT, and Princeton gave the incorrect intuitive answer. More than 80% of the students gave the incorrect answer at less elite universities. Kahneman finds the failure to check the answer to be remarkable because it takes only a few seconds. He reports that people apparently place too much faith in their intuitions and avoid cognitive effort as much as possible.

Keith Stanovich at the University of Toronto has constructed a detailed model of the interaction between three stages that involve relevant knowledge, detection of errors from System I processing, and overriding those errors through System II processing. Knowledge is an initial prerequisite for detecting System I errors. A respondent who has no conception of a base rate will not detect a base-rate error when answering the first question in Table 10.3 because of a lack of knowledge. The second stage—detection of errors from System I processing—is illustrated by Kahneman's analysis of the bat-and-ball problem. Students know the simple arithmetic procedures to check their answer but did not use them. The third stage occurs when a person realizes a System I answer is incorrect but does not know how to use System II to correct it. Students may learn from the software in Figure 8.1 that the average speed of a round trip is not simply the arithmetic average but do not know how to calculate the correct answer.

Another aspect of Stanovich's analysis is that not all fast responses are incorrect and not all slow responses are correct. A fast, correct response occurs when an expert automatically generates a quick response based on her expertise. A slow, incorrect response occurs when a nonexpert realizes a System I response is incorrect but fails to generate a correct System II response.

Biases Versus Competencies

Heuristics are typically defined as strategies that often work but do not guarantee success. Kahneman and Tversky decided to study those situations in which the strategies did not work. They identified biases that would help us make better decisions if we understood and corrected these biases. In contrast, a group at the Max Planck Institute for Human Development in Berlin, Germany, has studied situations in which strategies do work.

Gerd Gigerenzer has directed the Institute and contributed many techniques that have proven effective. He defines a "heuristic" in his book *Risk Savvy* as a conscious or unconscious strategy that ignores part of the information to make better judgments. It enables us to make a decision fast, with little search for information, but nevertheless with high accuracy. The Berlin group has often labeled such heuristics "fast and frugal."

One of their examples is "imitate your peers." If you do not know what to do in an unfamiliar environment, a good strategy is simply to follow what others are doing. This strategy worked for me as I was standing on a platform in the western suburbs waiting for the Metra to take me into Chicago. The platform was almost a block long, and I was surprised to see that people were waiting in two long lines rather than distributing themselves along the platform. I saw no markings or signs that indicated where people should wait but I thought it was a good idea to get in one of the lines. The strategy worked as only some of the doors on the Metra opened to let us board.

One of the studies discussed in *Risk Savvy* asked Germans about the populations of cities in Germany and in the United States; for instance, which city has a larger population, Detroit or Milwaukee? Many of the Germans had not heard of some of the cities in the United States such as Milwaukee. I had to recover from my shock before I could read further. I grew up near Milwaukee, and Germans made the city. They built German-speaking schools, contributed to its intellectual culture, opened fine German restaurants, ate bratwurst, and established commercial breweries such as Pabst Brewing Company, Schlitz Brewing Company, and Miller Brewing Company. Saying that Germans had not heard of Milwaukee is like saying that Americans had not heard of Berlin after President Kennedy claimed he was a Berliner and President Reagan ordered Mr. Gorbachev to take down the Berlin wall.

The lack of knowledge about smaller American cities nonetheless was an advantage because Germans could apply a recognition heuristic that states the recognized city (Detroit) is likely the larger city. Only 60% of Americans correctly answered that Detroit is larger than Milwaukee because they had heard of both cities while 90% of the Germans were correct. I am proud of the 40% of Americans who answered that Milwaukee is the larger city because it gives Milwaukee the credit it deserves. The 2020 Democratic Convention is scheduled to be held in Milwaukee. It should be interesting and it should put Milwaukee on the map.

Fast-and-frugal methods can also be helpful in providing guaranteed correct solutions such as in the following problem posed in Kahneman's *Thinking Fast and Slow*:

Adam switches from a gas-guzzler of 12 mpg to a slightly less voracious guzzler that runs at 14 mpg. The environmentally virtuous Beth switches from a 30 mpg car to one that runs at 40 mph. Who will save more gas by switching if both drivers drive equal distances over a year?

I concur with Kahneman that thinking about the problem intuitively suggests that Beth will save more gas and that his provided analytic solution—based on 10,000 miles—shows that Adam will save more gas. However, I took a fast-and-frugal approach by assuming that each driver drove 120 miles in a year because I could do the division in my head. Beth would reduce her gas requirements from 4 gallons to 3 gallons while Adam would reduce his requirements from 10 gallons to 8.6 gallons. The fast-and-frugal method answers the question with simpler mathematics. The method is an efficient algorithm in this case because, unlike a heuristic, the method guarantees a successful solution if I correctly perform the math. If I then scale up to from 120 to 12,000 miles to obtain a more realistic number Beth would reduce her gas requirements from 400 gallons to 300 gallons while Adam would reduce his requirements from 1000 gallons to 860 gallons.

Nudges Versus Boosts

In their book *Nudge: Improving Decisions about Health, Wealth, and Happiness*, Richard Thaler and Cass Sunstein at the University of Chicago advocate an approach that they label "libertarian paternalism." The first word implies that people should be free to make their own choices. The second word implies that institutions should steer people's choices in directions that will improve their lives. Libertarian paternalism will not prevent people from smoking cigarettes, eating unhealthy food, and failing to save for retirement. It will, however, attempt to nudge them in a direction that will be more beneficial.

One of my favorite examples of nudges in *Nudge* slows drivers as they navigate dangerous curves on Chicago's Lake Shore Drive. A sign that warns drivers to slow down is followed by a series of white stripes on the road. The stripes are evenly spaced but become closer as drivers approach a dangerous curve. The closer stripes give an impression of increasing speed that causes the drivers to reduce their speed.

One temptation that many of us struggle with is avoiding too many calories. Would a nudge push us in the right direction? What if we choose the dessert first rather than last? A research team investigated this question at a university cafeteria with a fixed-price menu consisting of a soup, main dish, side dish, bread, and either an indulgent (lemon cheesecake) or a healthy (fresh fruit) dessert. When the indulgent or the healthy dessert was presented first, approximately two thirds of the participants who chose the lighter main dish were in the indulgent-dessert condition. They compensated for the unhealthy dessert by selecting a main dish that had lower calories. The same results occurred when participants made selections online. Those participants who were initially assigned chocolate cake as their dessert were more likely to select a healthier entrée than those participants who were assigned fruit salad as their dessert.

An alternative to nudging is boosting. Ralph Hertwig in Berlin's Max Planck Institute for Human Development and Till Grune-Yanoff in Stockholm's Royal Institute of Technology argue that nudging steers good decisions whereas boosting empowers good decisions. The goal of boosting is to create competencies through enhancing skills, knowledge, and decision tools. Hertwig and Grune-Yanoff classify nudging as Type I processing because nudges do not require critical thinking. They classify boosting as Type II processing because instruction creates new procedures and mental tools to help people make better decisions. Boosts require active cooperation and investment in time, effort, and motivation. Individuals decide whether to engage or not to engage with a boost.

Nudging and boosting are clearly two different approaches to changing behavior. I can see merits in both. The stripes on Lake Shore Drive are an ingenious solution to correct speeding in a particular situation. A course on the dangers of speeding offers the possibility of reducing speed in a wide range of situations, but who would voluntarily enroll? Traffic tickets for speeding sometimes require attending such classes, creating an opportunity for boosting. We are fortunate that both the advocates of nudging and the advocates of boosting have provided us with options for improving behavior. We can take advantage of boosting to carefully decide which option best fits a particular situation if the advocates on both sides do not try to nudge us in their direction.

Novices Versus Experts

I spent the summer of 1993 as a Summer Faculty Fellow at the Navy Personnel Research and Development Center on Point Loma overlooking the San Diego Harbor. My assignment was to assist Josephine Randall and Larry Pugh on a project that studied the effect of expertise on the performances of 28 electronic warfare technicians from the U.S. Navy. The technicians proceeded through a 35-minute training scenario involving an accurate simulation of military action in the North Pacific. They performed their jobs as they would on ship, reporting and recording friendly, unknown, and hostile radar contacts and tracking the movements of friendly and enemy ships on a radar screen. Operator actions, verbal reports, and interactions with the software were videotaped.

Providing a theoretical framework for analyzing these data would have been unmanageable if we had conducted the study a year earlier. We were lucky. A book titled *Decision Making in Action: Models and Methods*, edited by Klein, Orasanu, Calderwood, and Zsambok, was hot off the press. The central argument of the book is that the traditional models and methods for studying decision-making are not very helpful in explaining what people do in emergency situations. The reason is that the traditional approach focuses on a single event in which the decision maker evaluates a fixed set of alternatives to select the best alternative. In contrast, emergency situations have a number of characteristics that distinguish them from more traditional decisions:

1. Emergency situations typically involve ill-structured problems in which the decision maker has to do significant work to generate hypotheses about what is happening.
2. Decision-making occurs within an uncertain, dynamic environment. Information about what is happening is often incomplete, ambiguous, and of poor quality.

3. There may be shifting or competing goals as the situation changes.
4. Responses to emergency situations require reacting to a sequence of events rather than to a single event. This creates action–feedback loops in which the decision maker has to react to the consequences of each action before determining the next action.
5. There is often considerable time pressure. Lack of time will typically produce less complicated reasoning strategies and perhaps high levels of personal stress.
6. There are high stakes, particularly in life threatening situations.
7. Often there are multiple players. Although there is usually a single person in charge, the leader interacts with others to solve the problem.
8. Organizational goals guide the decision-making.

All of these characteristics applied to our project on military engagement and now apply to the coronavirus pandemic.

One of the chapters in *Decision Making in Action* by Gary Klein proposed a recognition-primed decision model based on his interviews of commanders who fight forest fires. Rather than evaluate many alternatives, they reported that they used their prior experience to immediately generate and modify plans in reaction to the changing situation. Klein's model is called "recognition-primed" because of its emphasis on situation assessment and recognition of what is occurring. Once the situation is recognized, experienced decision makers can usually quickly identify an acceptable course of action rather than consider multiple options.

We measured situation awareness during the Navy training exercise by blanking the computer screen (Figure 10.1) and asking the electronic warfare technicians to reconstruct from memory the location of the ships they had been tracking. Experience was a major factor in their accuracy. Experts correctly drew the locations for

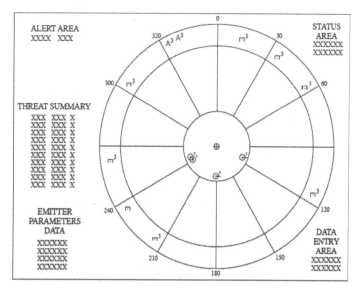

Figure 10.1. Computer screen for the electronic warfare task.

From J. M. Randel, H. L. Pugh, & S. K. Reed, 1996, Differences in expert and novice situation awareness in naturalistic decision making, *International Journal of Human-Computer Studies, 45,* 579–597.

95% of the hostile ships, compared to 78% for intermediates, and 51% for novices. They correctly located 74% of the friendly ships, compared to 53% for intermediates, and 21% for novices.

I wondered in 1993 when we were collecting our data whether such complex naval battles would still occur. A lack of training and situation awareness, however, can also lead to loss of life during peaceful maneuvers. On the morning of June 17, 2017, the *USS Fitzgerald* collided with a container ship bound for Tokyo, killing seven of the crew while injuring several others. A report by the Navy concluded that its "crew was unprepared for this situation in which they found themselves through a lack of preparation, ineffective command-and-control, and deficiencies in training and preparations for navigation." Another collision followed on August 21, 2017, off the coast of Singapore in which 10 crew members of the *USS John S. McCain* loss their lives. The Navy found there was "a loss of situational awareness" while responding to mistakes in one of the world's busiest shipping lanes. New directives now require Navy ships to broadcast their positions in crowded shipping lanes and make it more difficult for ships to leave port if their crews lack basic navigation skills.

Institutions, like people, have limited lives. A base closure unfortunately extinguished the research at the Navy Personnel Research and Development Center.

PART IV
PROBLEM-SOLVING

11

Problems

Problems frequently occur in our daily and professional lives. My wife and I encountered one such problem when we acquired a two-month-old puppy. We had previously avoided puppies when my wife smartly acquired our three previous dogs after they had outgrown the puppy stage. But on this occasion she became enamored by watching labradoodle puppies on a website. I reluctantly agreed to this new adventure and had to admit that our new puppy was cute. I include her picture so you can judge for yourself (Figure 11.1).

We had done our homework by reading the book *Puppies for Dummies*. The book informed us that puppies are born with an innate sense of mischief and the best remedy is patience. Peaches loss no time in confirming the book's predictions by creating a playpen without bars on our back patio where she dragged her toys and any other objects that fit into her mouth, including bathroom rugs. On one occasion I followed a trail of unrolled toilet paper from our bathroom through our master bedroom to Peaches's favorite location on the patio. I didn't see who did it, but I have a suspect.

I particularly wanted to protect my shoes so vowed to keep my closet doors closed. However, this obvious solution failed because I was frequently distracted by projects such as writing this book. On two occasions, the stolen objects included one of my shoes, but she lured me into a false sense of security by not harming them. On the third occasion I discovered a badly damaged shoe. I quickly developed a counterplan by hiding my four remaining pairs in the back of my closet and placing the damaged shoe at the front to serve a decoy. I knew I was in trouble the next day when I discovered

Cognitive Skills You Need for the 21st Century. Stephen K. Reed, Oxford University Press (2020). © Oxford University Press. DOI: 10.1093/oso/9780197529003.001.0001.

Figure 11.1. A troublemaker.
Photographed by Tian Reed.

three shoes on the patio, including another destroyed one. The two destroyed shoes were both parts of pairs that differed only in color so there remained the possibility of polishing the two remaining shoes the same color. Peaches, however, had anticipated and blocked this move by destroying two left shoes so I had only two right shoes left. I finally solved the problem by finding shelf space in the guest bedroom that was out of her reach.

At least Peaches was not as bad as Marley. As documented in a book and in a movie, Marley was the world's worst dog. Our family fled Boca Raton, Florida, before Marley's arrival so I emailed a friend to enquire about Marley sightings. He replied that Marley and his family had been neighbors. One day he discovered an article of clothing on the ground that had been hanging on the clothesline. He did not know how it got there, but he had a theory.

In his 1973 article "The Structure of Ill Structured Problems," Herbert Simon compared ill-structured with well-structured problems. Puzzles such as the missionaries and cannibals problem are good examples of well-structured problems. The problem requires transporting missionaries and cannibals across a river with the constraint that cannibals cannot outnumber missionaries in the boat or on either side of the river. It is well structured because both the goal and the constraint on actions are clearly defined. An example of an ill-structured problem for Simon was designing a house in which the actions and final design slowly evolve. An ill-structured problem for me was trying to outwit a determined puppy.

I became interested in revisiting the topic of ill-structured problems because most of the research on problem-solving continued to focus on well-structured problems. I decided to update research on both types of problems within a taxonomic framework.

A Strategy × Problem Taxonomy

I mentioned in Chapter 9 on imperfect knowledge that I would discuss five types of imperfections in that chapter and later discuss inert and conditional knowledge in this chapter. Inert knowledge is knowledge stored in long-term memory that is relevant for interpreting a situation but goes unnoticed. It confronted me head on as I wrote the manuscript on the distinction between ill-structured and well-structured problems by comparing puzzles, insight puzzles, classroom problems, and ill-structured design problems. I had experience in creating taxonomies based on matrices, but matrices require two dimensions, and I had only a single dimension that identified the four types of problems. My

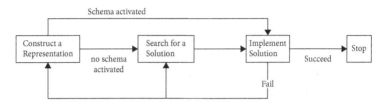

Figure 11.2. Problem-solving strategies.
From M. Gick, 1986, Problem-solving strategies, *Educational Psychologist, 21*, 99–120.

manuscript was rejected for a lack of organization that one reviewer appropriately described as meandering.

Improving the manuscript required finding a second dimension that would apply to the four types of problems. After much unproductive reflection, I finally found one after recalling a general model of problem-solving strategies that had been proposed by Mary Gick at Carleton University (Figure 11.2). It enabled me to effectively organize the manuscript, which was then quickly accepted by an excellent journal.

It amazes me, however, that I had not thought of this organization much earlier. I include Figure 11.2 in my cognitive psychology textbook and lectured on it in class. Discovering methods to bring inert knowledge to the surface would have both theoretical and practical significance. I will present one such method later in the chapter.

Table 11.1 presents my strategy × problem taxonomy that combines the four strategies discussed by Gick with the four problem types. The problem solver begins by constructing a representation to understand the problem by focusing on the goal, the constraints, and provided information. This construction may activate a schema if the problem is familiar. We learned in Chapter 4 that schemas provide generic knowledge structures for encoding and interpreting particular experiences.

In her book *Schemas in Problem Solving*, Sandra Marshall began by reviewing the historic development of schemas as a theoretical

Table 11.1 A Strategy × Problem Taxonomy

Strategy	Puzzle	Insight Puzzle	Classroom	Design
Representation				
Schema				
Search				
Analogy				

Based on Reed (2016). The structure of ill-structured (and well-structured) problems revisited. *Educational Psychology Review, 28,* 691–716.

construct by tracing the ideas of Plato, Aristotle, Kant, Bartlett, and Piaget. In her working definition, a schema is a memory organization that can (a) recognize similar experiences; (b) access a general framework that contains essential elements of those experiences; (c) use the framework to draw inferences, create goals, and develop plans; and (d) provide skills and procedures for solving problems in which the framework is relevant.

If the problem is unfamiliar and schematic knowledge is not activated, the problem solver must search for a solution by using general search methods such as means–end analysis and subgoals. Means–end analysis guides the search process by identifying moves that reduce the difference between the current problem state and the goal state. Subgoals are intermediate problem states between the initial and goal state that also guide the search process. Analogy is another general search process that works by attempting to find and then adapt a solution of a similar problem. These general strategies are typically labeled "heuristics" because they apply to many types of problems but do not guarantee success. If initial attempts to solve the problem are unsuccessful, the problem solver can attempt to construct a new representation of the problem or switch strategies.

I will use the taxonomy in this chapter to compare how representation, schema activation, search, and analogy apply to the

Box 11.1 Sample Problems

1. Produce the number 56 by combining four 7s with the standard arithmetic operations of adding, subtracting, multiplying, dividing, and using parentheses. There are no constraints on the arithmetic operations, but you need to use all four 7s.
2. Move a single stick in the problems below to turn an incorrect arithmetic statement into a correct one. The stick cannot be discarded but must occupy a new position in the equation.
3. Plant four small trees so they are exactly the same distance from the others.
4. A medical procedure requires using radiation to destroy a tumor without destroying the healthy tissue that surrounds it. Devise a procedure.
5. Estimate the concentration of a mixture of if three pints of a 20% acid solution are mixed with seven pints of a 40% acid solution.

three types of relatively well-structured problems—puzzles, insight puzzles, and classroom problems. Box 11.1 contains five problems that appear in this chapter. It will help you better understand the chapter if you try to solve them. The next chapter completes the taxonomy by focusing on ill-structured design problems.

Puzzles

The initial interest in programming computers to solve puzzles required them to produce, rather than simulate, intelligent behavior. The 1969 book *GPS: A Case Study in Generality and Problem*

Solving by George Ernst and Allen Newell contain early examples of these activities. GPS is an abbreviation for General Problem Solver, which had the goal of using general principles to solve a variety of puzzles including the Tower of Hanoi, missionaries and cannibals, and logical proofs. The General Problem Solver was not completely general because it focused on problems that could be solved by using means–end analysis. Means–end analysis attempts to successively eliminate differences between the initial problem state and the goal state until the program arrives at the goal state. This strategy is often successful on problems with a well-defined goal state: all disks moved to another peg in the Tower of Hanoi or all missionaries and cannibals moved across the river.

These early artificial intelligence programs provided possible theories of how people solve problems. In their 1972 book *Human Problem Solving*, Allen Newell and Herb Simon described their application of computer programs to simulate intelligent behavior of humans. They accomplished this by asking people to think out loud as they worked on the problem. They next translated the thoughts into a computer program and then executed the program to determine whether it could simulate human problem-solving. Programming a computer requires a detailed specification of the operations, which enabled them to evaluate whether the operations were sufficient to produce the behavior. It thereby avoided the vagueness that limited many other theories of higher mental processes.

The construction of logical proofs is an example. Problem solvers were given 12 rules that allowed them to modify logical expressions until they transformed the initial problem state into the goal state. For instance, transforming the initial state, A ⊃ B, into the goal state – B ⊃ – A, requires eliminating differences in both the sign and the position of the letters. Many aspects of their thinking corresponded to the means–end analysis used in the General Problem Solver.

A limitation of heuristics is that they are not always helpful. For instance, means–end analysis is of limited use in solving the problem of producing the number 56 by combining four 7s with the standard arithmetic operations of adding, subtracting, multiplying, dividing, and using parentheses. There are so many combinations of these symbols that it is difficult to find the correct one. Another heuristic—working backwards—is more effective when there are many possibilities leading from the initial state and relatively few possibilities connected to the goal state. The factors of 56 (the goal state) are 28×2, 14×4, and 7×8. The latter is particularly promising because it uses one of the 7s, creating the subgoal of combining three 7s to make the number 8. The answer is $7 \times (7 + 7/7)$.

Insight Puzzles

Many of the puzzles studied in the 1970s such as missionaries/cannibals and the Tower of Hanoi were transformation problems that required changing the initial state of the problem into the goal state by making a sequence of moves. Before scientists constructed computer programs to model transformation problems, Gestalt psychologists in Germany studied arrangement problems that could be solved quickly in one or two steps if the solver could identify those steps. They used the term "insight" to describe the sudden discovery of a correct arrangement of the parts following a succession of incorrect arrangements.

Janet Metcalfe and David Wiebe empirically evaluated this claim by giving students arrangement problems such as planting four trees exactly the same distance from the others. Every 15 seconds the participants had to indicate on a 7-point scale how close they believed they were to solving the problem. Although the highest rating was the most frequent rating at the solution, the lowest rating was still the most frequent rating 15 seconds before the solution.

The findings supported the construct of insight in which solutions occur very suddenly following a perceived lack of progress.

One interpretation of these findings is that insight occurs when solvers remove self-imposed constraints. For example, people typically attempt to solve the four-trees problem (Box 11.1) in two dimensions although this constraint is not mentioned in the problem. The solution requires a three-dimensional pyramid. Gunther Knobich and his coauthors evaluated the theory of constraint relaxation by asking participants to rearrange matchsticks. The objective was to move a single stick to turn an incorrect arithmetic statement into a correct one, as illustrated in Box 11.1.

Their findings confirmed the predictions based on constraint relaxation. Type a problems are solved by modifying the numerals (changing IV to VI) and were the easiest. Type b problems are solved by modifying arithmetic operations (moving a matchstick from the equals sign to the minus sign). Type c problems are solved by creating more than one equals sign and were the most difficult. The three types of problems became equally easy after participants learned what constituted legal moves.

You may have noticed that I have not mentioned schema activation when discussing either puzzles or insight puzzles. The reason is that schemas are organized knowledge structures, and puzzles are typically unique so people have to use general strategies to solve them. But instruction could encourage people to notice, and take advantage of, similarities between problems through schema abstraction—as demonstrated in a classic study by Mary Gick and Keith Holyoak in 1983. Three years earlier they had published research that demonstrated the difficulty of spontaneously noticing analogous solutions. Their goal in this earlier research was to increase the number of convergence solutions to Duncker's radiation problem mentioned in Box 11.1. The convergent solution divides the radiation to converge on the tumor without destroying the healthy tissue. Participants read an analogous problem in which a general wanted to capture a fortress but could not attack along one road because it was mined. The general therefore divided his army into small groups that simultaneously converged on the fortress from different roads. Very few participants, however, used the analogy to solve the radiation problem unless they were given a hint that the military problem would help them.

To spontaneously notice an analogy, people need to think about analogous solutions at a more abstract level so differences in the objects, such as a fortress and a tumor, would not be a hindrance. Gick and Holyoak therefore asked participants to compare the similarities between two stories, the military problem and a story about Red Adair whose crew put out fires in oil derricks by using multiple hoses that converged on the site of the fire. Comparing two stories helped participants spontaneously notice the analogy and solve the radiation problem by creating a more abstract convergence schema. Simply reading the two stories was insufficient; abstraction depended on making the comparison.

Classroom Problems

The transition from the study of puzzles to the study of classroom problems in the 1980s resulted in investigations of how knowledge of mathematics and science influenced problem-solving. Ed Silver asked good, average, and poor problem solvers to sort arithmetic word problems into groups based on common solution procedures. The better problem solvers excelled at this assignment, but the weaker problem solvers sorted by story content. For example, they placed coin problems into the same category although the problems required different solutions.

Silver's finding has been confirmed for many domains and for many levels of expertise. Chi, Glaser, and Reese at the University of Pittsburgh asked eight undergraduates and eight advanced physics doctoral students to sort 24 physics problems into categories based on similar solutions. Undergraduates tended to classify problems on the basis of common objects such as inclined planes and springs. Experts tended to classify problems based on physics principles such as the conservation of energy or Newton's second law $(F = MA)$.

One approach for improving knowledge in the classroom is to assist students in learning a new topic by drawing an analogy to a familiar topic. Consider the task of estimating the concentration of a mixture when three pints of a 20% acid solution are mixed with seven pints of a 40% acid solution. These kinds of questions proved difficult for students unfamiliar with chemistry. They are another example of a weighted average problem like the average speed problem discussed in Chapter 8. The answer requires weighting the two acid concentrations by the proportion used. The answer is 0.3 × 20% + 0.7 × 40% = 34%. Now consider the related task of estimating the temperature of a mixture when three pints of a 20°C water solution are mixed with seven pints of a 40°C water solution. Arthur Evans and I found that students performed very well on this more familiar task and were able to transfer this knowledge to improve their estimates on the unfamiliar chemistry problems.

Another helpful instructional method was based on Gick and Holyoak's finding that comparing two analogous solutions helped people formulate a schema to identify similar problems. Gentner, Lowenstein, Thompson, and Forbus applied this finding in a negotiation-training program at Northwestern University for management consultants who had approximately 15 years of work experience. The consultants initially had difficulty describing the principles of a contingent contract. They then studied two cases of a contingent contract that depended on the outcome of some future event. In one case, either a buyer in the United States or an Asian manufacturer would pay the cost of freight depending on whether a boat shipment arrived on time. In another case, the distribution of profit between two brothers from selling the family farm depended on whether the price of the main crop would rise or fall. One group studied the two cases separately, and another group compared the similarities of the two cases. As found in laboratory studies, the comparison aided schema abstraction. The comparison group was more successful in describing the principles of a contingent contract and in recalling previously inert examples of contingent contracts from their own experiences.

Although expert-defined schemas are usually very helpful, they can occasionally constrain innovative solutions. David Robson provides numerous examples in his book *The Intelligence Trap*, including Edison and Einstein. Thomas Edison refused to abandon his belief that direct current is superior to alternating current even after one of his own engineers, Nikola Tesla, strongly argued in favor of alternating current. Albert Einstein refused to abandon his theory of general relativity after mounting scientific evidence against the theory. Both men exhibited cognitive entrenchment.

Erik Dane defines "cognitive entrenchment" as a high level of stability in knowledge schemas that can cause experts to be inflexible in their thinking. Cognitive entrenchment increases the likelihood of problem-solving fixation and blocks the generation of novel ideas. Dane proposes two factors that can reduce cognitive entrenchment. The first is working in a dynamic environment in which one must remain open to a wide range of possibilities and options. The second is focusing attention on outside-domain tasks in which counterexamples and exceptions can increase the flexibility of one's beliefs. We will look at an example of cognitive entrenchment, and its avoidance, in the next chapter on design problems.

12

Design

Don Norman, a cognitive scientist at the University of California in San Diego (UCSD), raised our awareness about bad design in his 1988 book *The Psychology of Everyday Things*. Norman wrote the book for a general audience as an introduction to design. One of his goals was to make us more aware of poor design, particularly involving modern technology. He also wanted to make us more aware of good design, which is more difficult to recognize because it works well and therefore does not attract attention.

One of my favorite examples of poor design is the instructions on a towel dispenser on the UCSD campus (Figure 12.1). The instructions begin with the worthy objective of using only one towel to prevent waste. They next recommend shaking one's hands 10 to 12 times over the sink. I have used this dispenser on many occasions and can attest to the fact that one towel is more than sufficient without shaking my hands. The instructions conclude by telling users to fold the towel in half. I also ignore this advice because I would then have only half a towel to dry my hands. The instructions are so bizarre that I wondered whether a psychologist had designed an experiment to determine if anyone follows them. I can imagine that if someone did, the psychologist would immediately emerge from behind the door and hand that person a personality questionnaire.

Twenty-five years later, Norman published a revised and expanded edition of his book (*The Design of Everyday Things*) based on new examples and his experiences as an executive at companies such as Apple. He also added a greater emphasis on emotion as a key component of product satisfaction.

Cognitive Skills You Need for the 21st Century. Stephen K. Reed, Oxford University Press (2020). © Oxford University Press. DOI: 10.1093/oso/9780197529003.001.0001.

Figure 12.1. A towel dispenser without a clue.
Photographed by the author.

My favorite example of providing emotional support (from another book) is that designers of Terminal 5 at Heathrow Airport in London added an "up" button in an elevator even though the elevator could only travel in one direction and to one floor. When pushed, the button lit but did not connect to anything. Its sole purpose was to keep people from panicking after entering the elevator and discovering no way to control it.

Characteristics of Design Problems

Box 12.1 summarizes the major characteristics of design problems formulated by Vinod Goel and Peter Pirolli. Many of these characteristics reflect the characteristics of ill-structured problems described by Herb Simon. The initial, goal, and intermediate states are incompletely specified. There are no right or wrong answers, only better and worse ones. The size and complexity of the problems require decomposition into smaller problems or

---

Box 12.1   Characteristics of Design Problems

---

1. The three components of design problems—the start state, the goal state, and the intermediate states—are incompletely specified.
2. There are typically physical, social, economic, political, and legal constraints on the design.
3. The problems are large and complex.
4. Decomposition into smaller parts is determined more by the designer than by the structure of the problem.
5. There are many contingent interactions among the components.
6. Design problems do not have right or wrong answers, only better and worse ones.
7. Functional information mediates in many ways between the input and output information.
8. Feedback must be simulated or generated by the designer during the problem-solving process.
9. The cost of errors can be high.
10. The product is required to function independently of the designer.
11. There is a distinction between specification of the product and its construction.
12. Specification precedes delivery of the product.

Based on Goel and Pirolli (1992). The structure of design problem spaces. *Cognitive Science, 16,* 395–429.

---

modules. Constraints come from a variety of sources: physical, social, legal, and economic. The designer must request feedback, and the cost of errors can be high.

Research by Goel and Pirolli required three experts to either design a post office, a bank teller machine, or technical training material. The experimental protocols revealed that not only did the experts interpret the problem situation through their personal experiences, but they would also occasionally try to explicitly change the problem to more closely fit their expertise, knowledge, and experience. They would attempt to negotiate changes in the initial state and goal state that would be more easily achievable or might lead to a more effective design. The detailed verbal protocols were instrumental in identifying the characteristics of design problems listed in Box 12.1.

To provide a basis for comparison with nondesign problems, Goel and Pirolli also asked undergraduates to solve well-structured problems that had been studied by Newell and Simon. A major difference between the design and nondesign verbal protocols regarded the incremental development of knowledge. Abandoning an unproductive attempt in the nondesign problems seldom required reusing the knowledge gained from the abandoned attempt.

In contrast, Goel and Pirolli found considerable incremental development when experts returned to a previous module within the design. For instance, the designer of a post office divided the task into four modules that included an outdoor site plan. The location of seats went through several phases that placed the seats (a) below the evergreens, (b) next to the building structure, (c) away from the building, and (d) along the borders. These findings support Simon's claim that the same information-processing framework developed for puzzles also apply to design problems. Simon proposed that design consists of a combination of using means–end analysis to guide search on well-structured subproblems and continually modifying the search by retrieving from long-term memory new constraints, new subgoals, and new design alternatives.

A difference between design and nondesign tasks concerns the Gestalt concept of insight. Goel later listed two differences between classic insight problems and insight in real-world design problems. First, insight in Gestalt problems typically reveals the solution whereas insight in the more complex design problems typically reveals only an important step toward achieving the solution. Second, insight problems are usually well structured while design problems have both well-structured and ill-structured components. As the designer progresses from the preliminary to the final design, the problem becomes more structured.

Discovering Nature's Design

We typically think of a designer when reflecting on design but let's shift perspectives for a moment to consider the perspective of the scientist. Many of the characteristics of design problems in Box 12.1 also apply to the quest by scientists to discover nature's design. This is the topic of Mario Livio's book *Brilliant blunders: From Darwin to Einstein— Colossal Mistakes by Great Scientists That Changed Our Understanding of Life and the Universe.* I summarize one of his case studies—the race to discover the structure of DNA between Linus Pauling at the California Institute of Technology and the team of James Watson and Francis Crick in the Cavendish Laboratory at Cambridge University.

According to Livio, any knowledgeable person betting on the winner of the DNA race should have picked Linus Pauling. He was the most brilliant structural chemist of his day. In September 1951 *Life* magazine contained a picture of a smiling Linus Pauling standing next to his physical model of the alpha helix molecule. The title of the article is "Chemists Solve a Great Mystery: Protein Structure Is Determined."

At approximately the same time, James Watson and Francis Crick's theorizing had sufficiently advanced for them to present their structural model of DNA to a group at King's College, London, where Maurice Wilkins and Rosalind Franklin were taking X-ray diffraction pictures of nucleic acid. The Watson and Crick model, then based on three helical strands, had a number of inconsistencies with the research at Kings College. Their presentation was a total disaster. Pauling was also working on the structure of DNA so Watson and Crick eagerly awaited the arrival of his manuscript. They were surprised to discover that his three-strand model with the bases (adenine, thymine, guanine, cytosine) on the outside was similar to the model that they had already abandoned as completely wrong. But only Watson and Crick discarded their initial faulty model. Why?

Livio proposes that two memory lapses contributed to Pauling's incorrect construction. One was Erwin Chargaff's discovery regarding the relative amounts of the bases in DNA. The number of adenine (A) molecules equaled the number of thymine (T) molecules and the number of guanine molecules (G) equaled the number of cytosine (C) molecules. Pauling's model ignored these ratios. The second memory lapse concerned Pauling's own prior remarks. Four years earlier he proposed in a lecture that if genes consisted of two parts that were complementary to each other, the two parts could serve as a mold for replication. This principle strongly supports two strands and would be difficult to accomplish with three strands.

Pauling continued to rely too much on his previously successful alpha-helix protein structure in his search for the structure of DNA. It is a good example of cognitive entrenchment, defined in the previous chapter as a high level of stability in knowledge schemas that can cause experts to be inflexible in their thinking. A contributing factor was likely that Pauling worked in relative isolation whereas Watson and Crick benefited from the Kings College criticism of their initial faulty proposal. In addition, Livio argues that the Watson and Crick had equal seniority and therefore were open to frequently criticizing each other's ideas.

Another key difference is that Watson and Crick had quicker access to Franklin's X-ray diffraction photos of DNA. There still remained the difficult task of building a model but Watson and Crick utilized information that Pauling had ignored. Chargaff ratios showing an equal amount of the A and T bases and of the G and C bases suggested a possible pairing of A with T and of G with C, as shown in Figure 12.2. The final structure was the now-famous double helix consisting of two helical strands of alternating

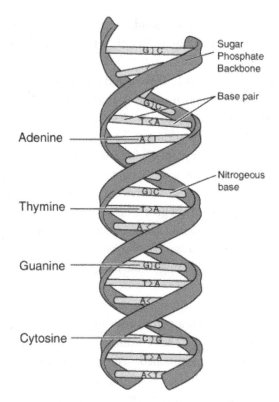

Sugar
Phosphate
Backbone

Base pair

Adenine

Nitrogeous
base

Thymine

Guanine

Cytosine

Figure 12.2. DNA structure and bases.
From Wikimedia Commons.

phosphates and sugars with the paired bases forming the rungs. Watson and Crick recognized the functional advantage of their proposed structure. The pairing of the two strands suggested a possible copy mechanism for genetic material.

The Geisel Library

Like Herb Simon, many of us associate the word *design* with buildings. I love architecture and am fortunate to have lived in three of the most beautiful communities in United States—Shaker

Heights, Ohio; Boca Raton, Florida; and now La Jolla, California. One of my favorite buildings in La Jolla is the Geisel Library on the UCSD campus.

In June 1965, William L. Pereira and Associates were asked to design the central library to serve as a key building for the entire campus and subsequently prepared a 91-page report. The firm began by studying existing campus libraries. Four designs looked promising: a multitower plan, a subterranean plan, a gateway plan, and a compound plan. A tower would reduce floor size and provide poor connections between stacks. A subterranean plan would have extensive floors but not proclaim the library as the heart of the University. A gateway would make a significant design statement but restrict future expansion. A compound that consisted of several buildings in a park setting would have poor circulation among stacks.

The final design, shown in Figure 12.3, consisted of raising a spherical structure from a plaza above the ground floor. Donald Davidson, chairman of the California Librarian Association buildings committee, commented, "Pereira has dramatically done the aesthetic task within the scope of library needs. I wish I could talk with my hands on paper to describe the 'sculptural tour de force' building being considered at San Diego." In my opinion, the library perfectly supplements other iconic buildings by Pereira such as the LAX Theme Building at the Los Angeles International Airport and the Transamerica Pyramid in San Francisco.

In 1995, the university changed the name of the library to the Geisel Library after Audrey Geisel's generous contribution of money and original works of her late husband Ted Geisel. If you don't recognize his name, it is because he wrote under the pen name "Dr. Seuss." The plaza level includes a life-size statue of Dr. Seuss working at his desk with a cat in a hat peering over his shoulder (Figure 12.4). The statue and the building behind it are lasting legacies that honor two brilliant designers. I visit the library three days a week and always enjoy the view as I approach it from the

Figure 12.3. The Geisel Library.
From https://www.flickr.com/photos/belisario/2700271091/

central walkway. Its only defect is that it contains the infamous towel dispenser shown in Figure 12.1.

Cathedrals of Culture

Cathedrals of Culture is a collection of buildings filmed by six acclaimed filmmakers. The film's website informs us that the buildings are material manifestations of human thought and action: the National Library of Russia, a kingdom of thoughts; Halden Prison, the world's most humane prison; the Salk Institute, an institute for breakthrough science; the Oslo Opera House, a futuristic symbiosis of art and life; the Centre Pompidou, a modern culture machine; and the Berlin Philharmonic, an icon of modernity.

Figure 12.4. Dr. Seuss at his desk.
Photographed by the author.

The Berlin Philharmonic concert hall, designed by German architect Hans Scharoun, was completed in 1963 as a futuristic replacement for the previous concert hall that was destroyed in World
War II. I attended a concert in the new hall in 1964 as a 20-year-old
student spending a week in Berlin. I was more interested in the new

building than in the music and was thrilled by its interior. It was an impressive example of the rebuilding of West Berlin.

I met a young journalist from Hamburg during my stay in Berlin, and we decided to venture into East Berlin. The Berlin wall had been constructed three years earlier, but it was possible to take a train directly into East Berlin where we disembarked at Friederichstrasse. The contrast between East and West Berlin could not have been more striking as we walked down streets of bombed buildings. I was nonetheless grateful to see the remnants of old Berlin. The rebuilding of West Berlin had made it reassemble an American city and therefore less interesting to a student from America.

The mastermind behind Cathedrals of Culture hoped to recruit Robert Redford as one of the film directors so offered him the choice of selecting any building in the United States. Redford selected the Salk Institute in La Jolla.

The Salk Institute

Many others share Redford's admiration. The Salk Institute for Biological Studies occupies a bluff overlooking the Pacific Ocean, not far from the Geisel Library. It was established in 1960 by Jonas Salk, developer of the first safe and effective polio vaccine. Salk selected the internationally renowned architect Louis Kahn to design spacious laboratory spaces that could be adapted to the changing needs of science. The building had to be simple, durable, and as maintenance-free as possible.

Architectural critic Paul Goldberger wrote about the majesty of the design in a 1996 article in the *New York Times*. He described the buildings as consisting of two identical four-story structures of concrete and teak, set parallel to each other and perpendicular to the Pacific. Goldberger was particularly impressed with the travertine-paved courtyard separating the two buildings, which he designated as the greatest outdoor room in American architecture since Thomas Jefferson's lawn at the center of the University of Virginia campus.

It was expected that the site would need to be expanded at some point, and that's when the trouble began as explained by Goldberger. Salk began by hiring two architects who had worked on the original design with Kahn, who had died in 1974. They had the almost impossible task of designing a new East building that would not infringe upon the rest of the Institute. Numerous critics protested the plans, which resulted in some modifications that included moving the new building further from the existing structures.

I attended a lecture in the East Building shortly after its completion and was pleased to discover that the building was set back from the rest of the Institute. A few minutes before the lecture began, Francis Crick walked down the aisle and sat in the seat in front of me. He had joined the Salk Institute in 1976 and was now its acting director. I divided my attention between the lecturer and the back of Dr. Crick's head, wondering what he was learning from the presentation that I was missing. As we left the lecture hall, I asked Dr. Crick whether there was still a controversy about the new building. He replied that, with only a few exceptions, most people were very satisfied.

Paul Goldberger gave it his mixed blessing:

> Approaching the Salk Institute is now nothing like what it was, but it is still possible to stand at the head of Kahn's great space, facing the sea, and almost put out of your mind what hovers behind. Kahn made architecture not only out of concrete but out of fusing the earth, the sea and the sky into a composition of incomparable strength and grace. The majesty of that has not been destroyed by the sycophantic fussing beside it, though it surely has been diminished. The Salk Institute remains intact—almost.

Seeing the expansion for myself was both enjoyable and informative but it was overshadowed by my brief conversation with Francis Crick. I was ecstatic the rest of the day. I had talked to a person who had contributed to one of the greatest discoveries in the history of science.

13

Dynamics

My office at San Diego State University was located in the Center for Research in Mathematics and Science Education. We had several office managers during the 26 years that I occupied it. One of them, Judith Leggett, informed me that her brother is a physics professor at the University of Illinois and he is very good. I did not know how objective her assessment was until one morning she excitedly exclaimed that her brother had won the Nobel Prize in Physics. I was convinced.

Designs occasionally create structures that move, and the 2003 Nobel Prize in Physics was awarded jointly to Alexei Abrikosov, Vitaly Ginzburg and Anthony Leggett for pioneering contributions to the theory of superconductors and superfluids. According to the Nobel Prize website, certain metals at low temperatures (a few degrees above absolute zero) allow an electric current to pass without resistance. Some allow superconductivity and magnetism to exist at the same time and remain superconductive in high magnetic fields. Alexei Abrikosov succeeded in explaining this phenomenon by expanding on a theory of superconductors by Vitaly Ginzburg and others. Although formulated in the 1950s, these theories have gained renewed importance in the rapid development of materials with new properties. Materials can now be made superconductive at increasingly high temperatures and strong magnetic fields. The decisive theory explaining how atoms interact in the superfluid state was formulated in the 1970s by Anthony Leggett. Recent studies show how this interaction passes into chaos or turbulence, which is one of the unsolved problems of classical

Cognitive Skills You Need for the 21st Century. Stephen K. Reed, Oxford University Press (2020). © Oxford University Press. DOI: 10.1093/oso/9780197529003.001.0001.

physics. Change over time, including transitions into new states, is the topic of this chapter.

Facilitating Flow

As someone interested in the organization of knowledge, I am delighted when I discover unifying theories that integrate diverse topics. Adrian Bejan, an engineering professor at Duke University, has spent much of his career developing such a theory based on his constructal law. A very readable summary of his theory appears in an interview published in the February 2–3, 2019 weekend edition of *The Wall Street Journal*.

The key idea is that design in nature evolves in a manner that facilitates the movement of the substances that flow through it by forming tree-like structures. This principle applies to both physical systems such as rivers and biological systems such as the circulatory system. Networks of brooks, streams, and large tributaries efficiently move water to the mouth of the major rivers such as the Mississippi and the Danube. The circulatory system has a similar structure in which a main channel, the aorta, pumps blood throughout the body through networks of arteries, veins, and capillaries. Highways move large number of vehicles through networks of freeways, toll roads, avenues, streets, and lanes.

These ideas are clearly explained in the book *Design in Nature* by Adrian Bejan and J. Peder Zane. The left circle in Figure 13.1 shows the structural similarity between the branching of rivers and the circulatory system. Bejan does more than show analogies between designs; he applies the principles of physics to predict how designs optimize flow. For instance, resistance is minimized when the rate of inhaling and exhaling is proportional to the mass of the animal raised to power of 0.24. Smaller animals should therefore breathe more rapidly than larger animals, which is consistent with numerous measurements. Also, regardless of size, the rate of inhaling should be the same as the rate of exhaling.

The middle circle shows the branching structure of trees, a flow system that transports water from the ground to the air. In addition to overcoming friction and gravity to move water upward, a tree must stabilize itself against stress caused by the wind. The constructal law reveals that every aspect of its design—the shape of its roots, trunk, branches, and leaves—facilitates the movement of water and reduces the effects of stress. I was not surprised to learn that trees have a tree-like structure, but I was surprised to learn that this same structure occurs across many systems, including the ones in the left circle.

The right circle in Figure 13.1 depicts the evolution of animals from the water to the land to the air. Fish are buoyant when they float but must push against the water when they swim. The only place where the displaced water can go is to the surface. Runners push against the ground to move forward while birds push against the air to fly. At each stage of biological evolution, changes occurred

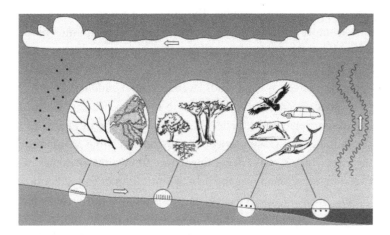

Figure 13.1. The physics of design facilitates flow in nature.
From A. Bejan & J. P. Zane, 2013, *Design in Nature*. New York: Random House. Courtesy of Adrian Bejan.

that enhanced movement. Land animals require less work to cover a certain distance than the sea animals that came before them. Insects and birds, similarly, require less work to cover the same distance than land animals of the same weight. The design principles illustrated in Figure 13.1 are only a few of the many discussed by Bejan and Zane.

Resolving Conflicts

Although nature is designed to facilitate flow, people are not. Conflicts often result in stalemates, and one does not have to search far to find one. The year 2019 began with conflicts on both sides of the Atlantic. In the United States, much of the federal government was shut down in an attempt by President Trump to gain congressional funding for a border wall between the United States and Mexico. In the United Kingdom, Prime Minister May was unsuccessfully seeking approval for her Brexit plan for the United Kingdom's exit from the European Union.

In their *American Psychologist* article "Rethinking Intractable Conflict: The Perspective of Dynamical Systems," Robin Vallacher, Peter Coleman, Andrzej Nowak, and Lan Bui-Wrzosinska propose that the dynamical systems perspective provides a coherent theory of conflict resolution. A key aspect of their proposal is that conflict is influenced by attractors that are difficult to escape.

A spatial metaphor of an attractor is a valley in a hilly landscape. The width of the valley represents the range of states that converge on the attractor. The depth of the valley represents the strength of the attractor—its resistance to change. Figure 13.2 illustrates this spatial metaphor for two attractors that correspond to (a) constructive relations and (b) destructive relations. Attractor *A* in this example has a wide, shallow basin. It attracts a wide range of states but the low strength of these states makes it easy to move to another attractor. Attractor *B* in this example has a relatively deep basin

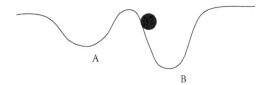

Figure 13.2. A dynamical system with two attractors corresponding to constructive relations (A) and destructive relations (B).

From R. R Vallacher, P. T. Coleman, A. Nowak, & L. Bui-Wrzosinska, 2010, Rethinking intractable conflict: The perspective of dynamical systems, *American Psychologist, 65,* 262–278.

indicating its strength but is relatively narrow. It attracts a smaller range of states than attractor *A*, but the strength of these states makes it more difficult to escape.

The width and depth of a basin can vary independently across attractors. The basin of any attractor can be wide and deep, narrow and deep, wide and shallow, or narrow and shallow. For instance, marital discord could be caused by a potentially large number of annoying acts such as forgetting to turn off lights, inefficiently stacking dishes in the dishwasher, and leaving the toilet seat up. These acts should not be very harmful, resulting in the broad, shallow basin of attractor *A*. In contrast, an act such as infidelity would likely result in the narrow, deep basin of attractor *B*.

The theory proposed by Vallacher and his co-authors distinguishes among several types of attractors—positive attractors, negative attractors, and latent attractors. Positive attractors facilitate progress toward a positive outcome such as reducing stress, building confidence, or resolving a conflict. Negative attractors impede progress toward a positive outcome. For example, a person's self-evaluative thoughts may give rise to chronically low self-esteem or a group may develop a conspiracy theory that maintains tension and mistrust toward other groups.

But an understanding of attractor dynamics can be beneficial because attractors are dynamic and susceptible to change. There are two general ways in which an attractor can change and promote a search for strategies that better optimize problem solving. One scenario is to disassemble the attractor so it can be more productively reassembled. Examples in the book *Groupthink* illustrate how removing the constraint of group coherence fosters greater flexibility. A positive attractor for mutual respect and feelings among the group members may inadvertently interfere with constructive analysis. Groupthink can be overcome, however, by removing the constraint of group coherence that blocks diverse ideas. In this approach, a member of the group is appointed to be the devil's advocate whose role is to question or challenge the specifics of proposals. The critiques may remove the initial constraint of group coherence so the group can select among a greater variety of plans for solving the problem.

A second scenario for changing an attractor is to utilize a latent attractor that has receded to the background but can supplant the original attractor under the right set of conditions. In a system with multiple attractors, only one is manifest at a particular time. The other latent attractors are not present and may not even be suspected. Latent attractors are nonetheless important because they determine possible stable states to which the system could converge when conditions change. An article in the April 17, 2019 issue of *The Wall Street Journal* announced that Apple and Qualcomm had ended a long legal battle by dismissing all litigation related to their battle over patent royalties. The article reported that the emergence of fifth-generation (5G) wireless speeds likely drove the agreement as both companies would benefit through future cooperation. In such cases, the original attractor is not disassembled but rather loses its salience in favor of an alternative frame for thinking and acting.

Compromising

I began discussing conflict resolution by pointing to political turmoil within both the United States and the United Kingdom. The conflicts did not go away. Prime Minister May later announced her resignation after repeated failures to seek approval for a plan regarding United Kingdom's exit from the European Union. President Trump failed to gain congressional funding for a border wall between the United States and Mexico. Congress did build a wall, but it was down the center aisle separating Democrats from Republicans. This was possible because Republicans sit on one side of both the House and the Senate while Democrats sit on the other side. It reminds me of the awkwardness of early school dances in which the girls congregated on one side of the room and the boys on the other side. At least these two groups were trying to cooperate.

One consequence of this wall occurred later in the year when the House of Representatives passed a resolution to investigate President Trump's dealing with Ukraine, setting in motion an agenda that resulted in the fourth presidential impeachment investigation in United States history. The 232–196 vote in favor of the investigation illustrated the sharp partisan divide in which only two of the House members crossed party lines. It would be difficult to find a better example of Groupthink.

A lack of interaction among members of opposing parties because of their physical separation may be partially to blame for such divisions. A recent article in the *Academy of Management Review* discusses research on how the design of office space can either foster or constrain work relationships. Spatial design influences three aspects of communication: face-to-face communication frequency, communication duration, and communication content. Closer spatial proximity encourages the exchange of work-related knowledge and enhances problem-solving. Informal interactions help different groups resolve differences and develop a shared understanding of problems that can make it easier to collaborate, share information, and develop trust.

Although the authors limited their analysis to office space, their conclusions should be relevant to other workspaces such as the halls of Congress. The spatial separation of opposing parties does not occur for institutions such as the United Nations General Assembly in which nations are seated alphabetically rather than by political affiliation. I recommend that members of Congress should also be seated alphabetically by their last name. It would cost very little to reorganize seating, and it may help reduce conflicts. At the very least, it would eliminate plotting against people seated across the aisle.

It is easy to wave a finger at the failure of others to compromise. It is more difficult to point a finger at oneself. In Figure 11.1, I labeled a puppy named Peaches a troublemaker. I was so focused on protecting my own turf from destruction that it required several months before I even considered Peaches's perspective. From her perspective, she was not a troublemaker. She was a little puppy who was trying to find some adventure in the quiet home she shared with a retired couple.

One of Peaches's favorite activities was to drag rugs from our two bathrooms out to her favorite spot on the patio. My wife and I decided to let her continue with this activity. Every few days we would retrieve the chewed rugs from the patio and replace them in the bathrooms so Peaches could return them to their proper location on the patio. It was a small price to pay to bring a bit more joy into the life of a puppy.

Comparing Theories

I accidently discovered the "Rethinking Intractable Conflict" article as I was searching for articles by Robin Vallacher and Dan Wegner on action identification theory. Robin and I were colleagues at Florida Atlantic University when they published their initial article in 1987. Another colleague, Scott Kelso, founded the Center for Complex Systems and Brain Sciences at Florida Atlantic University two years earlier. The laboratory was developing empirical and conceptual frameworks to explain how coordinated patterns form, persist, adapt, and change. I attended fascinating lectures on dynamical systems at the Center but did not perceive a connection between their interests in motor behavior and my interests in problem-solving.

"Rethinking intractable conflict" reveals how dynamical systems theory applies to problem solving so I invited Robin to collaborate on a manuscript to compare the similarities and differences between dynamical system constructs and the information-processing constructs that I had been using to model the puzzle, insight, classroom, and design problems described in Chapter 11. Table 13.1 reveals our attempt to find corresponding theoretical constructs that can serve as a basis for this comparison.

Comparing the characteristics of a problem space and a state space provides a starting point for identifying similarities and differences between the two perspectives. The problem space shows all the legal moves for solving a problem while the state space (Figure 13.2) shows only a few key problem states. Unlike a problem space, we do not know the details of the operations for moving about in the state space. A problem space would look more like a state space if problem solvers abstracted from the details in solving a problem, leaving only a few key subgoals. Research has revealed situations in

Table 13.1 A Mapping of Dynamical System Constructs to Information-Processing Constructs

Dynamical System	Information Processing
State space	Problem space
Positive attractor	Productive subgoal
Negative attractor	Impasse
Latent attractor	Implicit cognition
Nonincremental change	Insight

From Reed and Vallacher (2020). A comparison of information processing and dynamical systems perspectives on problem solving. *Thinking & Reasoning*, 26, 254–290.

which problem solvers remember only plans and subgoals rather than the detailed actions of a solution. A state space would look more like a problem space if problem solvers represented actions at a more detailed level, as discussed in Chapter 3. For instance, the joyful anticipation of a wedding is usually accompanied by many details for its successful execution as the date approaches.

Positive attractors in our comparison represent productive subgoals that are on the solution path and bring the problem solver closer to the solution. A similarity between subgoals and attractors is that both attract. A difference between subgoals and attractors is that attractors are more permanent than subgoals. A subgoal, however, can continue to be an attractor in more complex design tasks as we saw in the previous chapter on design. Decomposition of a design into subproblems is similar to forming subgoals in which planning can include leaving, and then returning to, previous subproblems for further development. An example was the design of a post office in which the architect repeatedly returned to the subgoal of planning outdoor seating as the design of the building progressed.

Our mapping equates a negative attractor with an impasse. According to Stellan Ohlsson, an impasse occurs when the problem solver cannot think of how to proceed. He proposed that elaboration, constraint relaxation, and re-encoding are possible mechanisms for escaping an impasse. Elaboration is needed when the initial representation of the problem is incomplete. Elaboration adds missing information rather than modifies existing information. Constraint relaxation is needed when the problem solver has imposed unnecessary constraints that block the solution. I purchased a flash drive as I wrote this chapter and could not pull off the plastic cap that protected the plug. After failing to find instructions on the packaging I pulled even harder until it finally occurred to me that pushing might be more effective. It worked. Re-encoding is needed when the initial encoding of the problem is insufficient, requiring a new interpretation. The Gestalt construct of "functional fixedness" blocks solutions that require finding novel uses of objects such as using a hammer as a pendulum weight.

The next correspondence in Table 13.1 maps a latent attractor onto implicit cognition. Implicit cognition is an idea, perception, or concept that may be influential in the cognitive processes or behavior of an individual even though the person is not explicitly aware of it. Implicit representations play an important role in social cognition, but most theories agree that these representations can be made explicit by directing attention to them. This view is consistent with the construct of a latent attractor in the dynamical systems perspective. As noted earlier, latent attractors provide a means for resolving conflicts through revealing alternative courses of action.

The final correspondence pairs nonincremental change in dynamic systems with insight in information-processing formulations. Nonincremental change occurs when the change is sudden and substantial such as in critical transitions or in suddenly discovering the solution to a problem. The inclusion of insight puzzles in Chapter 11 contains evidence for sudden discoveries of a solution.

Dynamical systems are examples of complex systems composed of interacting components. We will return to some of the concepts discussed in this chapter in Chapter 18 on complex systems. Blocking our path are four chapters on the use of computers to organize knowledge: the data sciences, explanatory artificial intelligence, the information sciences, and general artificial intelligence.

PART V

ARTIFICIAL INTELLIGENCE

14

Data Sciences

You may recall that the survey conducted by the World Economic Forum's *Future of Jobs Report 2018* revealed an accelerating demand for new specialist roles related to understanding and using the latest emerging technologies such as artificial intelligence (AI) and machine learning specialists, big data specialists, process automation experts, information security analysts, human–machine interaction designers, and robotics engineers. Section V on AI brings us to a hot topic that I discuss in the next four chapters. My goal in these chapters is to provide an overview of the current successes and limitations of AI.

Let's begin with four questions about AI that were part of an eight-question quiz in *The Wall Journal*. Box 14.1 contains the questions.

I took the quiz myself and got off to a quick start. I would have lost all credibility as the author of this section if I missed the first question but correctly answered B, C, D, and A in that order. I took an educated guess on the second question but correctly answered E. Then it started going downhill. I guessed Isaac Asimov for question 3 because science fiction writers are sometimes ahead of scientists in inventing terms or trends. The correct answer, John McCarthy, would have been my third choice behind Alan Turing even though I had already planned to quote John McCarthy in Chapter 17. One would have to be a trained economist specializing in AI to know the answer to question 4. I guessed $16 trillion, which matched the correct answer of $13 trillion, give or take a few trillion. You can tell I am not a trained economist.

Cognitive Skills You Need for the 21st Century. Stephen K. Reed, Oxford University Press (2020). © Oxford University Press. DOI: 10.1093/oso/9780197529003.001.0001.

Box 14.1 A Quiz on Artificial Intelligence

1. The following are definitions for *artificial intelligence, deep learning, machine learning,* and *natural language processing.* Match each term to its definition:
   A. Takes text or speech as input and can "read" or extract meaning from it.
   B. Encompasses techniques used to teach computers to learn, reason, perceive, infer, communicate and make decisions similar to or better than humans.
   C. Is a powerful statistical technique for classifying patterns using large training data sets in multilayer neural networks.
   D. Is the science of getting computers to act intelligently without being explicitly programmed.
2. Which of the following sectors is spending the most on AI systems?
   A. Banking
   B. Discrete manufacturing
   C. Healthcare
   D. Process manufacturing
   E. Retail
3. Who invented the term *artificial intelligence*?
   A. Science-fiction writer Isaac Asimov
   B. Dartmouth College mathematician John McCarthy
   C. Mathematician and computer scientist Alan Turing
   D. Computer scientist Grace Hopper
   E. Former IBM chairman Thomas J Watson
4. How much global economic activity will AI deliver between now and 2030?
   A. $4 trillion
   B. $9 trillion
   C. $10 trillion
   D. $13 trillion
   E. $16 trillion

Based on McCormick (2019). Test your knowledge of artificial intelligence. *The Wall Street Journal*, p. R3.

An earlier article in the November 2, 2018 edition of *The Wall Street Journal* stated that the University of California at Berkeley announced plans to create a new Division of Data Science and Information. The ability to make inferences and predictions from information requires both modeling skills from statistics and programming skills from computer science. It also requires expertise about a particular topic, which is why the attraction to the field is so broad. At that time nearly 1,300 students were enrolled in an introductory class called Foundations of Data Science.

Machine learning is at the center of this revolution. In his book *The Master Algorithm: How the Ultimate Learning Machine Will Remake Our World*, computer scientist Pedro Domingos provides many examples demonstrating that machine learning is all around us. It decides what information to show us when we type a query into a search engine. It filters spam from our emails. It makes recommendations when we buy a book from Amazon or select a video from Netflix. It helps pick stocks for our mutual funds. Domingos describes five "tribes" of machine learning: the Analogizers, Bayesians, Connectionists, Evolutionaries, and Symbolists. His book gives readers a clear introduction to these methods and their applications. It encourages them to think about how combining the methods can make them more effective.

Cognitive psychologists have also contributed to these methods when constructing models of human learning and categorization. I summarized some of their efforts in my article "Building Bridges Between AI and Cognitive Psychology" in *AI Magazine*. One might expect that there would be many bridges connecting AI implemented in computers with natural intelligence implemented in people. However, I have been both surprised and disappointed by the lack of cross-references between these two fields. The objective of my article was to demonstrate common methods used in both fields.

With the exception of the Evolutionaries who simulate natural selection in computer programs, members of the other four camps can be easily found among psychologists. The following sections on the Analogizers, Bayesians, Connectionists, and Symbolists begin with a description of each group, followed by examples of psychological contributions.

The Analogizers

The Analogizers in Domingos's terminology develop methods to categorize patterns based on their similarity to other patterns. We encountered one measure of similarity—family resemblance scores—in Chapter 3 on categorization. Family resemblance scores measure similarity based on the number of shared attributes.

This measure is well suited for attributes that have only two values such as male/female or alive/dead. However, it is less successful in measuring similarity when the attributes are continuous such as age. Children who are two, four, and five are not the same age but we expect the behavior of the five-year-old to be more similar to the four-year-old than to the two-year-old. The values of continuous measures can be plotted on a continuous scale in which points near each other are more similar than points far from each other.

These spatial measures of similarity have resulted in productive techniques for both machine learning and psychological modeling. Figure 14.1 shows the similarity of birds plotted in a multidimensional space. Stanford undergraduates received pairs of the words in Figure 14.1 and were instructed to rate the similarity of each pair on a 4-point scale. Psychologists Lance Rips, Ed Shoben, and Ed Smith then fed these ratings to a multidimensional scaling program that produced the plot. The scaled measure of similarity is the distance between two points. Goose and duck are very similar, but goose and robin are not.

Multidimensional scaling programs make three valuable contributions. First, scaled measures of similarity are better measures of similarity than the occasionally inconsistent similarity judgments. Second, visual displays of data reveal patterns that would be difficult to detect in a table of numbers. We can immediately see that goose, duck, and chicken form a cluster and that a sparrow is a more typical bird than an eagle as depicted by their distances from the concept of a "bird." Third, an interpretation of the dimensions of the solution may reveal the attributes that most influence the ratings. The horizontal dimension is influenced by size as revealed by the larger birds in the left half of Figure 14.1. The vertical dimension is influenced by the distinction between domestic (top half) and wild (bottom half) birds.

The Master Algorithm informs us that these spatial representations are an important tool for categorizing information in machine learning. Cognitive psychologists have also frequently constructed multidimensional models of how people categorize patterns. I used them while comparing a variety of categorization models to determine which models best predicted how people classify patterns

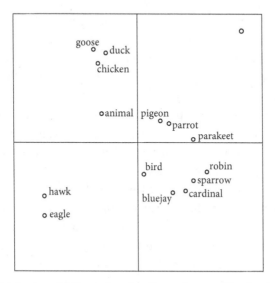

Figure 14.1. A multidimensional scaling solution of birds.

From L. J. Rips, E. J. Shoben, & E. E. Smith, 1973, Semantic distance and the verification of semantic relations, *Journal of Verbal Leaning and Verbal Behavior, 12,* 1–20.

into two categories such as the ones shown in Figure 14.2. The task required UCLA undergraduates to select a category for each of approximately 25 test faces that were similar to the category faces.

One model based on the distance between patterns is an exemplar model in which the classifier compares the distance of the test pattern to the examples in both categories. If the average similarity to the patterns in Category 1 is higher, select Category 1; otherwise, select Category 2. An alternative model is a prototype model in which the classifier creates an average face—a prototype—to represent each category as infants did for phonological categories. My findings indicated that comparing the test patterns to the category prototypes was the most frequent strategy for classifying faces into the categories in Figure 14.2.

Another finding was that classifiers emphasized some features more than others when making classifications because features differ in their information value. Imagine an adult who has blue eyes, an IQ of 110, and enjoys walking. Is that person a male or a female? The features are not very revealing, but if I told you the person is five feet tall, you would likely decide "female." You can demonstrate the differential value of features for yourself by selecting the most helpful and the least helpful feature for distinguishing between the categories in Figure 14.2.

I used a mathematical procedure called a class-separating transformation to find an optimal set of feature weights for distinguishing between the two categories. Applying the procedure to the faces in Figure 14.2 produced weights of 0.46 for eye height, 0.24 for eye separation, 0.24 for nose length, and 0.06 for mouth height. Eye height was very helpful for distinguishing between the two categories whereas mouth height was essentially worthless. The weighted-feature distances improved the prediction of both the prototype and exemplar models, indicating that classifiers placed more emphasis on the discriminating features when making their decisions.

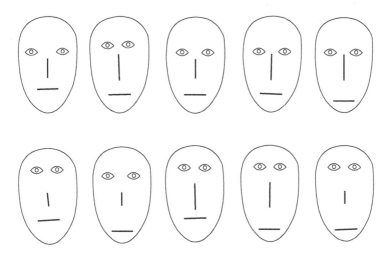

Figure 14.2. Two categories of schematic faces shown in the upper and lower row.

From S. K. Reed & M. P. Friedman, 1973, Perceptual vs. conceptual categorization, *Memory & Cognition, 1,* 157–163.

I do not believe that classifiers always use a prototype strategy, and another one of my experiments indicated that they did not. The upper two prototypes in Figure 14.3 are for the two categories in Figure 14.2, and the lower two prototypes are for another problem. The similarity of the lower prototypes would make it difficult to use this strategy. My findings indicated that classifiers emphasized a simple heuristic (take the best) that Gerd Gigerenzer describes in his book *Risk Savy.* This strategy bases a decision on the best predicting feature, such as classifying faces on the basis of eye separation in this particular case.

The Bayesians

Domingos informs us that Bayes's theorem is named after Thomas Bayes, an 18th-century English clergyman. Bayes described a new

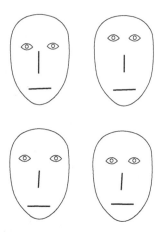

Figure 14.3. Prototypes for the categories in Figure 14.2 (above) and for another problem (below).

From S. K. Reed, 1972, Pattern recognition and categorization, *Cognitive Psychology, 3,* 382–407.

way to think about probability but it was the great French mathematician, Pierre-Simon de Laplace, who subsequently developed the mathematics and the foundations of probability theory.

An excellent overview of the many recent accomplishments of the Bayesians is the article in *Science* titled "How to Grow a Mind: Statistics, Structure, and Abstraction" by Joshua Tenenbaum, Charles Kemp, Thomas Griffiths, and Noah Goodman. The authors point out that the success of Bayesian applications in AI and machine learning have encouraged use of Bayesian methods in psychology.

Bayes rule provides a method for revising beliefs based on new evidence. It states that the "Probability of an Hypothesis based on the Data" is proportional to the "Probability of obtaining the Data if the Hypothesis were correct" multiplied by the "Probability of the Hypothesis." This looks complicated, but the authors of "How to Grow a Mind" provide a clarifying example based on medical diagnosis. The data are that John is coughing, and three possible hypotheses are that John has either (a) a cold, (b) lung disease, or (c) heartburn.

The first hypothesis is the most promising, and Bayes's rule provides an explanation. The first two hypotheses are consistent with the data. Both a cold and lung disease cause coughing, but a cold is much more common than lung disease (before the coronavirus pandemic). The probability of the hypothesis is therefore higher for a cold than for lung disease. Physicians typically begin by considering frequent causes of a symptom before considering infrequent ones. The probability of the hypothesis is also high for heartburn because of its frequency. However, heartburn usually does not cause coughing so the probability of the hypothesis based on the data is low for heartburn. It is likely that John has a cold because colds are frequent and are often accompanied by coughing.

The theme of *The Master Algorithm* is discovering productive combinations of machine-learning methods. Psychologists Charles Kemp and Joshua Tenenbaum combined the Analogizer and Bayesian approaches by using Bayesian methods to evaluate different graph representations of similarity. The method is called hierarchical Bayesian analysis because it selects a structure for representing similarity and then arranges the data within the structure. For instance, although two dimensions are required to show the similarities among birds in Figure 14.1, a single dimension is sufficient for representing voting similarities among Supreme Court justices on 1,596 cases. The single dimension in Figure 14.4 organizes the judges from liberal beliefs (Marshall and Brennan) to conservative beliefs (Thomas and Scalia).

The networks in Chapter 6 offer another structure for representing similarity that can be very effective, as depicted in Figure 14.5 for animals. The animals consist of birds, insects, two classes of mammals, and water animals such as a dolphin, salmon, and alligator. The data are embedded in a matrix at the bottom of the figure that show biological and ecological features of these animals. The number of shared features is a measure of the similarity between two animals, which is represented in a network constructed through Bayesian methods. The length of the path

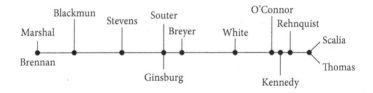

Figure 14.4. Voting similarities among Supreme Court justices.
From J. B. Tenenbaum, C. Kemp, T. L. Griffiths, & N. D. Goodman, 2011, How to grow a mind: Statistics, structure, and abstraction, *Science, 331,* 1279–1285.

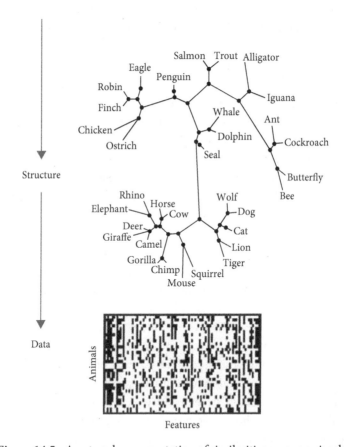

Figure 14.5. A network representation of similarities among animals.
From J. B. Tenenbaum, C. Kemp, T. L. Griffiths, & N. D. Goodman, 2011, How to grow a mind: Statistics, structure, and abstraction, *Science, 331,* 1279–1285.

between animals depicts their similarity in the network. Short path lengths reveal clusters of familiar categories such as birds, fish, insects, and mammals.

The Connectionists

The Master Algorithm informs us that Connectionists reverse-engineer what the brain does by adjusting the strength of connections between "neurons." Their software compares the obtained output to the desired output and then changes connection weights in layers of neurons to reduce the amount of error. Connectionist learning differs from symbolic learning because concepts are distributed across "neurons" rather than represented by a one-to-one correspondence between concepts and symbols. The classic psychological research on neural networks was done by Dave Rumelhart and Jay McClelland at the University of California, San Diego.

A finding labeled the "word superiority effect" motivated their theory. Gerald Reicher, in his dissertation at the University of Michigan, had investigated whether it is possible to recognize a letter in a four-letter word in the same amount of time as it takes to recognize a single letter. To answer this question, he designed an experiment in which observers were shown extremely brief displays of either a single letter or a four-letter word. For example, one case contrasted the word WORK with the letter K. Observers in the letter condition had to decide whether they saw the letter D or K and observers in the word condition had to decide whether the last letter in the word was a D or a K. A finding that surprised many people (including me) was that observers were more accurate in identifying a letter when it was part of a word.

In 1981–1982, McClelland and Rumelhart published two articles that described a neural network model called the interactive activation model. It provided an explanation of the word superiority effect by assuming that recognition occurs simultaneously at

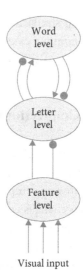

Visual input

Figure 14.6. An interactive-activation model of letter perception.

From J. L. McClelland, and D. E. Rumelhart, 1981, An interactive-activation model of context effects in letter perception: Part 1, An account of basic findings, *Psychological Review, 88,* 375–407.

the three different levels shown in Figure 14.6. A key assumption of the model is that the feature, letter, and word levels interact to determine accuracy. This is illustrated by the arrows in Figure 14.6, which show that the letter level receives information from both the feature level and the word level.

There are two kinds of connections between levels: excitatory connections and inhibitory connections. Excitatory connections provide positive evidence and inhibitory connections provide negative evidence about the identity of a letter or word. For example, a diagonal line provides positive evidence for the letter K (and all other letters that contain a diagonal line) and negative evidence for the letter D (and all other letters that do not contain a diagonal line). The information coming from the feature level is called "bottom–up learning" based on data from the environment.

Excitatory and inhibitory connections also occur between the letter level and the word level. Recognizing that the first letter of a word is a W increases the activation level of all words that begin with a W and constrains the other letters to be consistent with four-letter words that begin with that letter. It is these additional constraints from the word level that produce the word superiority effect. The information coming from the word level is called "top–down learning" based on information stored in memory. The interactive activation model had a major effect on encouraging the development of other models based on neural networks.

Fast forward to 2019 and we find that connectionist models based on deep neural networks are taking the world by storm. Deep neural networks utilize the same principles of simpler networks but have added multiple layers of connections to fine-tune the weights of thousands of connections. Figure 14.7 illustrates the application of deep neural networks to image recognition. The input begins with pixels from the image and the output classifies the image as one of 1,000 possible pictures. In between are many hidden layers in which each layer receives input from a small number of units in the previous layer to establish more global connectivity.

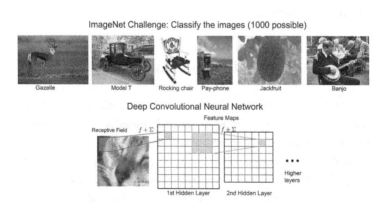

Figure 14.7. Application of a deep neural network to classify images.

From R. A. Jacobs & C. J. Bates, 2019, Comparing the visual representations and performance of humans and deep neural networks, *Current Directions in Psychological Science, 28,* 34–39.

The authors of this article, Robert Jacobs and Christopher Bates at the University of Rochester's Department of Brain and Cognitive Sciences, review evidence that we the people are nonetheless still superior at recognizing images under adverse conditions. Here's an example that occurred when I saw the letters MTA as I approached a café window inside an office building. I could not figure out the meaning of the letters until I realized they were a reflection from the glass and therefore a mirror image. The vertical symmetry of each letter implied that the shape of the letters would not change when reflected, but the reflection would reverse their order. My hypothesis was confirmed when I looked behind me and saw a sign for an ATM machine.

The authors list several reasons for our perceptual advantage over machines. We learn to recognize objects in perceptually rich, dynamic, interactive environments whereas networks are trained on static images. We can take advantage of three-dimensional features whereas networks are more limited to two dimensions. A disadvantage for people, however, is capacity limits because we cannot visually perceive and represent all aspects of a scene. These limits can nonetheless occasionally be an asset when we focus on the more discriminative features.

The Symbolists

Symbolic approaches in Domingos's framework are associated with knowledge engineering in which knowledge is programmed into the computer by experts rather than discovered by learning algorithms. Knowledge for the Symbolists occurs by manipulating symbols that replace expressions with other expressions. Manipulating symbols to solve problems typically occurs by learning rules that combine different pieces of pre-existing knowledge. Rules can be expressed in logic such as "If gene A is expressed and gene B is not, then gene C is expressed."

Sebastien Heile and Ron Sun combined the connectionist and symbolic approaches in the hybrid cognitive architecture CLARION to develop an explicit–implicit interaction theory to model the four stages of problem-solving proposed in Wallas's influential book *The Art of Thought*. Preparation is the initial search for a solution, incubation is a period of inactivity following an impasse, illumination (or insight) is a sudden discovery of a possible solution, and verification is a determination of whether the discovered solution is valid. The implementation of CLARION assumes that the initial preparation phase is predominately rule-based as people respond to verbal instructions, form a representation of the problem and establish goals. In contrast, the second (incubation) stage is predominately implicit processing in which people may not consciously think about the problem. CLARION uses a connectionist network to model implicit processing. The third stage, insight, occurs when the activation level crosses a threshold that makes the output available for verbal report. The final verification stage, like the initial stage, requires explicit processing to evaluate the potential of the discovered solution. Hybrid architectures demonstrate how Analogizer, Bayesian, Connectionist, and Symbolist methods can work together.

Kenneth Forbus, Chen Liang, and Irina Rabkina argue that the Connectionist approach, despite its many successes, has limitations as models of human reasoning. One limitation is that this approach requires massive amounts of data to learn—far more than required by people. A second limitation is that all of the data must be available at the beginning, which does not capture the incremental nature of human learning. A third limitation is that it is not always apparent what is being learned in distributed representations. They argue that these limitations indicate that symbolic representations should continue to play a central role in efforts to explain human cognition. I concur and therefore elaborate on symbolic representations in the next two chapters.

15

Explainable AI

In their recent chapter on artificial intelligence (AI) in *The Cambridge Handbook of Intelligence*, Ashok Goel and Jim Davies distinguish between two major paradigms. Engineering AI attempts to design the smartest possible intelligent systems regardless of whether the systems reflect intelligence found in people. The vast majority of AI research on robotics and machine learning falls into this category. In contrast, psychological AI attempts to design systems that think like people.

A goal of AI is to make engineering AI more transparent. Goel and Davies use machine learning based on multilayer networks (deep learning) as an example. Although this method has become very successful, it is unclear how learning occurs. The interactions among thousands of connections are too complex to understand by looking at the computer code. Other machine learning algorithms such as reinforcement learning can also be opaque. The program Alpha Go Zero became a world champion in the game of Go by identifying and rewarding sequences of successful actions. Rewarding sequences of actions, however, makes it difficult to determine which actions in the sequence were most productive.

My impression from reading recent articles on AI is that, following the successes of engineering AI, the pendulum is now swinging toward psychological AI. Part of the motivation may be that people outside of AI are becoming increasingly concerned about the threat of AI. In his book *Valley of Genius: The Uncensored History of Silicon Valley*, Adam Fisher quotes Marissa Mayer, Google's first female engineer and subsequent CEO of Yahoo:

Cognitive Skills You Need for the 21st Century. Stephen K. Reed, Oxford University Press (2020). © Oxford University Press. DOI: 10.1093/oso/9780197529003.001.0001.

I am incredibly optimistic about what AI can do. I think right now we are just in the early stages, and a lot of fears are overblown. Technologists are terrible marketers. The notion of artificial intelligence, even the acronym itself, is scary. If we'd had better marketing, we would have said "Wait, can we talk about enhanced intelligence or computer-augmented intelligence, where the human being isn't replaced in the equation."

A dilemma in using the output of machine learning, according to David Gunning and David Aha, is the trade-off between predictive accuracy and explainability. The best performing methods are the least explainable. A program supported by the U.S. Defense Advance Projects Agency (DARPA) is striving to correct this imbalance by developing programs that are both effective and explainable. The goal is to develop AI systems that can explain their reasoning to a human user, characterize the method's strengths and weaknesses, and convey an understanding of its future behavior.

A major component of the research agenda is to evaluate the effectiveness of explanations (Figure 15.1). Users rate both the clarity and usefulness of the systems in providing answers to questions such as

- Why did you do that?
- Why not do something else?
- When can I trust you?
- How do I correct an error?

Evaluations are also based on task performance to measure the effectiveness of the explanations in improving decisions.

The multiple projects supported by Defense Advance Projects Agency are still a work-in-progress so I will provide examples of other projects that support explanations. The first example is the application of IBM's WatsonPaths to medical diagnosis. A second example is the organization of biological and psychological

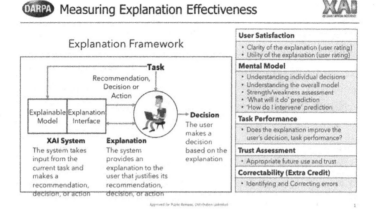

Figure 15.1. Explainable AI.

From D. Gunning & D. W. Aha, 2019, DARPA's explainable artificial intelligence program. *AI Magazine, 40*(2), 44–58.

knowledge to support the National Institute of Mental Health's (NIMH) Research Domain Criteria initiative discussed in Chapter 5. Both of these examples rely on semantic networks discussed in Chapter 6.

Applying AI to Medical Diagnosis

We would likely be apprehensive if we were told that a computer diagnosed our medical problem, and the doctors had no idea how it did it. Computers can nonetheless provide valuable assistance if patients and doctors understand how the program arrived at its decision. WatsonPaths is an example of such a program. It expands on IBM's Watson question-answering program that became famous on the quiz show *Jeopardy* by defeating two of the best human players. Watson takes natural language questions as input and produces answers with probabilities (confidence estimates) as output. WatsonPaths builds on Watson by reasoning from scenarios that are more elaborate than the *Jeopardy* questions. Its application to medicine begins with a patient summary and ends with the most likely diagnosis or most appropriate treatment.

Guiding the diagnosis in WatsonPaths is a network of entity types and relations that connect symptoms to hypotheses. Figure 15.2 shows an example in which a 63-year-old patient has a resting

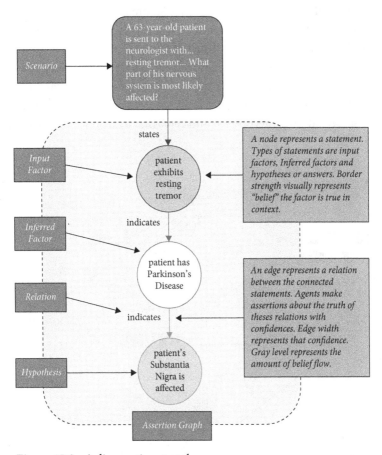

Figure 15.2. A diagnostic network.

From A. Lally, S. Bagchi, M. Barborak, D. W. Buchanan, J. Chu-Carroll, D. A. Ferrucci, ... J. M. Prager, 2017, WatsonPaths: Scenario-based question answering and inference over unstructured information. *AI Magazine, 38,* 59–76.

tremor, and the problem is to identify which part of the nervous system is most likely involved. WatsonPaths makes a medical diagnosis before answering the question. The diagnosis suggests that the patient has Parkinson's disease and that the substantia nigra area of the brain is affected. The diagnosis and the hypothesis regarding the nervous system are both accompanied by confidence estimates.

Beneath the surface of this brief summary is a sophisticated use of methods that combine semantics and statistics. Figure 15.3 displays a semantic network of the relations among diseases, demographics, possible causes, anatomical structures, biological functions, and test results that are crucial for making a diagnosis. Statistical contributions come from the data sciences. Parkinson's disease, Huntington's disease, and cerebellar disease are all possible

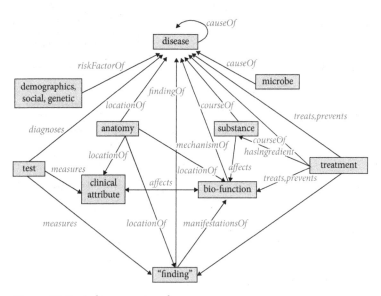

Figure 15.3. A disease network.
From A. Lally, S. Bagchi, M. Barborak, D. W. Buchanan, J. Chu-Carroll, D. A. Ferrucci, . . . J. M. Prager, 2017, WatsonPaths: Scenario-based question answering and inference over unstructured information. *AI Magazine, 38,* 59–76.

diagnoses for a patient who has a resting tremor that began two years ago, an unexpressive face, and difficulty walking. Probabilistic-driven deductive inferences connect these input symptoms to the hypotheses. For instance, a resting tremor indicates Parkinson's disease with probability 0.8 and difficulty in walking indicates Parkinson's disease with probability 0.4. The Bayesian methods in the previous chapter combine these probabilities to provide evidence for alternative hypotheses.

The authors report that the biggest gains in performance will come from improvements in Watson to select important information and not become overwhelmed with irrelevant details.

The initial goal of Watson was to answer trivia questions on *Jeopardy*, but real-world applications are not as concise. Medical records contain large amounts of detail that is irrelevant for answering a specific question. This hurdle brings us back to the select–organize–integrate framework in Chapter 1 in which the selection of critical information is the initial step toward successful organization and integration.

Another challenge identified by the developers is to make WatsonPaths' reasoning transparent to physicians who need to make the final decisions and then explain those decisions to their patients. I argue in the next chapter that formal ontologies provide assistance for tackling both of these challenges. I next describe a collaboration that creates a transition between the semantic networks discussed in this chapter and the ontologies discussed in Chapter 16.

A Biological Network

I spent my first year in retirement as a visiting scholar at the Center for the Study of Language and Information at Stanford University. My office in the center served as a home base for attending several lab meetings across the campus. One of these was the

Bioinformatics Research Group in the School of Medicine. There I met Michel Dumontier, the lead designer of the Semanticscience Integrated Ontology (SIO) for organizing knowledge about molecular biology. It was also at this time that I read an article about the new initiative at the NIMH to establish a biological basis for mental illness that I described in Chapter 5. The project requires formulating a biological basis at multiple levels that range from genes to emotional and cognitive behavior. Michel Dumontier and I decided to explore if an ontology about molecular biology could be extended upward to include these higher levels in the NIMH initiative. An advantage of extending SIO to cognition is that its four top-level categories— "object," "process," "attribute," "and relation"—also correspond to the building blocks of knowledge in cognitive psychology.

Figure 15.4 shows how SIO entities and relations organize a portion of molecular biology including organs, cells, and molecules. The overlap of one concept on another indicates a subclass relation, such as a gene is a subclass of a DNA region. Many other relations, such as "is attribute of" and "has part," are also frequently used to organize knowledge. A phenotype is an "attribute of" an organism and an organism "has part" cells.

An important relation in molecular biology is "encodes," defined by SIO as a relation between two objects in which the first object contains information that is used to produce the second object. Figure 15.4 distinguishes between two types of encoding used in genetics—"translated from" and "transcribed from." Transcribed is a relation in which the information encoded in one object produces an exact or similar kind of object. DNA and RNA are structurally quite similar in terms of their nucleotide composition but have different roles in the cell regarding information storage and transfer. Translated describes a relation in which a completely different kind of entity is generated. For instance, RNA molecules produce proteins.

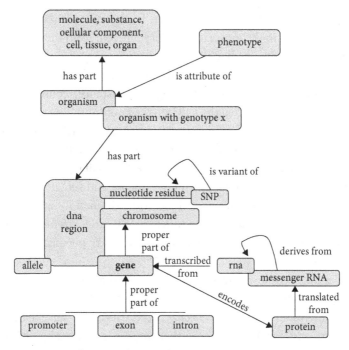

Figure 15.4. A biological network.

From M. Dumontier, C. J. O. Baker, J. Baran, A. Callahan, L. Chepelev, J. Cruz-Toledo, . . . R. Hoehndorf, 2014, The Semanticscience Integrated Ontology (SIO) for biomedical research and knowledge discovery, *Journal of Biomedical Semantics,* 5(4), 1–11.

A Cognitive Network

We selected reading as a case study for applying concepts in SIO to a cognitive process. Reading is a good example, not only because of its importance but because it requires a number of component processes. We read by transferring words on a page into internal speech, which is often referred to as subvocalization. We also need to activate the meaning of the words. Activation of meaning may be accompanied by visual images if the sentence consists of concrete words. You may have had the experience of reading a book and then seeing a movie based on the book, only to discover that the characters in the movie looked very different from the way you visualized them in the book. There is extensive psychological research on how each of these components contributes to reading. For instance, consider the sentences, "She pounded the nail into the floor" and "She pounded the nail into the wall." When participants had to verify whether a picture of an object was mentioned in the sentence, their verification times were faster for a picture of a vertical nail if given the first sentence and a horizontal nail if given the second sentence. There is now extensive evidence that these visual simulations are highly flexible and, like sensory-motor interactions, can focus on specific modalities, change according to context, and take perspective into account.

Figure 15.5 shows the application of SIO theoretical constructs to an information-processing model of reading. We were particularly interested in the word *encodes* because its importance in both biology and psychology. Recall that *encodes* is defined by SIO as a relation between two objects in which the first object contains information that is used to produce the second object. This is a very general definition that applies across many domains. More problematic are extending the two types of genetic encoding— transcribed and translated. We decided that all of the cognitive encodings in Figure 15.5 are translations because the second code differs substantially from the preceding code. The text on the page (a textual entity) is translated into internal speech (a verbal language entity) and into meaning (propositions). The meaning may then be translated into visual images (an iconic mental representation).

Figure 15.5 also shows that working memory is required for reading. We need to store words in working memory to combine them into meaningful phrases. The phonological loop and the visuospatial sketchpad are two components of a very influential model of working memory developed by Alan Baddeley. The phonological

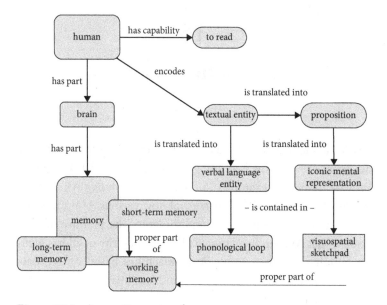

Figure 15.5. A cognitive network.
From S. K. Reed & M. Dumontier, 2019, Adding cognition to the Semanticscience Integrated Ontology, *Edelweiss: Psychiatry Open Access, 3,* 4–13.

loop stores internal speech and the visuospatial sketchpad stores visual simulations.

The figures in this chapter illustrate how networks capture semantic entities and their relations. They explicitly represent knowledge in a symbolic format that provides a foundation for constructing explanations. However, additional tools from the information sciences are needed to reason from this knowledge. The next chapter discusses these tools, beginning with an explanation of how the theoretical constructs in Figures 15.4 and 15.5 form the foundation for logical reasoning within the Semanticscience Integrated Ontology.

16

Information Sciences

Artificial intelligence (AI) has made impressive advances but these advances are only the beginning. Gary Marcus and Ernest Davis provide numerous examples in their book *Rebooting AI: Building Artificial Intelligence We Can Trust* of how various AI projects are still very limited in their accomplishments. The premise of their book is that AI is on the wrong path if the majority of efforts focus on building relativey unintelligent machines based on big data rather than deep understanding. Sound familliiar? It was the topic of the last chapter.

Marcus and Davis argue that a coherent understanding of the world requires organizing facts, and logic offers a promising approach. Logic is a key ingredient of formal ontologies—a major tool of the information sciences. Table 16.1 summarizes how this chapter relates to the previous two chapters on using AI to organize knowledge. The information sciences provide tools for deductive reasoning to supplement the classifications made by the data sciences and the explanations made by explanatory models. The data sciences seek organization. The information sciences impose organization. Explanatory models connect them.

The importance of combining the data and information sciences is emphasized in a chapter on linking neuroscience to cognition by Russell Poldrack at Stanford University and Tal Yarkoni at the University of Texas. They discuss the contributions of the data sciences in analyzing large databases but also highlight "the underappreciated but critical role for formal ontologies in helping to clarify, refine, and test theories of brain and cognitive function." This role is critical because of the complexity of the topic. The

Table 16.1 Computer Science Tools

Chapter	Primary Purpose	Tools
Data sciences	Classification	Statistics
Explanatory models	Explanation	Semantic networks
Information sciences	Reasoning	Formal ontologies

authors believe that it is unlikely that any single gene, neuron, brain region, or network will neatly map onto psychological constructs such as phonological rehearsal or working memory. The development of formal ontologies can provide a unifying framework for organizing definitions, research findings, and theories.

Poldrack and Yarkoni state that we can think of a good ontology "as a kind of universal language that dramatically reduces the likelihood of miscommunication between researchers by enabling statements to be defined in more formal and less ambiguous terms, even when the mapping between terms and the referents is still not perfect." The authors conclude by predicting that the combination of the data and information sciences will become increasingly common in psychology, as it has in biology, and provide a new path for discovering how neural processing results in mental life.

Applying SIO to the NIMH Research Domain Criteria

The integration of biology and psychology requires a shared language, as discussed in the previous chapter, but a shared language is insufficient for answering questions. Here is where ontologies come to the rescue because one of the primary purposes of a formal ontology is to use deductive reasoning to provide answers. When you query a computer, the computer does not have the answers directly stored for many of these questions. However, it may be able to figure out the answer based on the logical relations stored in the database. Scientific queries are often about causal relations. Answering these queries becomes challenging when the answer depends on a sequence of deductions, particularly when the causes require integration across different projects and units of analysis. To illustrate this process, let's begin with an article titled "Studying Hallucinations Within the NIMH RDoC Framework." The lead author is Judith Ford with the San Franciso VA Medical Center and Department of Psychiatry at the University of California, San Francisco. I knew nothing about auditory hallucinations other than that they are imagined voices but was curious to learn how the authors linked them to the National Institute of Mental Health's Research Domain Criteria (RDoC) dimensions. There are many links but let me mention a few. One is the lack of cognitive control because hallucinations are often described as unintentional and intrusive. Another involves memory because people diagnosed with schizophrenia often report hearing voices that are identical or similar to previously heard voices. A third link is to negative valence because the voices described in treatment settings are typically threatening and derogatory. I list this last attribute—negative emotion—in Box 16.1 to subsequently integrate it with other research findings.

A second article by Sheldon Cohen, Peter Gianaros, and Stephen Manuck in Pittsburgh proposed a stage model of disease that links stressful life events and negative emotional responses to increased risk of disease. The stages are (a) life events such as job loss or legal problems (b) that are appraised as stressful result in (c) a negative emotional response causing (d) disease related physiological changes. A third article by Maya Opendak and Elizabeth Gould at Princeton reports that stressful experiences have been shown to decrease the number of new neurons in the brain's hippocampus. Stress is known to reduce the effects of a molecule that enhances cell survival, which is a likely contributing factor. I also add this finding to Box 16.1.

Box 16.1 Integration of Research Findings

---

1. An attribute of abnormal auditory hallucination is negative emotion.

   Ford, J. M., Morris, S. E., Hoffman, R. E., Sommer, I., Waters, F., McCarthy-Jones, S., . . . Cuthbert, B. N. (2014). Studying hallucinations within the NIMH RDoC framework. *Schizophrenia Bulletin, 40* (Suppl 4), S295–S304.

2. Negative emotion causes stress.

   Cohen, S., Gianaros, P. J., & Manuck, S. B. (2016). A stage model of stress and disease. *Perspectives on Psychological Science, 11,* 456–463.

3. Stress reduces a molecule that enhances cell survival.

   Opendak, M., & Gould, E. (2015). Adult neurogenesis: a substrate for experience-dependent change. *Trends in Cognitive Sciences, 19,* 151–161.

   Deduction: Auditory hallucinations reduce a molecule that enhances cell survival.

Now consider the question "Do abnormal auditory hallucinations reduce cell survival?" The statements in Box 16.1 result in the conclusion that abnormal auditory hallucinations do influence cell survival. The first states that an attribute of abnormal auditory hallucinations is negative emotion. The second states that negative emotion causes stress. The third states that stress reduces a molecule that enhances cell survival, resulting in the deduction that abnormal auditory hallucinations reduce a molecule that enhances cell survival.

My coauthor Michel Dumontier formulated these statements in the Semanticscience Integrated Ontology (SIO) and, using its deductive reasoning powers and a Ontology Web Language

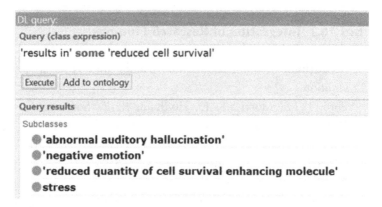

Figure 16.1. A query that uses SIO to connect causal relationships across RDoC categories.

From S. K. Reed & M. Dumontier, 2019, Adding cognition to the Semanticscience Integrated Ontology. *Edelweiss: Psychiatry Open Access, 3*, 4–13.

interpreter, received a response to the query "Which entities result in reduced cell survival?" The answer in Figure 16.1 reveals multiple causes. Abnormal auditory hallucination, negative emotion, reduced quantities of cell survival enhancing molecule, and stress are components of the causal change established by the statements in Box 16.1. Abnormal auditory hallucinations cause a negative emotion that causes stress that causes a reduction in the cells that enhance cell survival. This brief overview of SIO demonstrates the use of ontologies to formalize statements for reaching deductive conclusions that can serve as hypotheses for empirical evaluation.

The Suggested Upper Merged Ontology

Ontologies such as SIO describe a particular domain such as biomedical knowledge. Combining knowledge across the many cells in the RDoC matrix will require many domain ontologies. A recent survey of 17 domain ontologies that are relevant for RDoC reveals their contributions to behavior, emotions, genetics, health, and neuroscience. A general (or upper) ontology is needed to integrate these and other domain ontologies. I recommend the Suggested Upper Merged Ontology (SUMO).

I was surprised when I began my study of ontologies approximately 10 years ago that, with only a few exceptions, there had not been more advocates of their importance for psychology. I began to understand the reason when I began my own explorations of this field. There were few tutorial articles on ontologies, and many of the contributions were buried in the proceedings of engineering conferences. Then a book, *Ontology: A Practical Guide*, came to my rescue. Its author, Adam Pease, is the technical editor of the SUMO, a large-open source ontology. Adam and I subsequently collaborated on the article "A Framework for Constructing Cognition Ontologies Using WordNet, FrameNet, and SUMO" to describe information science tools to cognitive scientists.

SUMO is a large collection of 20,000 concepts with definitions in both English and formal logic. It covers a broad range of topics at a high level of generality but also includes details of many specific domains as diverse as finance, biological viruses, and geography. Box 16.2 shows the hierarchical organization of some major terms in SUMO, in which the indentions depict levels in the hierarchy.

I previously mentioned that an advantage of using SIO as a biomedical foundation for cognition is that its four top-level categories—object, process, attribute, and relation—correspond to fundamental components of knowledge in psychology. Notice that these components are also part of SUMO although they appear below SUMO's top-level categories of physical entities and abstract entities. "Object" and "process" are physical entities in SUMO; "attribute" and "relation" are abstract entities.

There are obvious parallels between the organization of knowledge in Box 16.2 and important theoretical concepts in psychology. For instance, SUMO partitions the top entry "entity" (not shown) into "physical" and "abstract"—a distinction made in

Box 16.2 A Part of the SUMO Hierarchy in Which Indentions Show Hierarchical Levels

Physical Entities
  Object
  Process
    Psychological process
    Perception
      Seeing
      Looking
      Hearing
      Listening
Abstract Entities
  Quantity
  Attribute
  Relation
  Proposition

previous chapters. A physical entity has a location in space/time and is partitioned into "object" and "process." An "object" is a physical thing like a chair or a glass of water. A "process" is an action that occurs over time like a lecture. An abstract entity cannot exist at a particular place in space/time without some physical encoding or embodiment. Subcategories of "abstract" include "quantity," "attribute," "relation," and "proposition."

The partitioning of "process" in Box 16.2 shows finer divisions within the hierarchy. A "psychological process" is one type of "process" that includes "perception." "Seeing" and "hearing" are subclasses of "perception." "Looking" is an intentional act of "seeing" and "listening" is an intentional act of "hearing." Some husbands are accused of hearing but not listening. Fortunately, I am not one of them.

Logical Reasoning

We learned in Chapter 7 that a hierarchical network model was one of the first models of semantic memory (Figure 7.1). The model proposes that the categories lower in the hierarchy inherit properties from categories higher in the hierarchy. Formal ontologies use this property of hierarchies to make deductions. Consider the question "Is vision used in looking?" The answer to the query is "yes" because vision is included in the definition of "seeing" and "looking" is a special case (subclass) of "seeing."

Another use of logic to represent knowledge is to identify contradictions. We encountered a hypothetical example in Table 9.2 in the chapter on imperfect knowledge. Box 16.3 contains another example regarding incidental learning. A logical deduction based on Premises 1 and 2 results in the inference that incidental learning (I) requires mental effort (M). A logical deduction based on Premises 3 and 4 results in the inference that incidental learning (I) does not require mental effort (–M). Removal of Premise 2 would eliminate the contradiction. It is not easy to detect contradictions, even in a very small knowledge base. You can imagine the helpfulness of computers in examining a large knowledge base for contradictions.

Although all formal ontologies use logical reasoning to answer questions and search for contradictions, they differ in the types of logic included in the ontology. The trade-off is between simpler logics that are easier to learn and complex logics that are more capable. The higher-order logic used in SUMO is more expressive than the logics used in many other ontologies such as the Ontology Web Language. More powerful logics require more computational power but advances in both hardware and software enable their use. A more powerful logic is one of the reasons why Adam Pease and I argue for the use of SUMO as a general ontology for organizing knowledge.

Box 16.3 Premises That Result in a Logical Contradiction

Premises
1. Incidental learning (I) stores information (S).
2. Storing information (S) requires mental effort (M).
3. Incidental learning (I) requires automatic processing (A).
4. Automatic processing (A) does not require mental effort (M).

Inference 1
1. I implies S (Premise 1).
2. S implies M (Premise 2).
3. I implies M (deduction).

Inference 2
1. I implies A (Premise 3)
2. A implies –M (Premise 4)
3. I implies –M (deduction)

From Reed Pease (2015). A framework for constructing cognition ontologies using WordNet, FrameNet, and SUMO. *Cognitive Systems Research, 33,* 122–144.

Connecting SUMO to WordNet

Another advantage of SUMO over other ontologies is its coordination with two other primary tools in the information sciences, WordNet and FrameNet. WordNet is a large, electronic dictionary that, although initially developed by psychologist George Miller to study language acquisition, has become the major source of linguistic definitions for the information sciences. Using WordNet requires selecting the relevant definition (sense) of each word when there is more than one definition. For instance, the word *attention* has six senses in WordNet. Two of them are psychological distinctions made by William James in his 1890 book *Principles of Psychology*. The first refers to the faculty or power of mental concentration. The second refers to the process whereby a person concentrates on some features of the environment to the relative exclusion of others.

SUMO has been manually mapped to all of the 117,000 definitions in WordNet by linking each word in WordNet to an equivalent or superordinate category in SUMO. Table 16.2 shows five senses of "see" with their links to SUMO classes. The WordNet definition of *see* as perceiving by sight is equivalent to SUMO's definition of *seeing*. The WordNet definition of *see* as watching is classified as looking in SUMO. Other senses of *see* are classified into the SUMO categories of interpreting, intentional process, and social interaction. Once classified, SUMO's hierarchical structure and deductive reasoning capabilities can be applied to the words.

A limitation of a general dictionary such as WordNet is that it may lack definitions of important theoretical constructs in a particular knowledge domain. For instance, the term *chunk* is one of the major theoretical constructs in cognitive science related to organizing knowledge. In his classic 1956 article "The Magical

Table 16.2 Senses of the Word *See* in WordNet

WordNet Sense	Example	SUMO classification
Perceive by sight		Seeing
See or watch	See a movie.	Looking
Perceive an idea mentally	I just can't see your point.	Interpreting
Take charge of or deal with	Could you see about lunch?	Intentional process
Date regularly	She is seeing an older man.	Social interaction

SUMO = Suggested Upper Merged Ontology.

Number Seven, Plus or Minus Two: Some Limits on Our Capacity for Processing Information," George Miller proposed that the capacity of short-term memory varies from five to nine chunks of information. A chunk consists of several items, such as KGB, that are stored together as a unit in long-term memory.

You can perform a quick experiment to illustrate the power of chunking. Ask someone to recall a string of letters and then read the letters FB–IJF–KC–IAIB–M with pauses at the hyphens. Watch the person struggle because the 12 letters greatly exceed the limited capacity of short-term memory. If the person believes they are your intellectual superior, stop the experiment at that point and walk away with a smirk on your face. If the person is a friend, give them another chance by changing the pauses to FBI–JFK–CIA–IBM. The order is the same but changing the pauses groups the letters into four familiar chunks that fit into the limited capacity of short-term memory.

The George Miller who wrote *The Magic Number Seven* is the same George Miller who developed WordNet. Nonetheless, his definition of *chunk* does not appear in WordNet. I had to consult the *APA Dictionary of Psychology* to find a definition of chunking as the process by which the mind sorts information into small, easily digestible units (chunks) that can be retained in short-term memory. I have generally been pleased with the definitions in the *APA Dictionary of Psychology*. I hope other knowledge domains have a specialized dictionary when a suitable definition of a word is not in WordNet.

Connecting SUMO to FrameNet

Daniel Mirman, Jon-Frederick Landrigan, and Allison Britt provide us with an extensive literature review that partitions semantic knowledge into taxonomic and thematic relations. Taxonomic relations capture similarities based on shared features. Rosch's

---

Box 16.4 Taxonomic (Columns) Versus Thematic (Rows) Categories

DOG	BONE	LEASH
HORSE	APPLE	SADDLE
MOUSE	CHEESE	TRAP

From Mirman, Landrigan, and Britt (2017). Taxonomic and thematic semantic systems. *Psychological Bulletin, 143*, 499–520.

---

subordinate, basic, and superordinate categories in Chapter 3 are a good example. Thematic categories capture co-occurrences in events or scenarios. Schank and Ableson's scripts in Chapter 4 are a good example. The matrix in Box 16.4 illustrates this distinction. The columns are taxonomic categories and the rows are thematic categories.

The literature review examines differences between the two types of categories. Taxonomic relations consist of relatively static features such as color and shape that describe objects. In contrast, thematic relations consist of action features that determine how objects interact with each other. The different feature sets have implications for neurological connections. Object information is provided by the "what" visual pathways that integrate features such as color and shape. Relations between objects are provided by the "where/how" visual pathways. Individuals with Alzheimer's disease show greater impairment of thematic relations whereas individuals with semantic dementia show greater impairment of taxonomic relations.

The co-occurrence of objects in thematic relations provides a context in which objects occur. Eiling Yee and Sharon Thompson-Schill argue that semantic memory is neither context-free nor independent of specific events. Concepts are so linked to their contexts that the dividing line between a concept and its context may be impossible. Their literature review indicates that concepts are fluid, influenced not only by the environment but by the experiences of individuals. Just as our interactions with objects in the world are defined by the contexts in which they are embedded, so is the conceptual system in which these objects are represented. FrameNet is an information science tool for representing these contexts.

Frames have a different structure than both dictionaries and ontologies because they capture co-occurrence and thematic relations among linguistic concepts. The Berkeley FrameNet project provides a useful tool for representing this type of knowledge. FrameNet is based on a theory of frame semantics developed by the Berkeley linguist Charles Fillmore and later by Colin Baker. They define cognitive frames as organized packages of knowledge that enable people to perceive, remember, and reason about their experiences. Examples include event schemas such as going to a hospital. The basic assumption of frame semantics is that words require a link to background frames to understand their meaning. FrameNet provides a tool for representing their context.

Many frames in FrameNet, such as for the word *remembering*, are relevant to cognition. The FrameNet distinction between *remembering_experience* and *remembering_information* captures the cognitive distinction between remembering personal experiences and remembering facts. Frames consist of core frame elements—the most essential components—and less essential noncore frame elements. Core frame elements in a person's *remembering_experience* frame are the person, experience, impression, and saliency. Noncore frame elements are context, duration, manner, time, and vividness.

An example of a linkage between FrameNet and SUMO is an attack frame in which an assailant physically attacks a victim. The core frame elements are assailant and victim. There are numerous noncore frame elements including circumstances, direction, duration, manner, purpose, and time. In the statement "As soon as he stepped out of the bar he was set upon by four men in ski masks," the phrase "As soon as he stepped out of the bar" specifies a time and location, "he" specifies the victim, "set upon" specifies a manner, and "four men in ski masks" specifies the assailants. Frame elements can be linked to classes in SUMO such as spatial relation, temporal relation, sentient agent, and group.

Together, WordNet, FrameNet, and SUMO provide an integrated linkage of three major information science tools. WordNet supplies definitions, FrameNet supplies a context for the thematic aspects of knowledge, and SUMO supplies a formal ontology for reasoning from this knowledge. I believe that the greatest contribution from the information sciences will come from linking these components.

17

General AI

We can congratulate ourselves. All of the advances in artificial intelligence (AI) still fall far behind our own general intelligence. We can use our cognitive skills to solve a wide range of problems whereas computers solve only a limited range of specific problems. They are forced to watch us in envy.

Thomas Griffiths at Princeton University, with the help of five coauthors, contrasts the differences between computers and people. The current trend in AI is to combine more computational power with more training data—doing more with more. In contrast, people do more with less. They have both limited data and limited computational powers. As a consequence, we have become efficient general-purpose learners by adapting to many different situations. The authors predict that doing more with less will become an increasingly important aspect of AI.

Alison Gopnik, a psychology professor at the University of California at Berkeley, argues that the ultimate learning machines are babies. The Defense Advance Projects Agency agrees. The mission of their new Machine Common Sense program is to design AI that understands the world as well as an 18-month-old child. The problem with many machine-learning algorithms is that they require enormous amounts of data, but only some of the data are relevant. Gopnik compares them to children with super-helicopter-tiger moms who dictate whether every step is correct.

Babies learn more general kinds of knowledge from much less and messier data. They are particularly good at learning by exploring, which their parents label "getting into everything." Gopnik is collaborating with her AI colleagues to build a system

Cognitive Skills You Need for the 21st Century. Stephen K. Reed, Oxford University Press (2020). © Oxford University Press. DOI: 10.1093/oso/9780197529003.001.0001.

named MESS for model-building, exploratory, social learning system. Exploring and active learning are encouraged by rewarding the system whenever it creates unexpected events.

A paradox is that tasks that are relatively easy for computers, such as producing logical proofs and playing chess, are difficult for humans. Tasks that are relatively easy for humans such as perceiving, walking, and talking are difficult for computers. The goal of general AI is to make computers proficient at a wide range of tasks, including those that are relatively easy for humans. A step in this direction is to create a standard model of the mind to model the skills of both people and machines.

A Standard Model of the Mind

Participants in a symposium sponsored by the Association for the Advancement of Artificial Intelligence began to develop a standard model of the mind to provide a common framework for unifying AI, cognitive psychology, cognitive neuroscience, and robotics. Each of these fields contributes to our understanding of intelligent behavior but each from a different perspective. A standard model would help integrate these disciplines and guide practitioners in constructing a broad range of applications.

Figure 17.1 shows the proposed standard model in an article by John Laird, Christian Lebiere, and Paul Rosenbloom. The model is a stripped-down cognitive architecture that captures the basic components of cognition to encourage interdisciplinary cooperation. Perception converts sensory stimuli into representations that can be stored in working memory or directly converted into actions by the motor component. Attention limits the amount of available perceptual information in both situations. Working memory provides a temporary storage space where perceptual information can be integrated with information from long-term declarative and long-term procedural memory. Declarative memory is the store for

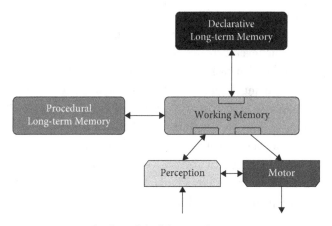

Figure 17.1. A standard model of the mind.

From J. E. Laird, C. Lebiere, & P. S. Rosenbloom, 2017, A standard model of the mind: Toward a common computational framework across artificial intelligence, cognitive science, neuroscience, and robotics, *AI Magazine, 38,* 13–26.

facts and concepts. Procedural memory contains knowledge about actions. The motor component executes the actions.

A standard model would provide a shared foundation for comparing human and machine reasoning. For instance, the explainable AI program discussed in Chapter 16 draws on extensive research on the psychology of human explanation that should help computers provide us with better explanations. This research has identified how different components in Figure 17.1 contribute to the effectiveness of human explanations. Limitations occur when we attend to irrelevant information, generate too simple an explanation because of the limited capacity of working memory, and retrieve superficial information from long-term memory.

The authors of the standard model hope that it will grow over time to include more data, applications, architectures, and researchers. This could happen in symposia and workshops in which the different disciplinary groups work together to provide incremental refinements to the model.

Robotics

Robotics is one of the four domains included in the standard model. An advantage of beginning with robotics is that robots require all components of the model including the perception and motor components. They are therefore uniquely suited for developing and evaluating general theories of cognition, such as grounded cognition. According to Giovanni Pezzulo and his co-authors, grounded cognition views all cognitive activities as emerging from a variety of bodily, affective, perceptual, and motor processes that occur within physical and social environments. Figure 17.2 shows these interrelationships.

The authors advocate for cognitive robotics as a research methodology for developing theories of grounded cognition. Cognitive

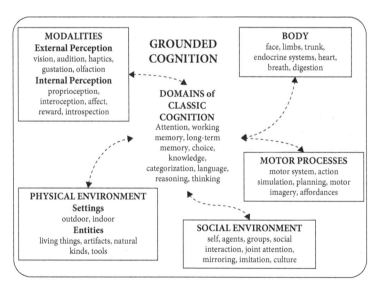

Figure 17.2. A grounded cognition field map.

From G. Pezzulo, L. W. Barsalou, A. Cangelosi, M. H. Fischer, K. McRae, & M. J. Spivey, 2013, Computational grounded cognition: A new alliance between grounded cognition and computational modeling. *Frontiers in Psychology, 3*(612).

robotics takes its inspiration from theories of human and animal cognition while attempting to build robots with comparable abilities. The theories require unified design principles to combine multiple psychological processes (attention, memory, action, control) within the context of a specific task. They are based on the principle that behavior and cognition are guided by goals that require actions to achieve them.

One of the most fundamental requirements for both robots and people is the ability to navigate in a spatial environment. An international collaboration is creating cognitively plausible spatial models to function in complex realistic environments. The project is developing Bayesian models for self-localization, object localization, map structuring, route planning, and map correction. Their goal is to construct computational models that (a) are implementable in brains, (b) can reproduce behavioral data, (c) be integrated within a cognitive architecture, and (d) navigate in realistic environments.

Navigating in realistic environments is needed for many practical applications such as warehouse management, medical care, home assistance, and transportation. Participants in a workshop sponsored by the National Science Foundation on robot planning concluded that achieving the full potential of robots will require improving their ability to process sensory data in real time, effectively utilize available resources, adapt to changes in the environment, and cooperate with humans. Cooperating with humans requires developing a shared language that both robots and people can understand.

To execute a command a robot needs to connect the command to its perception of the environment and its ability to act on the environment. The Language and Action Research group at Michigan State University is accomplishing this task by matching the nodes and links in a language network with the nodes and links in a vision network. The developers also utilized pointing gestures to increase the level of performance. Relying on human gaze patterns was less effective than pointing because looking can be unreliable in interactive environments. An ultimate goal is to enable robots to continuously learn from their human partners through lifelong interactions.

Language

I previously mentioned that I spent my first year in retirement as a visiting scholar at Stanford's Center for the Study of Language and Information. I used the Center as a base for attending various meetings on campus, and some of these meetings required walking through Stanford's impressive engineering campus. During one of my walks, I peeked into the lobby of the Gates Computer Science Building and read the quotes of faculty members printed on the walls. One in particular caught my attention: "In my opinion, getting a language for expressing general commonsense knowledge for inclusion in a general database is the key problem of generality in AI." John McCarthy, 1971. I had not realized that John McCarthy is credited with inventing the term *artificial intelligence* until I read the answers to the quiz in Chapter 14. However, I did know that he was one of the founders of the discipline and helped establish the Stanford AI Lab so I take notice when I read his proclamations.

Sergei Nirenburg addresses the greater challenge that in order for computer systems to communicate they must understand people's needs and motives, be aware of some of their beliefs, remember past experiences, and use these experiences in decision-making. Understanding requires not only recognizing the current situation but knowing the goals and plans of the participants. He argues that the ultimate criterion of success in building a computer system is whether the system behaves like a human and its behavior makes sense to the people who interact with it.

Progress in building such systems is discussed by Marjorie McShane. McShane states that language is important because it is often a prerequisite for reasoning about the knowledge, beliefs, and goals of others. Understanding requires learning words and concepts, interpreting indirect speech, managing ambiguity and incongruity, and pursuing implications. Context is often needed for resolving ambiguities to interpret referents, ontological scripts, the plans and goals of agents, and even perceptual information. I previously discussed the importance of context in several chapters including those on comprehension (Chapter 1), imperfect knowledge (Chapter 9), and information sciences (Chapter 15).

Nigel Ward and David DeVault inform us that the challenges in building highly interactive dialogue systems include surpassing human models, enabling exploration, integrating learned and designed behaviors, synthesizing multifunctional behaviors, modeling user variation, and making evaluation more informative. Solving these challenges will make conversations with artificial agents such as Siri and Erica more natural, efficient, and task-related. A final challenge is to engage social scientists. According to Ward and DeVault, today's dialog systems are seldom based on the findings of social scientists, and therefore the results of dialog systems research are rarely noticed by them.

Intelligence Tests

AI excels in performing specialized tasks but lacks the generality of human intelligence. A goal of AI is to build on its previous success in specific environments to advance toward the generality of human-level intelligence. Measuring progress in achieving this objective requires tests to measure intelligence.

Many examples of such measures occur in the Spring 2016 issue of *AI Magazine* on the topic "Beyond the Turing Test." The Turing test was the initial measure of machine intelligence, designed to fool people that they were conversing with a human rather than a machine. One problem with the Turing test was that it focused on deception rather than on intelligence. A second problem was that language is only one aspect of intelligence. The special issue contains 10 articles on other tests of machine intelligence that can be used as measures of general AI. I summarize five of the articles and encourage interested readers to view the others.

One of the articles proposed a multidimensional Turing test by using the Olympic decathlon for inspiration. The multidimensional test would require a computer to perform a variety of intelligence tests, as the Decathlon requires an athlete to perform a variety of track events. Figure 17.3 shows a large set of possible candidates. A practical group of tests should evaluate several dimensions of intelligence while allowing for objective scoring, automated scoring, and measures of incremental progress.

An example that requires a variety of skills is visual question answering in which a machine must understand the question, interpret an image, and reason about the answer. The test can be applied to a large database consisting of 760,000 human-generated questions about images. The questions span many age groups such as "Is this man wearing shoes?" for preschoolers to "Is this a vegetarian meal?" for high school students. The test has the advantages that it can be easily evaluated, and the questions vary across a wide range of difficulty.

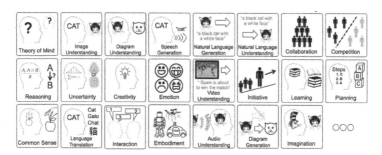

Figure 17.3. Candidates for intelligence tests.
From S. S. Adams, G. Banavar, & M. Campbell, 2016, I-athalon: Toward a multidimensional Turing test, *AI Magazine*, 2016(Spring), 78–84.

Performance on standardized tests provides another measure of machine intelligence. Peter Clark and Oren Etzioni give examples that can be used to directly assess the ability to answer actual questions found in education and science. This ability can range from answers based on common sense to answers based on sophisticated models of the world. Here are two of their examples:

- Can you make a watermelon fit into a bag by folding the watermelon?
- Fourth graders are planning a roller-skate race. Which surface would be the best for this race? (A) gravel (B) sand (C) blacktop (D) grass

Note that most children could answer these questions, but the answers nonetheless depend on both extensive knowledge and the ability to make inferences from that knowledge. Other questions require reasoning from diagrams such as finding the length of a line in a geometry exam or selecting the correct depiction of a life cycle in a biology exam.

An advantage of a physically embodied Turing test is that it would require the integration of four major aspects of AI research—perception, action, language, and reasoning. Charles Ortiz partitions this challenge into two tracks. The construction track requires using a combination of text and pictures to build predefined structures such as modular furniture or a tent. The exploration track requires improvising and experimenting with possible structures such as occurs when a child plays with Lego blocks.

Grand Challenges

I want to elaborate on a fifth article that introduces a grand challenge specified in its title: "Artificial Intelligence to Win the Nobel Prize and Beyond: Creating the Engine for Scientific Discovery."

According to the article's author, Hiroaki Kitano, grand challenges are a driving force in AI research. Examples include the IBM computer champion Deep Blue defeating world champion Gary Kasparov in 1997and IBM's Watson computer winning $1 million on the TV show *Jeopardy* in 2011. Kitano is the founder of another grand challenge, RoboCup, which has the goal of building humanoid robots that can defeat the World Cup soccer champions in 2050. A part of RoboCup that focuses on disaster rescue has already been deployed in real-life situations such as search-and-rescue operations following the attack on New York's World Trade Center.

Hitano proposes that scientific discovery should be the next grand challenge. He predicts, "In the near future, AI systems will make a succession of discoveries that have immediate medical implications, saving millions of lives, and totally changing the fate of the human race." He is uniquely qualified to make such a prediction. Hitano is the director of Sony Computer Science Laboratories, a professor at the Okinawa Institute of Science and Technology, and a group director for the Laboratory of Disease Systems Modeling. His research currently focuses on artificial intelligence for biomedical scientific discovery and application.

Hitano lists some fundamental difficulties that overwhelm the cognitive capabilities of researchers. The first is an overload of information. The amount of data is accumulating at a faster and faster pace based on a variety of new measurements. The publication of biomedical research is far beyond the capabilities of scientists to read these articles. A second problem is that papers frequently involve ambiguity, inaccuracy, and missing information. Readers therefore have to fill in gaps based on their own knowledge, resulting in an arbitrary interpretation of the content. A third problem is cognitive bias that occurs for both authors and their readers. Thought processes are biased as reflected in our use of language in reasoning and communication.

One way in which AI could assist in making scientific discoveries is by helping scientists ask the right questions. However, Katano argues that a more realistic use of AI is to more efficiently explore the extensive amount of accumulated knowledge. The importance of asking the right questions is reduced when computers contribute abundant time and resources. A critical aspect of scientific discovery is generating and testing many hypotheses, including those that seem highly unlikely. Figure 17.4 illustrates how computers can contribute throughout this process.

The report *Intelligence and Life in 2030* provides reflections about AI and its influence as the field advances. It covers the domains of transportation, robots, healthcare, education, low-resource communities, public safety and security, employment and workplace, and entertainment. We can expect to see more self-driving cars, healthcare diagnostics and treatment, and physical assistance for the elderly. Policy decisions made in the near future are likely

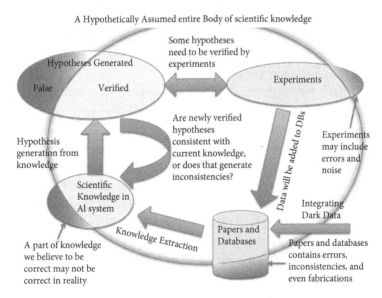

Figure 17.4. Scientific discovery and knowledge accumulation.

From H. Kitano, 2016, Artificial intelligence to win the Nobel prize and beyond: Creating the engine for scientific discovery, *AI Magazine, 37,* 39–49.

to have long-lasting influences on the direction of developments, making it important for AI researchers, developers, social scientists, and policymakers to balance innovation with social benefits that are broadly shared across society. The study panel produces the report every five years so we can look forward to periodic updates.

PART VI
EDUCATION

18

Complex Systems

I tried to avoid the letter C as a student but could not as a writer when I decided to finish the book with three chapters on learning 21st-century skills. I selected complex systems, computational and mathematical thinking, and continuing education as critical topics. In Chapter 13 on dynamics, I mentioned that Scott Kelso founded the Center for Complex Systems and Brain Sciences at Florida Atlantic University to develop empirical and conceptual frameworks to explain how coordinated patterns form, persist, adapt, and change. These changes create dynamical systems— complex systems that fluctuate over time. Vallacher, Coleman, Nowak, and Bui-Wrzosinska later applied dynamical systems theory to conflict resolution, which Robin Vallacher and I incorporated into our article on comparing the similarities and differences between dynamical-system and information-processing constructs. We began our article by referring to Jonathan Hilpert and Gwen Marchand's (2018) distinction between component-dominant and interaction-dominant systems. Figure 18.1 shows their diagram of the two systems.

The relationships between the components in component-dominant systems are primarily sequential as depicted in the left diagram. It has the structure of a flow chart in which information flows from left to right. Language is an example of a sequential process because one word follows another word. I mentioned in the chapter on design that I enjoy approaching the Geisel Library on the University of California at San Diego campus. Above the entrance to the library are the four words

Cognitive Skills You Need for the 21st Century. Stephen K. Reed, Oxford University Press (2020). © Oxford University Press. DOI: 10.1093/oso/9780197529003.001.0001.

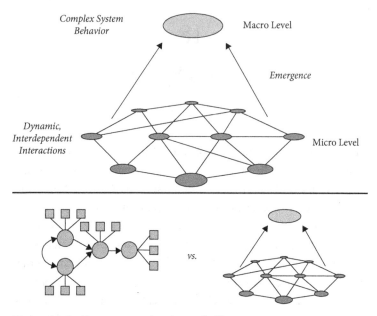

Figure 18.1. Component-dominant (left) versus interaction-dominant (right) systems.

From J. C. Hilpert & G. C. Marchand, 2018, Complex systems research in educational psychology: Aligning theory and method, *Educational Psychologist, 53,* 185–202.

READ WRITE THINK DREAM

I read from left-to-right so think of the words as sequential stages but then object to their order. Thinking and dreaming occur too late if delayed until after writing. My preferred order is

DREAM READ THINK WRITE

Writing begins with a dream that the author has something interesting to convey. It then requires reading and thinking before writing.

The upper part of Figure 18.1 reveals that the relationships between the components in interaction-dominant systems do not occur in a sequential order. The strength and direction of their relationships change over time and context. As writing progresses, it interacts with dreaming, reading, and thinking to create a more interactive-dominant system. Missing from the interaction is the word is ACT. John Keegan writes in his biography of Winston Churchill:

> In the end the personality of Churchill and the prose that inspired his being so interpenetrated each other as to be indistinguishable and mutually inextricable. The inner voice of words shaped his thought and determined his choices. Prose was deed, prose was outcome. Churchill the war leader was literature in action and written history in realization.

It is these dynamic qualities and interdependent relationships among variables that provide the foundation for the dynamical-systems approach to modeling behavior.

Critical Transitions

A characteristic of emergence, discussed in Chapter 13 on dynamics, is the sudden transition from one state to another state that occurs after reaching a tipping point. *The Tipping Point* was Malcom Gladwell's first bestseller in which he described the rapid spread of ideas that began with a slow progression. The tipping point in his examples depended on richly connected social networks like those shown in Figures 6.1A and D. It helps, of course, to have good ideas and enthusiastic people to promote them.

Transitions are also noteworthy in science as I discovered when browsing through a 2012 issue of *Science* magazine. I noticed an article that had many authors who came from many countries and many different departments. The departments included environmental sciences, limnology, economics, conservation ecology, and evolutionary studies. The title of their article is "Anticipating Critical Transitions."

The number and diversity of the authors demonstrates the importance of transitions in many types of complex systems. The left network in Figure 18.2 is composed of nodes that differ from the other nodes (heterogeneity) and are relativity independent (modularity). The consequence is that the network is more adaptive to stress and the changes are gradual. The right network in Figure 18.2 is composed of nodes that are similar to other nodes (homogeneity) and are more connected. This network is less adaptive to stress, causing critical transitions as a domino effect spreads throughout the network. Research is revealing how the structure of networks may cause ecological systems, financial markets, and other complex systems to collapse.

Multiple connections within a network help it survive small challenges but also give a false impression of its resilience to survive larger challenges. An example is the collapse of the Caribbean coral

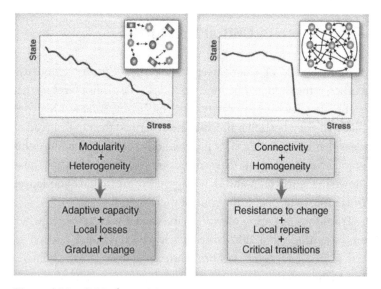

Figure 18.2. Critical transitions.

From M. Scheffer, S. R. Carpenter, T. M. Lenton, J. Bascompte, W. Brock, V. Dakos, . . . J. Vandermeer, 2012, Anticipating critical transitions, *Science, 338,* 344–348.

system in the 1980s caused by the outbreak of a sea urchin disease. The coral reefs had recovered repeatedly from devastating tropical storms but failed to meet the bigger challenge. The rate of recovery from smaller challenges may nonetheless serve as an early warning signal. Critical slowing down of recovery can indicate less resilience to survive greater degrees of stress. The authors of the *Science* article inform us that indicators of resilience have been discovered in ecology and climate change, but the social sciences and medicine are also promising fields for exploration.

An interdisciplinary group of scientists recently pooled their knowledge to consider how network resilience applies to mental health. They viewed resilience in maintaining mental health as a dynamic process that reacts to stress rather than as a unitary personality construct. As an example of a possible biological interaction, anxiety may lead to high levels of stress hormones that impair executive control that impairs social functioning that induces feelings of despair.

Figure 18.3 shows how an external stressor (E) could affect a symptom and resilience network. The symptoms are anxiety (S1),

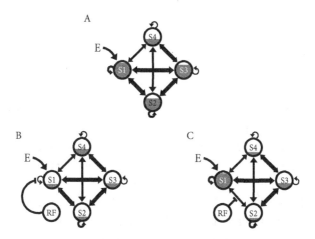

Figure 18.3. A symptom and resilience network.

From R. Kalisch, 2019, Deconstructing and reconstructing resilience: A dynamic network approach, *Perspectives on Psychological Science, 14*, 765–777.

social functioning (S2), depression (S3), and somatic feelings such as tension and exhaustion (S4). Examples of resilience factors (RF) are protective skills, coping styles, social resources, molecular feedback mechanisms, and gene-expression patterns. The interconnectivity of the network implies that increased anxiety increases other symptoms as revealed by the partially filled circles in Figure 18.3A. A resilience factor that reduces anxiety should therefore reduce other symptoms as illustrated in Figure 18.3B. Figure 18.3C shows the application of a resilience factor to a link in the network. Reducing the effect of anxiety on social functioning should also reduce depression and somatic symptoms.

Science Standards

The increasing importance of complex systems for understanding science requires excellent instruction. Excellent science instruction is the goal of a report titled *A Framework for K–12 Science Education*, published by the United States National Academy of Sciences. The core ideas of the Next Generation Science Standards are

1. Have broad importance across multiple sciences or engineering disciplines or be a key organizing principle of a single discipline.
2. Provide a key tool for understanding or investigating more complex ideas and solving problems.
3. Relate to the interests and life experiences of students or be connected to societal or personal concerns that require scientific or technological knowledge.
4. Be teachable and learnable over multiple grades at increasing levels of depth and sophistication. That is, the idea can be made accessible to younger students but is broad enough to sustain continued investigation over years.

Deborah Keleman at Boston University has made a strong case for teaching counterintuitive ideas such atomic theory much sooner in elementary school. Such instruction would take advantage of children's natural search for explanations as indicated by the "why" questions asked by two- and three-year-olds. Such questions often go unanswered because adults are preoccupied with other tasks or simply don't know the answers. She recommends focusing on unifying mechanisms that are likely a cause of misconceptions to reduce later academic struggles.

The science standards are goals that reflect what a student should know; they do not dictate the manner or methods by which the standards are taught. Teachers have flexibility to arrange the goals in any order within a grade level to satisfy the requirements of state and local districts. The framework identifies crosscutting themes to give students an organizational structure to connect ideas across disciplines and grades. The themes include finding patterns, establishing cause and effect, identifying structure and function, and studying the stability and change of systems. A challenge for distinguishing between sequential and emergent processes is that students typically classify phenomena as sequential because of their greater familiarity with sequential processes.

Dynamically emergent structures provide a helpful framework for helping educators react to students' fragmented knowledge and misconceptions discussed in Chapter 9. David Brown in the Department of Curriculum and Instruction at the University of Illinois proposes that in a dynamic systems perspective, misconceptions emerge from knowledge structures that change and evolve. Instruction aimed at genuine change and growth requires promoting change over an extended period of time rather than attempting a "quick fix." The unpredictability of interactive dynamics requires a flexible curriculum and attentive teachers to find effective paths for navigating these dynamic changes.

Instruction

Michael Jacobson and Manu Kapur are leaders in the study of instruction on complex systems. In one of their articles, they investigated the learning of emergent interactions by three groups of undergraduates who used the NetLogo modules Ants (social insects foraging for food), Traffic Jams (automotive transportation system), Slime Molds (self-organizing single cell organisms), Segregation (human social system) and Wolf–Sheep Predation (food web ecosystem). The NetLogo modules, developed by Northwestern's Center for Connected learning and Computer-Based Modeling, enable learners to give simple rules to individual "agents" and observe the combined results in a simulation of the agents' behavior. The models can be explored and revised as part of model-based inquiry in middle, secondary, and undergraduate classrooms.

To help students learn, the investigators included instructional support (scaffolds) such as "Contrast and compare how the concept of self-organization applies in the Slime Molds and the Wolf–Sheep Predation cases." All three groups, which differed in amount and type of scaffolding, demonstrated improved conceptual change scores for concepts such as "de-centralized," "random," and "emergent." All three groups additionally improved their problem-solving scores by exhibiting transfer to unstudied problems such as providing services in a large city.

Another of their projects focused on climate change—a disciplinary core idea in the Next Generation Science Standards. A group led by Michael Jacobson at the University of Sydney evaluated whether instruction based on both a complex systems model and a climate model would be more effective than instruction based only on a climate model. They conducted their study in the ninth-grade of an Australian all-girls school with high-achieving students.

Table 18.1 shows daily topics for the climate model and for the complex systems model. The one-model group studied only

NetLogo modules on climate change while the two-model group compared the climate modules with NetLogo modules on other types of complex systems. These modules, shown in the last column of Table 18.1, had topics that differed from climate change but shared common principles. For instance, on Day 3 both the Climate and the Ants Foraging topics illustrated the effect of feedback in complex systems. The potential advantage of comparing two topics is that students will learn to apply complex-systems principles across a greater variety of topics. A potential disadvantage of comparing two topics is the possibility of confusion created by the greater cognitive demands of the instruction.

Students in both groups did equally well on tests that required them to explain ideas about climate change (such as the carbon cycle) and about complex systems (such as emergent properties). The students also did equally well in solving a near-transfer problem that was closely related to the instruction. However, the two-model group did significantly better in solving a far-transfer problem that required them to apply their knowledge to a different domain—using robots to mine gold on a remote planet. Problem comparisons in other research projects have also often found that problem comparisons are helpful in creating the more general schematic knowledge discussed in Chapter 11 on problem-solving. Such schematic knowledge supports transfer to a broader range of problems.

The practical significance of instruction on climate change was dramatically illustrated by the fires raging in Australia when I read this article in January 2020. By the middle of January, bush fires had killed at least 26 people and burned thousands of homes. More than 13,000 head of cattle had been killed in the state of New South Wales where more than 20,000 square miles of land had burned. The fires threatened the country's unique wildlife, and scientists feared some species would be pushed to the brink of extinction.

Climate change, of course, threatens regions throughout the world. The Global Change Research Act of 1990 mandates that the

Table 18.1 Daily Activities for the Climate Model and Complex Systems Model

Day	Complex Systems Daily Topics	Climate Model	Complex Systems Model
1	Pre-test		
2	Dynamic equilibrium	Carbon Cycle Climate topics: Equivalent carbon, *carbon cycle, fossil fuel; carbon* sinks Complexity topics (both models): Equilibrium, dynamic *equilibrium, closed system*	Wolf–Sheep Predation Climate topics None
3	Feedback in dynamic systems	Climate with Feedback Climate topics: *Global temperature greenhouse effect,* amid cover Complexity topics (both models): *Input, output, positive feedback negative feedback, self-organization*	Ants Foraging Climate topics *None*
4	Emergence	Wind and Storm Climate topics: *Convection wind, greenhouse effect, enhanced greenhouse effect* Complexity topics (both models): *Emergence, micro level of systems, macro level of systems*	Birds Flocking *Climate* topics None
5	Tipping points and positive feedback	Climate with Water Feedback Climate topics: *Atmospheric water feedback albedo*	Forest Fire Climate topics *None*
6	Post-test	Complexity topics (both models): *Positive feedback, tipping points, linear* versus *non-linear effects*	

From M. J. Jacobson, M. Goldwater, L. Markauskaite, P. K. Lai, M. Kapur, G. Roberts, & C. Hilton, 2020, Schema abstraction with productive failure and analogical comparison: learning designs for far across domain transfer, *Learning and Instruction, 65,* 101222. Reprinted with permission from Elsevier.

U.S. Global Change Research Program deliver a report to Congress and the president at least every four years. The 2018 report reviewed national concerns such as water, energy, land use, ecosystems, coastal effects, oceans and marine resources, rural communities, urban systems, transportation, air quality, and human health. It also reviewed regional concerns within the United States. The many contributors should be proud of their efforts. The design and content make it the most impressive report that I have ever seen.

In an annual climate report discussed in the January 16, 2020 edition of *The Wall Street Journal* scientists at the National Aeronautical and Space Administration and the National Oceanic and Atmospheric Administration reported that the temperatures in 2019 were the second warmest since record keeping begin in 1880. In June and July, Europe recorded two of its most intense heat waves of modern history. In the United States, there were 14 weather-related disasters that each created more than $1 billion in damage.

Instructional Needs

Climate change is only one topic that would benefit from more instruction on complex systems. To determine whether complex-systems instruction aligned with the Next Generation Science Standards and reflected the research of real-world science investigations Susan Yoon, Sao-Ee Goh, and Miyoung Park reviewed 75 studies conducted between 1995 and 2015. Their review distinguished between structures, processes, and states. Structures refer to the physical features of the system such as the number and name of the variables and how the variables are connected to each other. Processes refer to the dynamics of the systems such as self-organization, the causal nature of the relationships, and emergence. States refer to how complex systems exist in the world as a result of shifts to existing structures and processes. The review revealed a need for more emphasis on system states that influence equilibrium, robustness, and resilience.

Another variable in their review was science content that distinguished between biology, chemistry, computer science, earth science, ecology, physics, and engineering. There was an abundance of studies in the domains of biology and ecology. Biological systems included circulatory and respiratory systems, cellular systems, and genetics. Topics from ecology included population growth, global warming, and effect of pollutants on ecosystems. The review revealed a need for more instructional research on knowledge domains outside of biology and ecology. The reviewers recommended that future research on improving complex-systems instruction should include its application to many other domains including psychology.

The review also revealed that the studies primarily represented early-stage exploratory research. Although the study of complex-systems instruction is relatively recent compared to established courses such as mathematics, some of its subfields are mature enough to justify more systematic comparisons of alternative instructional designs. The reviewers recommended that research should include exploring how to scale-up interventions for inclusion within a comprehensive curriculum.

19

Computational and Mathematical Thinking

Developing 21st-century skills would have a gaping hole if it did not include computational thinking. The report *Computational Thinking for a Computational World* begins with the observation that technology has fundamentally changed how we live in the world and perhaps even how we think.

Figure 19.1 shows the interrelationships between computational thinking, computer science, and coding. The report defines computational thinking as a way of solving problems, designing systems, and understanding human behavior that draws on concepts fundamental to computer science. Computer science is the study of computers and algorithmic processes including their principles, hardware, software, and applications to society. Coding is the practice of developing a set of directions that a computer can understand and execute.

Computational Thinking

In their 2013 article in *Educational Researcher* Suchi Grover and Roy Pea at Stanford University reviewed the status of instruction on computational thinking. They claimed that the approach to problem-solving based on computational thinking was a critical omission from the K–12 Science and Mathematics education curriculum. Early experiences with this type of problem-solving would not only subsequently help students in introductory computer

Cognitive Skills You Need for the 21st Century. Stephen K. Reed, Oxford University Press (2020). © Oxford University Press. DOI: 10.1093/oso/9780197529003.001.0001.

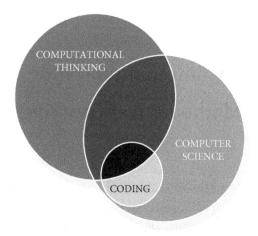

Figure 19.1. The relation between coding, computer science, and computational thinking.

From *Computational Thinking for a Computational World*. Retrieved from www. digitalpromise.org.

science courses but also generate interest and prime students for success in this growing field. As an example, they referred to a computer science course that the College Board was then developing with assistance from the National Science Foundation.

In 2016, the College Board's Advanced Placement (AP) Program oversaw the largest course launch in the program's 60-year history with the release of AP Computer Science Principles. The course introduces students to the foundational concepts of the field and challenges them to explore how computing and technology can impact the world. In the 2018–2019 school year more than 5,000 schools were offering the course. A second course, AP Computer Science A, focuses on computing skills related to programming in Java. The Principles course complements AP Computer Science A by teaching the foundational concepts of computer science to encourage broader participation. Its big ideas are creativity, abstraction, data and information, algorithms, programming, the Internet, and global impact. Unlike Computer Science A, it allows teachers to select a programming language for the course.

The College Board announced that nearly 100,000 students took the AP Computer Science Principles Exam in 2019, more than doubling participation since the course launched during 2016–2017 school year. During that period, the number of female students, Black/African American students, and Hispanic/Latino students more than doubled.

In their extensive literature review on demystifying computational thinking Valerie Shute, Chen Son, and Jodi Asbell-Clark discuss the characteristics, interventions, and assessment of computational thinking in studies ranging from kindergarten to undergraduate courses. Interventions include using programming tools, robotics, and game design. Characteristics include decomposition, abstraction, algorithms, debugging, iteration, and generalization. Table 19.1 defines each of these characteristics.

A challenge is to match the growing demand for computational skills with an increasing supply of prepared teachers. To meet this demand, Digital Promise, the organization that produced the report *Computational Thinking for a Computational World*, developed 10 competency-based micro-credentials to recognize specific skills. Five of the credentials focus on key elements of

Table 19.1 Characteristics of Computational Thinking

Characteristic	Purpose
Decomposition	Dissect a complex problem into manageable parts that collectively comprise the whole problem.
Abstraction	Identify patterns underlying the information. Construct models or simulations to represent how the system operates.
Algorithms	Design sequential instructions for solving the problem.
Debugging	Identify and fix errors when the solution does not work.
Iteration	Repeat the design process to refine solutions.
Generalization	Transfer computational thinking skills to a wide range of situations.

Based on V. J. Shute, C. Sun, and J. Asbell-Clarke (2017). Demystifying computational thinking. *Educational Research Review, 22*, 142–158.

computational thinking: working with data, creating algorithms, understanding systems with computational models, creating computational models, and developing computational literacies. The remaining five focus on instructional practices: creating an inclusive environment for computational thinking, integrating computational thinking into the curriculum, assessing computational thanking, using computers as tools for thinking, and selecting the appropriate tools.

Computer Programming

In a 1985 article in *Educational Researcher*, Marcia Linn at the University of California at Berkeley discussed the advantages of learning computer programming. At the most specific level, students learn a particular programming language such as Basic. At a more general level, they learn to design programs that consist of reusable patterns of code that Linn labels "templates." At the most general level students learn broad problem-solving skills that transfer to other problems. Linn advocates that introductory programing courses should explicitly identify those aspects of programming that generalize to other disciplines.

I took my first programming course in graduate school to learn Fortran and used it for my dissertation to calculate mathematical solutions to matrix problems. I later learned to program in Basic to create and evaluate instructional animation on my Apple II computer. I subsequently learned HyperCard to run an experiment. It was insightful to discover both similarities and differences between these computer languages. My experiences have been very consistent with Linn's list of advantages of learning programming skills. For me, programming represents the essence of problem-solving.

A recent article in the *Review of Educational Research* titled "Changing a Generation's Way of Thinking: Teaching

Computational Thinking Through Programming" justifies its broad title. The authors at the Universidad de los Andes in Bogota, Columbia, contributed an extensive review of teaching programming skills, including its relation to computational thinking. They define computational thinking as a way of reasoning that consists of high-level skills and practices that are at the heart of computing but applicable to many areas beyond computer science. The authors list the various ways in which computational thinking is applicable to biology, chemistry, physics, medicine, engineering, the arts, music, and the social sciences.

The Systems and Computing Engineering Department at their university assists students through an interactive platform that provides an extensive set of resources. The platform includes lectures, workshops, books, articles, lab exercises, concept maps, and tutorials. Students' lack of prior experience nonetheless limits their ability to learn specialized programming languages. The authors therefore proposed that high school students should be exposed to the development of logic, abstraction, decomposition, and comprehension of basic algorithmic design to facilitate the learning of programming languages in higher education. In addition, constructivist, social cultural, and pedagogical approaches are needed to create computational thinking skills in primary, middle, and high school. The article cites many references and provides a comprehensive overview that should be required reading for anyone interested in this topic.

Many articles and reports have praised the cognitive benefits of learning computer programming, but is there evidence? There is. A recent statistical analysis of 105 studies concluded that learning how to program a computer improves a variety of cognitive skills. The instruction improved reasoning, creative thinking, meta-cognition (managing cognition), spatial skills, and mathematical skills. Furthermore, improvement in cognitive skills occurred at all grade levels: kindergarten, primary school, secondary school, and college.

Mathematical Thinking

Computational thinking is supported by mathematics, a topic that would also benefit from a broad overview. I recommend the book *In Pursuit of the Unknown: 17 Equations that Changed the World* by Ian Stewart. The author, an Emeritus Professor of Mathematics at Warwick University in the United Kingdom, has written many books on mathematics that have been widely praised. For instance,

- "Stewart has a genius for explanation. . . . Mathematics doesn't come more entertaining than this."—*New Scientist*
- "Combines a deep understanding of math with an engaging literary style."—*The Washington Post*
- "Possibly mathematics most energetic evangelist."—*The Spectator* (London)
- "Stewart admirably captures compelling and assessable mathematical ideas along with the pleasure of thinking about them."—*Los Angeles Times*

Professor Stewart explains that there are two types of equations that on the surface look very similar. One type presents relations between different mathematical quantities and the task requires determining whether the equation is true. Equations in pure mathematics are usually of this type. The second type provides information about an unknown quantity, and the task is to solve for this unknown. Equations in applied mathematics and physics are usually of this type. Both types appear in the book, as listed in Box 19.1.

Stewart selected the equations because of their historical importance. Newton's Law of Gravity informed us about the motion of the planets and how to send space probes to explore them. Maxwell's equations helped launch radio, television, and communications. Shannon's information theory places limits on the effectiveness of communications. Chaos theory allows scientist to study many irregularities in nature without resulting to statistics by revealing

---

Box 19.1 Seventeen Equations That Changed the World

1. Pythagoras's Theorem	7. Normal Distribution	13. Relativity
2. Logarithms	8. Wave Equation	14. Shroedinger's Equation
3. Calculus	9. Fourier Transform	15. Information Theory
4. Newton's Law of Gravity	10. Navier–Stokes Equation	16. Chaos Theory
5. Square Root of Minus One	11. Maxwell's Equations	17. Black–Scholes Equation
6. Formula for Polyhedra	12. Law of Thermodynamics	

Based on I. Stewart (2012). *In pursuit of the unknown: 17 equations that changed the world*. New York: Basic Books.

---

patterns that characterize chaos. It is one of the ways in which modern dynamical systems theory is changing the way scientists think about the world.

Each of the short chapters on the 17 equations begins with a summary page that labels symbols in the equation and explains what it tells us, why it is important, and what it created. Figure 19.2 shows the first page of Chapter 1 of *In Pursuit of the Unknown* on Pythagoras's Theorem. Stewart includes in his historical overview that the Greek philosopher Thales used the geometry of triangles to estimate the height of the Giza pyramids about 600 BCE, the Dutch mapmaker Gemma Frisius helped launch surveying in 1533 by explaining how to use trigonometry to produce accurate maps, and in 1854 the German mathematician Georg Bernhard Riemann generalized Euclidean geometry to curved surfaces.

1 The squaw on the hippopotamus
Pythagoras's Theorem

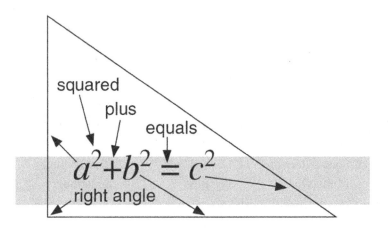

What does it tell us?

How the three sides of a right-angled triangle are related.

Why is that important?

It provides a vital link between geometry and algebra, allowing us to calculate distances in terms of coordinates. It also inspired trigonometry.

What did it lead to?

Surveying, navigation, and more recently special and general relativity – the best current theories of space, time, and gravity.

Figure 19.2. Introduction to Pythagoras's Theorem.

From I. Stewart, 2012, In pursuit of the unknown: 17 equations that changed the world. New York: Basic Books.

Perhaps the most infamous of the equations is the Black–Scholes equation in Chapter 17 of *In Pursuit of the Unknown* that describes how the price of a financial derivative changes over time. It is based on the principle that when the price is correct the derivative carries no risk, making it possible to trade the derivative as if it were a commodity. It is infamous because it led to a huge growth of the financial sector using ever more complex financial instruments until it precipitated the 2008–2009 financial crisis. The models used to place value on financial products and estimate their risk made simplifying assumptions that did not accurately represent actual markets. Stewart concludes that an equation is a tool that has to be used intelligently. "There is a danger that the financial sector may turn its back on mathematical analysis, when what it actually needs is a better range of models, and—crucially—a solid understanding of their limitations. The financial system is too complex to be run on human hunches and vague reasoning. It desperately needs *more* mathematics, not less." More mathematics requires greater emphasis on computational thinking as advocated in this chapter.

I would like to see *Pursuit of the Unknown* included in a university course for students majoring in mathematics education. It would provide them with an extensive background on the history and applications of mathematics that they could later incorporate into their own courses. The book would also be help high school students select mathematics courses in high school and later in college. I took three semesters of calculus in college. I do not regret taking calculus but have not used it in my career whereas I have used other mathematics courses such as abstract algebra, logic, matrices, and probability theory. Providing students with an overview of a broad range of mathematical topics should help them appreciate the discipline and assist them in selecting courses that provide the best fit for their interests.

Combining Computational and Mathematical Thinking

I mentioned in Chapter 8 on visuospatial reasoning that my initial crude attempts to program animation on my Apple II computer included two pixels that raced across the screen.

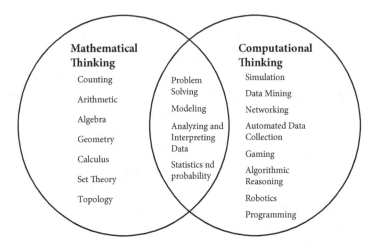

Figure 19.3. Venn diagram of mathematical and computational thinking.

From C. Sneider, C. Stephenson, B. Schafer, & L. Flick, 2014, Computational thinking in high school science classrooms, *The Science Teacher, 81,* 53–59.

I "moved" the pixels by turning off one pixel and turning on the adjacent one. My computer had to count from 1 to N before moving the pixel and the lower the value of N, the faster the speed. I measured how the value of N determined different speeds and stored these values in a table. I thought my program would be more elegant if I could find an equation that would produce each value of N without storing them. After finding a complex polynomial equation that could produce the correct value for each speed, my equation kicked my table out of my program and substituted itself.

Computational and mathematical thinking have much in common as illustrated in Figure 19.3. Problem-solving, modeling, analyzing and interpreting data, and statistics and probability are key components in developing skills for both domains.

Included in the article on computational thinking in high school science classrooms is material on implementing curriculum based on the recommendations of the Next Generation Science Standards. One activity is a six-unit lesson using StarLogo TNG simulation software that enables students to modify ecosystems involving carrots, rabbits, and wolves. The simulations reveal how increases or decreases in one component of the ecosystem influence the other components. The software encourages students to explore the dynamics of ecosystems by (a) using an existing simulation, (b) showing them how to modify the software, and (c) challenging them to apply their knowledge to design an entirely new simulation.

Another activity requires students to analyze geoscience data to make the claim that one change to the Earth's surface can create feedbacks that cause changes to other Earth systems. Interpreting data in grades 9–12 builds on K–8 experiences by introducing more detailed statistical analysis, comparison of data sets, and use of models to generate and analyze data. This and others activities are supported by the My NASA Data website that provides free activities for elementary, middle, and high school.

20

Continuing Education

The class motto of our 1962 Hartford High School graduating class was "The man who graduates today and stops learning tomorrow is uneducated the day after, " ascribed to Newton D. Baker. Newton D. Baker was the 27th mayor of Cleveland, Ohio, and served as the U.S. Secretary of War from 1916 to 1921. When I arrived in Cleveland to begin my first academic job at Case Western Reserve University I discovered the Newton D. Baker Building on campus. It housed the Office of Continuing Education. Replace the word "man" with the word "person" in Baker's quote, and it becomes even more valid today than it was in 1962.

This book's introduction reported predictions that much of the world's workforce will require extensive retraining. Articles in the media quickly confirmed these predictions. The title of a front-page article in the July 12, 2019 issue of the *Wall Street Journal* read "Amazon Prepares to Retrain A Third of its US Workforce" by spending $700 million over six years. "Technology is changing our society, and is certainly changing our work," said Jeff Wilkie, chief executive of Amazon's worldwide consumer business, describing the initiative as a way to help workers prepare for "the opportunities in the future."

To determine how respondents would prepare for a future that included artificial intelligence (AI), Gallup and Northeastern University surveyed more than 10,000 respondents over the age of 18 who resided either in the United States, Canada, or the United Kingdom. The resulting report "Facing the Future" revealed that 70% in the United States replied that they would look to their employers for training and only 28% responded that they would

Cognitive Skills You Need for the 21st Century. Stephen K. Reed, Oxford University Press (2020). © Oxford University Press. DOI: 10.1093/oso/9780197529003.001.0001.

seek licensing, certification, or a degree from a university. The percentage seeking university assistance was similar for Canada and the United Kingdom. In none of the countries did the majority of adults say they were confident in knowing which skills are required to adapt to AI. The report concluded,

> The current lack of confidence in institutions in the acceptance of the value of lifelong learning provides a clear opportunity for leaders in higher education. Partnering with governments and businesses to provide affordable, relevant, bite-sized, lifelong education to workers in all three countries could restore confidence, not just for higher education, but for the other institutions as well.

Universities

I consider myself extremely fortunate to have spent most of my life on university campuses. I was an undergraduate at the University of Wisconsin; a graduate student at University of California, Los Angeles; a postdoctoral fellow at the University of Sussex in Brighton, England; an assistant and associate professor at Case Western Reserve; a visiting associate professor at Carnegie Mellon and at the University of California, Berkeley; a professor at Florida Atlantic University and at San Diego State; and, most recently, a visiting scholar at Stanford University and at the University of California, San Diego. I want to share a few opinions based on these experiences and as an avid reader of *The Chronicle of Higher Education*.

An important decision that many high school graduates make before graduation is selecting a university to attend in the fall. I am dismayed whenever I learn that students are heartbroken because they were not accepted into a prestigious private university. I attended graduate school at University of California, Los

Angeles, but would likely had gone to Stanford had I been accepted there. I later had a chance to spend an inspiring academic year at Stanford as a visiting scholar following my retirement. I learned a lot by attending lab meetings in bioinformatics, education, and psychology.

I also realized during this time that living four years in Palo Alto would have been very mundane compared to the four exciting years I spent as a graduate student living in Los Angeles. I have many fond memories that include driving west in my convertible on Sunset Boulevard to the Pacific Coast Highway and then south to Santa Monica Beach; sitting 10 feet from the stage to hear Neil Diamond perform at the Troubadour when he could have easily sold out an entire arena; ushering at the Greek Theater with my fiancé; and looking up and up and up whenever Lew Alcindor walked past me near my apartment.

But tragedies occasionally penetrated the California sunshine. One morning I encountered my neighbor Vince who asked me if I had heard that Robert Kennedy had been shot. I replied that I had not. He then told that he had worked as a waiter at the Ambassador Hotel the previous evening and was in the kitchen when and where the shooting occurred. My initial knowledge of the assassination came from an eyewitness.

I believe that students can obtain a first-rate education at many universities and the most important criterion is selecting a university that provides a good fit with the student's abilities and aspirations. A September 5, 2019 issue of *The Wall Street Journal* contained a 10-page report on U.S. college rankings that provided a general ranking of 500 universities. It also ranked the top 10 schools for (a) resources, (b) student outcomes, (c) student engagement, (d) diversity, (e) best values, (f) small universities, (g) medium universities, and (h) large universities. Ranking universities according to these diverse criteria should help students make informed choices.

A second important decision for college students is selecting a major. An article in the August 16, 2019 issue of *The Chronicle of Higher Education* reported on how some colleges are helping freshman find their academic focus. In a closely watched move beginning in the fall of 2019, the entire University of Georgia system asked incoming freshmen to declare an academic focus area, if not a major. The purpose is to provide students with an initial direction to prevent wandering. The University of Houston has a similar program—Guided Pathways to Success—based on the same concept. These programs have been influenced by studies described in books such as Thaler and Sunstein's 2008 book *Nudge* that seeks to help people who are faced with an overwhelming number of options.

A third important decision is how to take full advantage of the many resources that the university offers. These can include participating in student government, writing for the student newspaper, entering art and photography competitions, and working in research labs. Attending conferences to listen and (more important) present is particularly illuminating. I donate my book royalties to student travel funds at my favorite universities and organizations. If you purchased this book, thank you for supporting a worthy cause.

Doctoral Training

I began Chapter 1 with my concern that people with PhDs are specialists who know a lot about very little. There is nothing wrong with being a specialist. Prominent faculty who receive major awards, large research grants, and distinguished professorships are invariably specialists who have become a world expert on their topic. They end their careers by investigating topics very similar to those at the beginning of their careers.

I am concerned, however, with the impact of specialization on doctoral training. Too often students in doctoral programs spend their entire graduate training in a single lab and are then expected to do an original research project as their dissertation. These dissertations are not always very original. Many simply continue ongoing research in the lab. An ideal dissertation from a professor's perspective is one that continues and cites the professor's research program after the student graduates. There is nothing wrong with this approach when it works.

I have witnessed many cases in which it does not work. Intelligent students from major doctoral programs can flounder in a tenure-track system after graduation because they cannot think of enough new ideas to sustain a career that requires innovative research. They did not have to think hard enough in graduate school about big ideas. One solution is that dissertation committees should require dissertations that demonstrate innovation rather than extrapolation.

Another solution is to require students to spend their graduate training in more than one laboratory so they achieve greater breadth of training. Broader training may even result in innovative projects that combine ideas across the two areas of research. The same recommendation applies to postdoctoral training to provide doctoral graduates with an opportunity to broaden, rather than merely extend, their training.

Obtaining an MA degree before a PhD provides another avenue to breadth of knowledge, particularly if there is a different focus in the two degrees. I mentioned that Arthur Evans and I worked together on evaluating mathematical instruction, and it became part of his MA thesis in experimental psychology at Florida Atlantic University. After next receiving his PhD in clinical/community psychology from the University of Maryland, he established a very successful career that led to his appointment in 2017 as the CEO of the American Psychological Association. As CEO, Evans became head of an organization with over 117,000 researchers, educators, clinician, consultants, and students as its members. It has 56 divisions organized around the interests of its members including addiction, clinical, community, consulting, consumer, counseling, comparative, developmental, educational, environmental, experimental, family, health, humanistic, international, media, military, pediatric, quantitative, rehabilitative, school, social, sport, and trauma psychology. The American Psychological Association provides guidance and continuing education to its diverse members.

Role Models

I have emphasized the importance of institutions in providing education and leadership but individuals are as important, particularly those who become role models. The heroes in 2020 are the brave men and women who have stood at the front lines in the battle against the coronavirus. Although most of us will never be as heroic we still have an opportunity to learn from, and become, role models.

Guidance can often be found within families. I dedicated my first book to my wife, my second book to my parents, and this book to my extended family. My late father-in-law, Dean Anderson, provides an exemplary role model for the value of continuing education. His expectation of graduating from Montana State University in 1944 with a BS degree in electrical engineering was interrupted when he was drafted into the U.S. Army Signal Corps in 1943. Following World War II, he joined Hazeltine Electronic Corporation in New York but continued his education through classes at New York University and correspondence courses from the University of Chicago. He eventually obtained a BS degree from Montana State and had a very successful career at North American Aviation in California, later incorporated into Rockwell International. He was honored with an IEEE Fellow Award "for contributions to optical waveguides and optical parametric amplification."

Educational, religious, service, professional, and social organizations provide another source for role models. My academic hero, Herb Simon (b. 1916–d. 2001), has influenced much of my work, including chapters in this book. Herb made many scholarly contributions across fields that included public administration, organization theory, AI, information processing, decision-making, and problem-solving. In 1978 he was awarded the Nobel Prize in Economics. One way of measuring academic impact is by number of citations. Anyone whose publications have been cited more than 25,000 times is an academic superstar in my opinion. There are not many scholars who exceed this number. According to Google Scholar, Herbert A. Simon's publications have received more than 360,000 citations.

The highlight of my academic career was the six months that I spent working with Herb in 1975 as a visiting associate professor at Carnegie Mellon University. His generosity matched his brilliance. He suggested that we list authors by alphabetical order when we submitted our manuscript "Modeling Strategy Shifts in a Problem Solving Task." The letter R does not win many alphabetic contests, but this time it did. I politely declined. Herb had all of the key ideas, and I would have felt guilty the rest of my life if listed as first author.

History provides us with another source for role models. Walter Isaacson begins his biography of Leonardo Da Vinci by summarizing a letter Leonardo wrote to the ruler of Milan that listed the reasons why he should be given a job. The first 10 paragraphs mentioned Leonardo's engineering skills that included designing bridges, waterways, cannons, armored vehicles, and public buildings. The eleventh paragraph mentioned that he could also paint. This claim would later be supported by two of the most famous paintings in history—The Last Supper and the Mona Lisa.

Although Leonardo Da Vinci epitomizes my idea of a universal genius, Isaacson argues that this label could oddly minimize his contribution by suggesting supernatural powers:

> In fact, Leonardo's genius was a human one, wrought by his own will and ambition. It did not come from being the divine recipient, like Newton and Einstein, of a mind with so much processing power that we mere mortals cannot fathom it. Leonardo

had almost no schooling and could barely read Latin or do long division. His genius was of the type we can understand and even take lessons from. It was based on skills we can aspire to improve in ourselves, such as curiosity and intense observation. He had imagination so excitable that it flirted with the edges of fantasy, which is also something we can try to preserve in ourselves and indulge in our children.

Leonardo Da Vinci demonstrated in the 15th-century cognitive skills that will endure forever in their importance.

Epilogue

The most surreal experience during my youth occurred during a family vacation to the east coast. We drove through New York City and found no signs of life after entering the financial district on a Sunday morning. The streets and sidewalks were empty. For a brief moment in time it appeared that humanity had vanished from the planet and only the vacant canyons created by the tall skyscrapers remained.

The lack of people on streets and sidewalks again is surreal as we experience the medical uncertainty that greeted the year 2020. By spring a coronavirus had created a global pandemic that required unprecedented action. In March I received an email from a family friend in northern Italy, one of the hardest hit regions:

We might be broke but find me another country that has:
- uniforms for doctors by Armani
- ventilators by Ferrari
- medical masks by Gucci
- disinfectant solution by Bulgari

We might go to hell but with style!

Major manufacturers were not the only ones who had to suddenly switch their agenda. Doctors and nurses had to maintain the front lines under threat to their own health. As the world began to shut down the newly unemployed had to figure out how to pay their bills. Educational institutions switched to on-line learning. Parents had to care for their children at home. People had to maintain social distancing. The most important cognitive skill in 2020 became adaptability.

I wrote this book before the pandemic but reviewed the proofs in mid-April. The cognitive skills attracted my renewed appreciation as I reread them within the context of the current world crisis. Fighting the pandemic requires situation awareness in the face of imperfect and uncertain knowledge. It requires data organization, the establishment of causality, scientific discovery, and the creation of disease models. It requires planning and persuasion. It requires coordination at the international, national, state, and municipal levels. Look again at the predicted trending skills by 2022 in Table I.1 of the Introduction. The World Economic Forum predictors in 2018 had no idea how much the world would change in 2020. Yet, all of the trending skills have been critical in fighting the global pandemic. Flattening the curve became the rallying cry of 2020, a cry that accelerated the need for the cognitive skills predicted in 2018.

In early April I saw a graph of the number of projected hospital beds needed on each day in California for Covid-19 patients. The projected number peaked in late April at 15,000 beds according to a March 26th prediction. The latest projection on April 5th lowered the peak to 5,000 beds in mid-April. Social distancing was beginning to flatten the curve.

That afternoon my editor sent me an image of the cover of this book for which I had previously selected the light bulb as a symbol of powerful thinking. I had remembered cartoons in which a light bulb above a person's head symbolized an insightful idea. I had recalled the use of light as a metaphor in words such as 'brilliant'. For the first time that afternoon I saw the light bulb in an alternative perspective. The rays emanating from it represented a beacon of hope. There is light at the end of the tunnel.

Notes

Introduction

ix. *Oxford & Cambridge: An Uncommon History* (Sager, 2005) is a fact-filled, entertaining history of the two institutions.

xi. Job advertisments list cognitive skills (Rios et al., 2020).

xi. *The Future of Jobs Report 2018* can be downloaded at http://www3. weforum.org/docs/WEF_Future_of_Jobs_2018.pdf.

xii. Computer algorithms impact many areas of our lives (Rahwan et al., 2019).

xii. *Only Humans Need Apply: Winners and Losers in the Age of Smart Machines* (Davenport & Kirby, 2016) discusses how technology will influence different segments of the workforce.

Chapter 1

4. Mayer (1996) proposed the select–organize–integrate framework to explain effective reading skills.

6. Purposeful reading requires managing goals during text comprehension (Rouet, Britt, & Durik, 2017).

6. Skimming the text can help determine what is important (Miyatsu, Nguyan, & McDaniel, 2018).

7. Abstract material impedes comprehension because it is difficult to organize (Bransford & Johnson, 1973).

8. Switching perspectives can be an effective retrieval cue (R. C. Anderson & Pichert, 1978).

9. Rittle-Johnson and Loehr (2017) evaluated when self-explanations aid learning.

11. Self-explanations are effective for a variety of outcome measures such as the ability to make inferences, recall information, solve problems, and transfer to new tasks (Bisra, Liu, Nesbit, Salimi, & Winne, 2018).

12. The Center for Disease Control and Prevention https://www.cdc.gov/ includes material on the spread of measles.

12. Weisman and Markman (2017) recommended guidelines for designing effective explanations.

13. The perceived quality of an explanation was positively influenced by its coherence, the extent to which most people would agree with the general principles, the quality of the articulation, and the ease of visualizing the principles (Zemla, Sloman, Bechlivanidis, & Lagnado, 2017).

Chapter 2

15. Barsalou (1999) proposed that perception and action are central components of cognition, which has been referred to as "embodied cognition" (Wilson, 2002).

15. The embodied approach has successfully been applied to reading instruction (Glenberg, Gutierrez, Levin, Japuntich, & Kaschak, 2004; Glenberg, Jaworski, Rischal, & Levin, 2007; Walker, Adams, Restrepo, Fialko, & Glenberg, 2017).

17. Combining actions and objects can occur physically, virtually, and mentally (Reed, 2018).

18. Lillard's (2005) book discusses Montessori's contributions with supporting research.

18. Laski, Jor'dan, Daoust, and Murray (2015) made recommendations for the effective use of manipulatives.

19. The Wii gaming system combines physical actions with virtual objects (Dogov, Graves, Nearents, Schwark, & Volkman, 2014).

19. Gestures are useful for learning arithmetic operations (Novack, Congdon, Hermani-Lopez, & Goldin-Meadow, 2014; Novack & Goldin-Meadow, 2017).

20. Performing surgical movements on the computer console require training unique actions that differ from those used in either open or laparoscopic surgery (Bric, Lumbard, Frelich, & Gould, 2016; Sridhar, Briggs, Kelly, & Nathan, 2017).

21. Studies (Klahr, Triona, & Williams, 2007; Triona & Klahr, 2003) demonstrate the effectives of virtual environments for learning experimental design.

21. An audio-based environmental simulator (Merabet, Connors, Halko, & Sanchez, 2012) helped the blind learn to navigate a virtual building and transfer learning to the physical building (Connors, Chrastil, Sanchez, & Merabet, 2014).

22. Brain computer interfaces record brain potentials to control robots (Spataro et al., 2017).
23. and a cursor on a computer screen (Ma et al., 2017).
23. A literature review summarizes the effect of different variables on mental simulations of sports activities (Cumming & Williams, 2014).
24. Research on putting is one example (Frank, Land, Poppp, & Schack, 2014).
24. Lanier's (2017) book documents his involvement in the design of virtual and augmented reality.
25. Dede (2009) discusses the advantages of virtual learning environments.
25. Virtual reality comes to the classroom (McMurtrie, 2019).
26. The APA journal *Monitor on Psychology* (Weir, 2018) contains an article on clinical applications of virtual reality.
26. An article in the *Wall Street Journal* (J. Greene, 2019) reports how tech giants are racing to develop augmented reality.

Chapter 3

27. The first chapter in *A Study of Thinking* (Bruner, Goodnow, & Austin, 1956) lists the advantages of forming categories.
28. Kuhl's articles (1991, 1992, 1993) investigated the development of phonological categories.
30. Rosch's lab (Rosch, Mervis, Gray, Johnsen, & Boyes-Braem, 1976) studied the hierarchical organization of categories.
31. A theory of typicality is based on family resemblance scores (Rosch & Mervis, 1975).
33. Cantor and Mischel (1979) applied Rosch's insights to social categories.
33. Twenge's (2017) book on the iGen documents how technology influenced those born after 1995.
33. A *Wall Street Journal* columnist (Zimmer, 2019) writes about labeling generations.
34. Actions such as crossing "event boundaries" influence our memory (Radvansky, 2012).
35. Richmond and Zacks (2017) discuss research on how low-level actions become organized into high-level actions.
36. Action identification theory (Vallacher & Wegner, 1987, 2012) proposes how attention is directed to different levels in an action hierarchy.

Chapter 4

38. The quote appears on page 127 of *Turing's Cathedral* (Dyson, 2012).
40. The *APA Dictionary of Psychology* (VandenBoss, 2006) is a valuable source for definitions.
41. A taxonomic analysis of abstraction contrasts concrete and abstract representations at the instance, attribute, and category levels (Reed, 2016b).
42. The book *Behaviorism* (Watson, 1924) discouraged the study of mental processes.
43. Paivio (1969, 1986) proposed a dual-coding explanation to account for the superiority of learning concrete words.
43. *Principles of Perceptual Learning and Development* (Gibson, 1969) emphasized the importance of learning visual features.
44. Highlighting distinctive features helped children make difficult discriminations (Egeland, 1975).
44. Participants demonstrated better recognition of caricatures (Mauro & Kubovy, 1992).
46. *Remembering* (Bartlett, 1932) describes the constructive aspects of memory.
46. *Scripts, Plans, Goals and Understanding: An Inquiry Into Human Knowledge Structures* (Schank & Abelson, 1977) describes the structure of events.
47. Readers best remembered the interruption of events (Bower, Black, & Turner, 1979).
48. Causal relations are another variable that influenced judged importance and memory (Trabasso & van den Broek, 1985).

Chapter 5

51. The Dewey Decimal System is an example of an institutional classification (Glushko, Maglio, Matlock, & Barsalou, 2008).
54. The quote is from pages 2 and 3 of *Periodic Tales: A Cultural History of the Elements from Arsenic to Zinc* (Aldersey-Williams, 2011).
55. The Periodic Table of Elements was downloaded from the Los Alamos National Laboratory website at https://www.lanl.gov/community/education/index.

56. The quote about the NIMH RDoC initiative appears on page 499 of Insel and Cuthbert (2015).
57. The NIMH RDoC framework can be found at https://www.nimh.nih.gov/ research-priorities/rdoc/constructs/rdoc-matrix.shtml
58. Carroll, Thomas, and Malhotra (1980) studied the use of matrices on design.

Chapter 6

60. The quote appears on page 425 of *The Square and the Tower: Networks and Power* (Ferguson, 2018).
60. *The Creative Priority* (Hirshberg, 1998) de-emphasized hierarchical organization at Nissan Design.
61. Hillary and Grafman (2017) explain the characteristics of networks.
63. *Complexity: A Guided Tour* (Mitchell, 2009) is a simple tutorial on complexity.
63. Watts and Strogatz (1998) studied the organization of small world networks.
64. Collins and Loftus (1975) proposed a spreading activation theory of semantic processing.
65. Activation of a word makes it easier to identify (Meyer & Schvaneveldt, 1976)
66. Learning more facts increases verification time (J. R. Anderson, 1976).
66. Subnodes create clusters of knowledge that aid verification (Reder & Anderson, 1980).
67. Brain injuries can result in hyperconnectivity (Hillary & Grafman, 2017).

Chapter 7

69. *The Square and the Tower: Networks and Power* (Ferguson, 2018) analyzes the relation between networks and power.
69. *The Book of Trees: Visualizing Branches of Knowledge* (Lima, 2013) contains many historical examples of how tree diagrams organize knowledge.
70. Collins and Quillian (1969) created the hierarchical network model of semantic memory.
74. Chi (2008, 2013) studied the organization of students' intuitive networks.
74. Intuitive networks do not always inherit properties of superordinate categories (Shtulman & Valcarcel, 2012).

75. Older children become more adept at appropriately transferring physics principles (Heyman, Phillips, & Gelman, 2003).
76. Gupta, Hammer, and Redish (2010) argue for a flexible perspective of physics knowledge.
76. The quote appears on page 96 of Carroll (2016).
77. Novick and Hurley (2001; Hurley & Novick, 2010) investigated students' ability to select the best diagram.

Chapter 8

81. *Thinking Visually* (Reed, 2010) reviews research on visual cognition.
81. Shepard (1988) discussed how visual thinking supported scientific discoveries.
82. It is difficut to discover novel parts in visual images (Reed, 1974).
83. The Animation Tutor (Reed, 2005) provides simulation feedback on students' estimates and calculations.
86. Newell (1973, 1990) designed the cognitive architecture SOAR to organize cognition.
86. Cognitive architectures integrate the major components that support cognition (Laird, Lebiere, & Rosenbloom, 2017).
87. Soar/SVS contains a visual buffer to model spatial reasoning (Lathrop, Wintermute, & Laird, 2011).
88. Reed (2019b) adapted and applied Soar/SVS to model human spatial reasoning.
88. People have difficulty reinterpreting an ambiguous image (Chambers & Reisberg, 1985).
89. People are better at the mental synthesis of geometric forms to create objects (Finke, 1990).
90. Students derive rules from the mental simulation of gears (Schwartz & Black, 1996).
90. Cognitive geography is the study of cognition about space, place, and the environment (Montello, 2009).
91. Hierarchical errors occur in geographic reasoning (Stevens & Coupe, 1978).
91. Tversky's (2005) chapter reviews visual/spatial reasoning.

Chapter 9

92. Reasoning from imperfect knowledge creates challenges for both people and computers (Reed & Pease, 2017).
92. Context reduces ambiguity (Swinney & Hakes, 1976). The example appears on page 686.
94. Swinney (1979) applied spreading activation theory to resolving ambiguities.
94. Collins and Loftus (1975) formulated a spreading activation model of semantic verification.
94. The limited capacity of workng memory constrains the resolution of ambiguities (Miyake, Just, & Carpenter, 1994).
95. Contradictions is one aspect of imperfect knowlege (Reed & Pease, 2017).
96. diSessa (2013; diSessa, Sherin, & Levin, 2014) proposed a knowledge-in-pieces theory of fragmentation.
97. Carey (2011) developed a theory of cognitive development.
97. Chi (2013) argued that students' scientific reasoning is based on intuitive ontologies.
97. Vosniadou (2013; Vosniadou & Skopeliti, 2014) accounts for the development of scientific knowledge in her framework theory.
98. The International Astronomical Union reclassified Pluto (Messeri, 2010).
99. *A Mind at Play: How Claude Shannon Invented the Information Age* (Soni & Goodman, 2017) is an engaging biography.
99. The New England Patriots have dominated the NFL (Gay, 2019).
100. Articles in *Sports Illustrated* (Baskin, 2019; D. Greene, 2019) discussed the top contenders for the final four.

Chapter 10

101. *Thinking Fast and Slow* (Kahneman, 2011) reviews research on how people reason.
101. *The Big Short: Inside the Doomsday Machine* (Lewis, 2011) discusses economic collapse.
101. *The Undoing Project: A Friendship That Changed Our Minds* (Lewis, 2016) discusses the collaboration of Daniel Kahneman and Amos Tversy.
102. Sloman (2002) contrasts associative versus rule-based reasoning.
103. Analytical thinking is important in everyday reasoning (Pennycook, Fugelsang, & Koehler, 2015).

104. The Cognitive Reflection Test (Frederick, 2005) measures individual differences in reasoning.
105. Stanovich (2018) contrasts System I versus System II processing.
106. *Risk Savvy* (Gigerenzer, 2014) demonstrates that simple heuristics can often be effective.
108. *Nudge: Improving Decisions About Health, Wealth, and Happiness* (Thaler & Sunstein, 2008) advocates how to help people reason.
109. An example of a nudge is to select a dessert first rather than last (Flores, Reimann, Castano, & Lopez, 2019).
109. Hertwig and Grune-Yanoff (2017) contrast nudging with boosting.
109. Governments need to decide when to invest in nudging (Benartzi et al., 2017).
110. Experts' greater situation awareness aids their decisions (Randel, Pugh, & Reed, 1996).
110. *Decision Making in Action: Models and Methods* (Klein, Orasanu, Calderwood, & Zsambok, 1993) contributed theoretical frameworks for studying action-based decision making.
111. Klein's (1993) recognition-primed decision model emphasized situation awareness as a critical component of action-based decision-making.
112. Naval reports (Hinks, 2017; Lubold & Youssef, 2017) identified causes of ship collisions.

Chapter 11

117. *Marley & Me* (Grogan, 2005) documents a dog's misadventures.
119. Simon (1973) compared strategies on ill-structured and well-structured problems.
119. Reed (2016a) constructed a problem × strategy taxonomy.
120. Gick (1986) formulated a general model of problem-solving.
121. *Schemas in Problem Solving* (Marshall, 1995) describes how organizied knowledge structures support problem solving.
123. *GPS: A Case Study in Generality* (Ernst & Newell, 1969) applied means–end analysis to many problems.
123. *Human Problem Solving* (Newell & Simon, 1972) is a landmark publication.
124. Insight problems are solved suddenly (Metcalfe & Wiebe, 1987).
125. Constraint relaxation may lead to a solution (Knoblich, Ohlsson, Haider, & Rhenius, 1999).
125. Schema induction identifies common principles (Gick & Holyoak, 1983).

126. Better problem solvers identify common principles in math problems (Silver, 1981)

126. Better problem solvers identify common principles in physics problems (Chi, Glaser, & Rees, 1982).

127. A familiar analogy helped students learn functional relations (Reed & Evans, 1987).

127. Schema induction helped professionals retrieve inert knowledge (Gentner, Lowenstein, Thompson, & Forbus, 2009).

128. *The Intelligence Trap* (Robson, 2019) describes how failure to abandon unproductive ideas limits progress.

128. Cognitive entrenchment creates inflexible thinking (Dane, 2010).

Chapter 12

129. *The Psychology of Everyday Things* (Norman, 1988) described good and poor designs.

129. *The Design of Everyday Things* (Norman, 2013) revised and expanded Norman's 1988 book.

130. Goel and Pirolli (1992) list the characteristics of design problems.

132. Insight during design problems typically solves only one aspect of the problem (V. Goel, 2014).

133. *Brilliant blunders: From Darwin to Einstein* (Livio, 2013) tells how even great thinkers make mistakes.

136. See Pereira (1969) for a report on design of the UCSD Geisel Library.

137. The Cathedrals of Culture website is https://vimeo.com/97424666.

139. Description of the Salk architecture is part of its website https://www.salk.edu/about/visiting-salk/about-salk-architecture/.

140. The quote is from page 40 of Goldberger (1996).

Chapter 13

142. The 2003 Nobel Prize in Physics is on its website https://www.nobelprize.org/prizes/physics/2003/summary/

143. Zane's (2019) article in *The Wall Street Journal* discusses the biological, economic, and physical consequences of flow.

143. *Design in Nature* (Bejan & Zane, 2013) describes physical principles that optimize flow.

145. Rethinking intractable conflict proposes a dynamical systems approach (Vallacher, Coleman, Nowak, & Bui-Wrzosinska, 2010).
147. *Groupthink* (Janis, 1982) discusses approaches to avoiding it.
147. Apple and Qualcomm end a long legal battle (Mickle & Fitch, 2019).
148. The partisan vote to impeach President Trump is an excellent case study of groupthink (Andrews & Salama, 2019).
148. Workspace design impacts communication (Khazanchi, Sprinkle, Masterson, & Tong, 2018).
150. Reed and Vallacher (2020) compare information processing and dynamical systems perspectives on solving problems.
151. Elaboration, constraint relaxation, and re-encoding are possible mechanisms for escaping an impasse (Ohlsson, 2018).

Chapter 14

156. A quiz on AI (McCormick, 2019) appeared in *The Wall Street Journal*.
157. Courses on data and information sciences are attracting students at Berkeley (Belkin, 2018).
157. *The Master Algorithm* (Domingos, 2015) introduces machine learning methods.
157. Psychologists use these methods to construct cognitive models (Reed, 2019a).
158. Multidimensional scaling plots similarities (Rips, Shoben, & Smith, 1973).
160. Emphasizing diagnostic features improves predictions of how students classify patterns (Reed, 1972).
161. The book *Risk Savvy* (Gigerenzer, 2014) emphasizes simple heuristics for making decisions.
162. The success of Bayesian methods in AI have encouraged their use in psychology (Tenenbaum, Kemp, Griffiths, & Goodman, 2011).
163. Kemp and Tennenbaum (2008) applied Bayesian methods to similarity scaling.
165. The word *superiority* effect (Reicher, 1969) demonstrates that identifying a letter is more accurate when it occurs in a word.
166. The interactive-activation model (McClelland & Rumelhart, 1981) is an influential connectionist model.
167. Deep neural networks consist of many layers of connections (Jacobs & Bates, 2019)

167. *The Deep Learning Revolution* (Sejnowski, 2018) reviews the history of these networks.
169. Helie and Sun (2010) model the effect of incubation on insight by combining connectionist and symbolic techniques.
169. Forbus, Liang, and Rabkina (2017) argue for the necessity of symbolic models.

Chapter 15

170. Goel and Davies (2020) distinguish between engineering and psychological AI.
171. The Marissa Mayer quote is on page 423 of *Valley of Genius* (Fisher, 2018).
171. The Defense Advance Projects Agency is developing programs that are both effective and explainable (Gunning & Aha, 2019).
173. An important application of WatsonPaths is to medicine (Lally et al., 2017)
176. The Semanticscience Integrated Ontology (Dumontier et al., 2014) organizes knowledge about molecular biology.
178. Adding cognitive processes to SIO requires both reusing and extending its organization (Reed & Dumontier, 2019).
178. There is evidence for visual simulations of text (Pecher, 2013) such as reading about hammering a nail (Stanfield & Zwaan, 2001).
178. A working memory model (Baddeley, 2001) provides short-term storage of different memory codes.

Chapter 16

180. The book *Rebooting AI* (Marcus & Davis, 2019) discusses the limitations of current AI projects and the need for symbolic reasoning.
180. Poldrack and Yarkoni (2016) argue for the critical role of formal ontologies in organizing knowledge.
181. One role of formal ontologies is to use deductive reasoning to answer questions (Reed & Dumontier, 2019).
182. A large working group (Ford et al., 2014) organized hallucinations within the NIMH RDoC framework.
182. Cohen, Gianaros, and Manuck (2016) developed a stage model of disease.
182. Some molecules enhance cell survival (Opendak & Gould, 2015).

185. Read *Ontology: A Practical Guide* (Pease, 2011) if you want to learn about ontologies.
185. The Suggested Upper Merged Ontology (SUMO) website is (http://www.adampease.org/OP/).
185. Reed and Pease (2015) construct a framework for cognition ontologies.
190. The website for WordNet (Fellbaum, 2015; Miller & Fellbaum, 2007) is https://wordnet.princeton.edu/.
190. Short-term memory is limited in capacity (Miller, 1956).
190. Mirman, Landrigan, and Britt (2017) review research on taxonomic and thematic categories.
191. Context is essential for understanding semantic memory (Yee & Thompson-Schill, 2016).
192. The website for the Berkeley FrameNet project is https://framenet.icsi.berkeley.edu.
192. Fillmore and Baker (2010) developed FrameNet to provide a context for understanding.

Chapter 17

194. General-purpose learners adapt to many different situations (Griffiths et al., 2019).
194. Babies learn by exploring (Gopnik, 2019).
195. A standard model of the mind provides a common framework for unifying artificial intelligence, psychology, cognitive neuroscience, and robotics (Laird et al., 2017).
197. Grounded cognition views all cognitive activities as emerging from a variety of bodily, affective, perceptual, and motor processes that occur within physical and social environments (Pezzulo et al., 2013).
198. Developing the robot Shakey was a key project in advancing robotics (Kuipers, Feigenbaum, Hart, & Nilsson, 2017).
198. An National Science Foundation workshop on robot planning identified future developments (Alterovitz, Koenig, & Likhachev, 2016).
198. The Language and Action Research group (Chai, Fang, Liu, & She, 2016) is linking vision and language networks.
199. Nirenburg (2017) addresses the many challenges for communicating with computers.
199. McShane (2017) reviews progress in meeting these challenges.
200. Social scientists need to participate in building interactive dialog systems (Ward & DeVault, 2016).

201. A multidimensional Turing test could evaluate general AI (Adams, Banavar, & Campbell, 2016).

202. Performance on standardized tests provides another measure of machine intelligence (Clark & Etzioni, 2016).

202. A physically embodied Turing test would require the integration of four major aspects of AI research (Ortiz, 2016).

203. Kitano (2016) shows how grand challenges have been a driving force in AI research.

204. The report *Artificial Intelligence and Life in 2030* can be downloaded at https://ai100.stanford.edu/sites/g/files/sbiybj9861/f/ai_100_report_0831fnl.pdf.

Chapter 18

209. Hilpert and Marchand (2018) contrast component-dominant and interaction-dominant systems.

211. The quote is from page 16 of Keegan's (2002) biography of Winston Churchill.

211. *The Tipping Point* (Gladwell, 2000) discusses how network interactions reach a major transition.

211. Critical transitions occur for many scientific domains (Scheffer et al., 2012).

213. An external stressor can affect a symptom and resilience network (Kalisch et al., 2019).

214. *A Framework for K-12 Science Education* (2012) report can be downloaded or purchased at https://www.nap.edu/catalog/13165/a-framework-for-k-12-science-education-practices-crosscutting-concepts.

215. Science should be taught much sooner in elementary school (Kelemen, 2019).

215. Curriculum design requires promoting change over an extended period of time (Brown, 2014).

216. NetLogo offers complex systems instruction (Jacobson, Kapur, So, & Lee, 2011).

216. NetLogo is part of the curriculum offered by Northwestern's Center for Connected Learning and Computer-Based Modeling: https://ccl.northwestern.edu/.

216. Climate change can be effectively embedded within instruction on complex systems (Jacobson et al., 2020).

217. Australia fires devastated the country in January, 2020 (Wright, 2020).
219. The 2018 climate report for the United States (Reidmiller et al., 2018) can be downloaded at https://nca2018.globalchange.gov/downloads/NCA4_Report-in-Brief.pdf.
219. Temperatures in 2019 were the second warmest recorded (Hotz, 2020).
219. Yoon, Go, and Park (2018) conducted a literature review on complex-systems instruction.

Chapter 19

221. *Computational Thinking for a Computational World* is available at https://digitalpromise.org/.
221. Grover and Pea (2013) reviewed computational thinking in grades K–12.
222. See https://ap.collegeboard.org/ for information about the College Board AP program.
222. AP course on computational thinking: https://www.collegeboard.org/releases/2019/participation-csp-nearly-doubles.
223. Characteristics of computational thinking include decomposition, abstraction, algorithms, debugging, iteration, and generalization (Shute, Sun, & Asbell-Clarke, 2017).
224. Linn (1985) wrote about the benefits of learning computer programming.
225. Computational thinking can be taught through programing (Florez et al., 2017).
225. Cognitive benefits of programming occurred at all grade levels (Scherer, Siddiq, & Viveros, 2019).
226. *In Pursuit of the Unknown: 17 Equations that Changed the World* (Stewart, 2012) describes the equations and why they are so important.
230. Mathematical and computational thinking overlap and support each other (Sneider, Stephenson, Schafer, & Flick, 2014).
230. The website for The Next Generation Science Standards is https://www.nextgenscience.org/.
231. My NASA Data website is https://mynasadata.larc.nasa.gov/.

Chapter 20

232. George Lucas captured the lives of another1962 HS graduation class in his 1973 movie *American Graffiti* whose talented cast included Richard

Dreyfyss, Ron Howard, Cindy Williams, Paul Le Mat, Mackenzie Phillips, Harrison Ford, Suzanne Somers, and Wolfman Jack.

232. Amazon plans to retrain a third of its U.S. workforce (Cutter, 2019).

232. A retraining survey revealed a lack of confidence in institutions (Schaffhausser, 2019). The survey can be downloaded at https://www.gallup.com/education/259514/northeastern-gallup-perceptions-preparing-to-meet-ai.aspx.

235. *The Chronicle of Higher Education* article (How some colleges are helping freshmen find their academic focus) can be downloaded at https://www-chronicle-com.libproxy.sdsu.edu/article/How-Some-Colleges-Are-Helping/246913.

238. Modeling strategy shifts (Simon & Reed, 1976) describes solvers' attempts to avoid a blind alley.

238. The quote from the book *Leonardo Da Vinci* (Isaacson, 2017) appears on pages 3 and 4.

References

Adams, S. S., Banavar, G., & Campbell, M. (2016). I-athalon: Toward a multidimensional Turing test. *AI Magazine*, 2016(Spring), 78–84.

Aldersey-Williams, H. (2011). *Periodic tales: A cultural history of the elements from Arsenic to Zinc*. London, England: Viking.

Alterovitz, R., Koenig, S., & Likhachev, M. (2016). Robot planning in the real world: Research challenges and opportunities. *AI Magazine*, *37*, 76–84.

Anderson, J. R. (1976). *Language, memory, and thought*. Hillsdale, NJ: Erlbaum.

Anderson, R. C., & Pichert, J. W. (1978). Recall of previously unrecallable information following a shift in perspective. *Journal of Verbal Learning and Verbal Behavior, 17*, 1–12.

Andrews, N., & Salama, V. (2019, November 1). House passes impeachment resolution. *The Wall Street Journal*, p. A1.

Baddeley, A. D. (2001). Is working memory still working? *American Psychologist, 56*, 851–864.

Barsalou, L. W. (1999). Perceptual symbol systems. *Behavioral & Brain Sciences, 22*, 577–660.

Bartlett, F. C. (1932). *Remembering: A study in experimental and social psychology*. New York, NY: MacMillan.

Baskin, B. (2019, March 25–April 1). Fight to the finish. *Sports Illustrated*, 118–123.

Bejan, A., & Zane, J. P. (2013). *Design in Nature*. New York: Random House.

Belkin, D. (2018, November 2). At Berkeley, big data on campus. *The Wall Street Journal*, p. A3.

Benartzi, S., Beshears, J., Milkman, K. L., Sunstein, C. R., Thaler, R. H., Shankar, M., . . . Galing, S. (2017). Should governments invest more in nudging? *Psychological Science, 28*, 1041–1055.

Bisra, K., Liu, Q., Nesbit, J. C., Salimi, F., & Winne, P. H. (2018). Inducing self-explanation: A meta-analysis. *Educational Psychology Review, 30*, 703–725.

Bower, G. H., Black, J. B., & Turner, T. J. (1979). Scripts in memory for text. *Cognitive Psychology, 11*, 177–220.

Bransford, J. D., & Johnson, M. K. (1973). Considerations of some problems of comprehension. In W. G. Chase (Ed.), *Visual information processing* (pp. 383–438). Orlando, FL: Academic Press.

Bric, J. D., Lumbard, D. C., Frelich, M. J., & Gould, J. C. (2016). Current state of virtual reality simulation in robotic surgery training: A review. *Surgical Endoscopy, 30*(2169), 2169–2178.

Brown, D. E. (2014). Students' conceptions as dynamically emergent structures. *Science & Education, 23*, 1463–1483.

Bruner, J. S., Goodnow, J. J., & Austin, G. A. (1956). *A study of thinking.* New York, NY: Wiley.

Cantor, N., & Mischel, W. (1979). Protoypes in person perception. In L. Berkowitz (Ed.), *Advances in experimental social psychology.* Orlando, FL: Academic Press.

Carey, S. (2011). Precis of the *The Origin of Concepts. Behavioral and Brain Sciences, 34*, 113–124.

Carroll, J. M., Thomas, J. C., & Malhotra, A. (1980). Presentation and representation in design problem solving. *British Journal of Psychology, 71*, 143–153.

Carroll, S. (2016). *The big picture: On the origins of life, meaning, and the universe itself.* New York, NY: Dutton.

Chai, J. Y., Fang, R., Liu, C., & She, L. (2016). Collaborative language grounding toward situated human–robot dialogue. *AI Magazine, 37*, 32–45.

Chambers, D., & Reisberg, D. (1985). Can mental images be ambiguous? *Journal of Experimental Psychology: Human Perception and Performance, 11*, 317–328.

Chi, M. T. H. (2008). Three types of conceptual change: Belief revision, mental model transformation, and categorical shift. In S. Vosniadou (Ed.), *Handbook of research on conceptual change* (pp. 61–82). Hillsdale, NJ: Erlbaum.

Chi, M. T. H. (2013). Two kinds and four sub-types of misconceived knowledge, ways to change it and the learning outcomes. In S. Vosniadou (Ed.), *International handbook of research on conceptual change* (2nd ed., pp. 49–70). New York, NY: Routledge.

Chi, M. T. H., Glaser, R., & Rees, E. (1982). Expertise in problem solving. In R. J. Sternberg (Ed.), *Advances in the psychology of human intelligence* (Vol. 1, pp. 7–75). Mahwah, NJ: Erlbaum.

Clark, P., & Etzioni, O. (2016). My computer is an honor student—But how intelligent is it? Standardized tests as a measure of AI. *AI Magazine, 37*, 5–12.

Cohen, S., Gianaros, P. J., & Manuck, S. B. (2016). A stage model of stress and disease. *Perspectives on Psychological Science, 11*, 456–463.

Collins, A. M., & Loftus, E. F. (1975). A spreading activation theory of semantic processing. *Psychological Review, 82*, 407–428.

Collins, A. M., & Quillian, M. R. (1969). Retrieval time from semantic memory. *Journal of Verbal Learning and Verbal Behavior, 8*, 240–248.

Connors, E. C., Chrastil, E. R., Sanchez, J., & Merabet, L. B. (2014). Virtual environments for the transfer of navigation skills in the blind: A comparison of directed instruction vs. video game based learning approaches. *Frontiers in Human Neuroscience, 8*(223). https://doi.org/10.3389/fnhum.2014.00223

Cumming, J., & Williams, S. E. (2014). The role of imagery in performance. In S. M. Murphy (Ed.), *The Oxford handbook of sport and performance psychology* (pp. 213–232). New York, NY: Oxford University Press.

Cutter, C. (2019, July 12). Amazon prepares to retrain a third of its U.S. workforce. *Wall Street Journal*, p. A1.

Dane, E. (2010). Reconsidering the trade-off between expertise and flexibility: A cognitive entrenchment perspective. *Academy of Management Review, 35*, 579–603.

Davenport, T. H., & Kirby, J. (2016). *Only humans need apply: Winners and losers in the age of smart machines*. New York, NY: HarperCollins.

Dede, C. (2009). Immersive interfaces for engagement and learning. *Science, 323*, 66–69.

diSessa, A. A. (2013). A bird's-eye view of the "pieces" vs. "coherence" controversy (from the "pieces" side of the fence). In S. Vosniadou (Ed.), *International handbook of research on conceptual change* (2 ed., pp. 31–48). New York, NY: Routledge.

diSessa, A. A., Sherin, B., & Levin, M. (2014). Knowledge analysis: An introduction. In G. Kaiser, H. Forgasz, M. Graven, A. Kuzniak, E. Simmt, & B. Xu (Eds.), *Invited lectures from the 13th International Congress on Mathematical Education*. ICME-13 Monographs (pp. 65–84). Cham, Switzerland: Springer.

Dogov, I., Graves, W. J., Nearents, M. R., Schwark, J. D., & Volkman, C. B. (2014). Effects of cooperative gaming and avatar customization on subsequent spontaneous helping behavior. *Computers in Human Behavior, 33*, 49–55.

Domingos, P. (2015). *The master algorithm: How the quest for the ultimate learning machine will remake our world*. New York, NY: Basic Books.

Dumontier, M., Baker, C. J., Baran, J., Callahan, A., Chepelev, L. L., Cruz-Toledo, J., . . . Hoehndorf, R. (2014). The Semanticscience Integrated Ontology (SIO) for biomedical research and knowledge discovery. *Journal of Biomedical Semantics, 5*(4), 1–11.

Dyson, G. (2012). *Turing's cathedral: The origins of the digital universe*. New York, NY: Pantheon Books.

Egeland, B. (1975). Effects of errorless training on teaching children to discriminate letters of the alphabet. *Journal of Applied Psychology, 60*, 533–536.

Ernst, G. W., & Newell, A. (1969). *GPS: A case study in generality and problem solving* New York, NY: Academic Press.

Fellbaum, C. (2015). WordNet: An electronic lexical resource. In S. Chipman (Ed.), *Oxford handbook of cognitive science* (Vol. 1, Oxford Handbooks Online). New York, NY: Oxford University Press. doi:10.1093/oxfordhb/9780199842193.001.0001

Ferguson, N. (2018). *The square and the tower: Networks and power from the freemasons to Facebook*. New York, NY: Penguin Press.

Fillmore, C. J., & Baker, C. F. (2010). A frames approach to semantic analysis. In B. Heine & H. Narrog (Eds.), *The oxford handbook of linguistic analysis* (pp. 313–340). Oxford: Oxford University Press.

Finke, R. A. (1990). *Creative imagery: Discoveries and inventions in visualization*. Mahwah, NJ: Lawrence Erlbaum Associates.

Fisher, A. (2018). *Valley of genius: The uncensored history of Silicon Valley*. New York, NY: Hachette Book Group.

Flores, D., Reimann, M., Castano, R., & Lopez, A. (2019). If I indulge first, I will eat less overall: The unexpected interaction effect on indulgence and presentation order on consumption. *Journal of Experimental Psychology: Applied, 25*, 162–176.

Florez, F. B., Casallas, R., Hernandez, M., Reyes, A., Restrepo, S., & Danies, G. (2017). Changing a generation's way of thinking: Teaching computational thinking through programming. *Review of Educational Research, 87*, 834–860.

Forbus, K. D., Liang, C., & Rabkina, I. (2017). Representation and computation in cognitive models. *Topics in Cognitive Science, 9*, 694–718.

Ford, J. M., Morris, S. E., Hoffman, R. E., Sommer, I., Waters, F., McCarthy-Jones, S., . . . Cuthbert, B. N. (2014). Studying hallucinations within the NIMH RDoC framework. *Schizophrenia Bulletin, 40*(Supplement 4), S295–S304.

A framework for K–12 science education. (2012). Washington, DC: National Research Council.

Frank, C., Land, W. M., Poppp, C., & Schack, T. (2014). Mental representation and mental practice: Experimental investigation on the functional links between motor memory and motor imagery. *PloS One, 9*(4), 1–12.

Frederick, S. (2005). Cognitive reflection and decision making. *Journal of Economic Perspectives, 19*, 25–42.

Gay, J. (2019, January 22). The angriest super bowl. *The Wall Street Journal*, p. A16.

Gentner, D., Lowenstein, J., Thompson, L., & Forbus, K. D. (2009). Reviving inert knowledge: Analogical encoding supports relational retrieval of past events. *Cognitive Science, 33*, 1343–1382.

Gibson, E. J. (1969). *Principles of perceptual learning and development*. Englewood Cliffs, NJ: Prentice-Hall.

Gick, M. (1986). Problem-solving strategies. *Educational Psychologist, 21*, 99–120.

Gick, M., & Holyoak, K. J. (1983). Schema induction and analogical transfer. *Cognitive Psychology, 15*, 1–38.

Gigerenzer, G. (2014). *Risk savvy*. New York, NY: Penguin/Viking.

Gladwell, M. (2000). *The tipping point: How little things can make a big difference*. New York, NY: Little, Brown.

Glenberg, A. M., Gutierrez, T., Levin, J. R., Japuntich, S., & Kaschak, M. P. (2004). Activity and imagined activity can enhance young children's reading comprehension *Journal of Educational Psychology, 96*, 424–436.

Glenberg, A. M., Jaworski, B., Rischal, M., & Levin, J. R. (2007). What brains are for: Action, meaning, and reading comprehension. In D. McNamara (Ed.), *Reading comprehension strategies: Theories, interventions, and technologies* (pp. 221–240). Mahwah, NJ: Lawrence Erlbaum.

Glushko, R. J., Maglio, P. P., Matlock, T., & Barsalou, L. W. (2008). Categorization in the wild. *Trends in Cognitive Sciences, 12*, 129–135.

Goel, A. K., & Davies, J. (2020). Artificial intelligence. In R. J. Sternberg (Ed.), *Cambridge handbook of intelligence* (2nd ed.). Cambridge, UK: Cambridge University Press.

Goel, V. (2014). Creative brains: Designing in the real world. *Frontiers in Human Neuroscience, 8*(241), 1–14.

Goel, V., & Pirolli, P. (1992). The structure of design problem spaces. *Cognitive Science, 16*, 395–429.

Goldberger, P. (1996, April 28). Imitation that doesn't flatter. *The New York Times*. Section 2, page 40. https://www.nytimes.com/1996/04/28/arts/architecture-view-imitation-that-doesn-t-flatter.html

Gopnik, A. (2019, October 12–13). The ultimate learning machines. *The Wall Street Journal*, pp. A1–A2.

Greene, D. (2019, March 25–April 1). A cut above. *Sports Illustrated*, 104–117.

Greene, J. (2019, February 25). Microsoft's HoloLens avoids the hype. *Wall Street Journal*, p. B5.

Griffiths, T. L., Callaway, F., Chang, M. B., Grant, E., Kruger, P. M., & Lieder, F. (2019). Doing more with less: Meta-reasoning and meta-learning in humans and machines. *Behavioral Sciences, 29*, 24–30.

Grogan, J. (2005). *Marley & Me*. New York: HarperCollins.

Grover, S., & Pea, R. (2013). Computational thinking in K-12: A review of the state of the field. *Educational Researcher, 42*, 38–43.

Gunning, D., & Aha, D. W. (2019). DARPA's explainable artificial intelligence program. *AI Magazine, 40*(2), 44–58.

Gupta, A., Hammer, D., & Redish, E. F. (2010). The case for dynamic models of learners' ontologies in physics. *Journal of the Learning Sciences, 19*, 285–321.

Helie, S., & Sun, R. (2010). Incubation, insight, and creative problem solving: A unified theory and a connectionist model. *Psychological Review, 117*, 994–1024.

Hertwig, R., & Grune-Yanoff, T. (2017). Nudging and boosting: Steering or empowering good decisions. *Perspectives on Psychological Science, 12*, 973–986.

Heyman, G. D., Phillips, A. T., & Gelman, S. A. (2003). Children's reasoning about physics within and across ontological kinds. *Cognition, 89*, 43–61.

Hillary, F. G., & Grafman, J. H. (2017). Injured brains and adaptive networks: The benefits and costs of hyperconnectivity. *Trends in Cognitive Sciences, 21*, 385–401.

Hilpert, J. C., & Marchand, G. C. (2018). Complex systems research in educational psychology: Aligning theory and method. *Educational Psychologist, 53*, 185–202.

Hinks, J. (2017, November 2). Two U.S. warships had deadly crashes this year. Here's what the navy says went wrong. *Time.* Retrieved from time.com/5006790/pacific-navy-collisions-avoidable/

Hirshberg, J. (1998). *The creative priority.* New York, NY: Harper Collins.

Hotz, R. L. (2020, January 16). Last decade was warmest on record. *The Wall Street Journal*, p. A3.

Hurley, S. M., & Novick, L. R. (2010). Solving problems using matrix, network, and hiearchy diagrams: The consequences of violating construction conventions. *Quarterly Journal of Experimental Psychology, 63*, 275–290.

Insel, T. R., & Cuthbert, B. N. (2015). Brain disorders? Precisely. *Science, 348*, 499–500.

Isaacson, W. (2017). *Leonardo Da Vinci.* New York, NY: Simon & Schuster.

Jacobs, R. A., & Bates, C. J. (2019). Comparing the visual representations and performance of humans and deep neural networks. *Current Directions in Psychological Science, 28*, 34–39.

Jacobson, M. J., Goldwater, M., Markauskaite, L., Lai, P. K., Kapur, M., Roberts, G., & Hilton, C. (2020). Schema abstraction with productive failure and analogical comparison: Learning designs for far across domain transfer. *Learning and Instruction, 65*, 101222.

Jacobson, M. J., Kapur, M., So, H.-J., & Lee, J. (2011). The ontologies of complexity and learning about complex systems. *Instructional Science, 39*, 763–783.

Janis, I. L. (1982). *Groupthink.* Boston, MA: Houghton Mifflin.

Kahneman, D. (2011). *Thinking fast and slow.* New York, NY: Farrar, Straus and Giroux.

Kalisch, R., Cramer, A. O. J., Binder, H., Fritz, J., Leertoouwer, I., Lunansky, G., . . . van Harmelen, A. (2019). Deconstructing and reconstructing resilience: A dynamic network approach. *Perspectives on Psychological Science, 14*, 765–777.

Keegan, J. (2002). *Winston Churchill.* New York, NY: Penguin Putnam.

Kelemen, D. (2019). The magic of mechanism: Explanation-based instruction on counterintuitive concepts in early childhood. *Perspectives on Psychological Science, 14*, 510–522.

Kemp, C., & Tenenbaum, J. B. (2008). The discovery of structural form. *Proceedings of the National Academy of Sciences, 105*, 10687–10692.

Khazanchi, S., Sprinkle, T. A., Masterson, S. S., & Tong, N. (2018). A spatial model of work relationships: The relationship-building and relationship-straining effects of workspace design. *Academy of Management Review, 43*, 590–609.

Kitano, H. (2016). Artificial intelligence to win the Nobel prize and beyond: Creating the engine for scientific discovery. *AI Magazine, 37*, 39–49.

Klahr, D., Triona, L. M., & Williams, C. (2007). Hands on what? The relative effectiveness of physical vs. virtual materials in an engineering design project by middle school children. *Journal of Research in Science Teaching, 44*, 183–203.

Klein, G. A. (1993). A recognition-primed decision (RPD) model of rapid decision making. In G. A. Klein, R. Orasanu, R. Calderwood, & C. E. Zsambok (Eds.), *Decision making in action: Models and methods* (pp. 138–147). Norwood, NJ: Ablex.

Klein, G. A., Orasanu, R., Calderwood, R., & Zsambok, C. E. (Eds.). (1993). *Decision making in action: Models and methods.* Norwood, NJ: Ablex.

Knoblich, G., Ohlsson, S., Haider, H., & Rhenius, D. (1999). Constraint relaxation and chunk decomposition in insight problem solving. *Journal of Experimental Psychology: Learning, Memory and Cognition, 25*, 1534–1555.

Kuhl, P. K. (1991). Human adults and human infants show a "perceptual magnet effect" for the prototypes of speech categories, monkeys do not. *Perception & Psychophysics, 50*, 93–107.

Kuhl, P. K. (1993). Infant speech perception: A window on psycholinguistic development. *International Journal of Psycholinguistics, 9*, 33–56.

Kuhl, P. K., Williams, K. A., Lacerda, F., Stevens, K. N., & Lindblom, B. (1992). Linguistic experience alters phonetic perception in infants by 6 months of age. *Science, 225*, 606–608.

Kuipers, B., Feigenbaum, E. A., Hart, P. E., & Nilsson, N. J. (2017). Shakey: From conception to history. *AI Magazine, 38*, 88–103.

Laird, J. E., Lebiere, C., & Rosenbloom, P. S. (2017). A standard model of the mind: Toward a common computational framework across artificial intelligence, cognitive science, neuroscience, and robotics. *AI Magazine, 38*, 13–26.

Lally, A., Bagchi, S., Barborak, M. S., Buchanan, D. W., Chu-Carroll, J., Ferruci, D. A., . . . Prager, J. M. (2017). WatsonPaths: Scenario-based question answering and inference over unstructured information. *AI Magazine, 38*, 59–76.

Lanier, J. (2017). *Dawn of the new everything: Encounters with realty and virtual reality.* New York, NY: Henry Holt.

Laski, E. V., Jor'dan, J. R., Daoust, C., & Murrray, A. K. (2015). What makes mathematics manipulatives effective? Lessons from cognitive science and Montessori education. *SAGE Open, 2*(5). doi:10.1177/2158244015589588

Lathrop, S. D., Wintermute, S., & Laird, J. E. (2011). Exploring the functional advantages of spatial and visual cognition from an architectural perspective. *Topics in Cognitive Science, 3*, 796–818.

Lewis, M. (2011). *The big short: Inside the doomsday machine*. New York: W. W. Norton.

Lewis, M. (2016). *The undoing project: A friendship that changed our minds*. London, England: Penguin.

Lillard, A. S. (2005). *Montessori: The science behind the genius*. Oxford, England: Oxford University Press.

Lima, M. (2013). *The book of trees: Visualizing branches of knowledge*. New York, NY: Princeton Architectural Press.

Linn, M. C. (1985). The cognitive consequences of programming instruction in classrooms. *Educational Researcher, 14*, 14–29.

Livio, M. (2013). *Brilliant blunders: From Darwin to Einstein—Colossal mistakes by great scientists that changed our understanding of life and the universe*. New York, NY: Simon & Schuster.

Lubold, G., & Youssef, N. A. (2017, November 2). Deadly navy collisions were avoidable. *Wall Street Journal*, A8.

Ma, T., Li, H., Deng, L., Yang, H., Lv, X., Li, P., . . . Xu, P. (2017). The hybrid BCI system for movement control by combining motor imagery and moving onset visual evoked potential. *Journal of Neural Engineering, 14*, 1–12.

Marcus, G., & Davis, E. (2019). *Rebooting AI: Building artificial intelligence we can trust*. New York, NY: Pantheon Books.

Marshall, S. P. (1995). *Schemas in problem solving*. New York: Cambridge University Press.

Mauro, R., & Kubovy, M. (1992). Caricature and face recognition. *Memory & Cognition, 20*, 433–440.

Mayer, R. E. (1996). Learning strategies for making sense out of expository text: The SOI model for guiding three cognitive processes in knowledge construction. *Educational Psychology Review, 4*, 357–371.

McClelland, J. L., & Rumelhart, D. E. (1981). An interactive-activation model of context effects in letter perception: Part 1. An account of basic findings. *Psychological Review, 88*, 375–407.

McCormick, J. (2019, April 2). Test your knowledge of artificial intelligence. *The Wall Street Journal*, p. R3.

McMurtrie, B. (2019). Virtual reality comes to the classroom. *The Chronicle of Higher Education*, A8–A11.

McShane, M. (2017). Natural language understanding (NLU, not NLP) in cognitive systems. *AI Magazine, 38*, 43–56.

Merabet, L. B., Connors, E. C., Halko, M. A., & Sanchez, J. (2012). Teaching the blind to find their way by playing video games. *PloS One, 7*(9).

Messeri, L. R. (2010). The problem with Pluto: Conflicting cosmologies and the classification of planets. *Social Studies of Science, 40*, 187–214.

Metcalfe, J., & Wiebe, D. (1987). Intuition in insight and noninsight problem solving. *Memory & Cognition, 15*, 238–246.

Meyer, D. E., & Schvaneveldt, R. W. (1976). Meaning, memory structure, and mental processes. *Science, 192,* 27–33.

Miller, G. A. (1956). The magical number seven, plus or minus two: Some limits on our capacity for processing information. *Psychological Review, 63,* 81–97.

Miller, G. A., & Fellbaum, C. (2007). WordNet then and now. *Language Resources & Evaluation, 41,* 209–214.

Mirman, D., Landrigan, J.-F., & Britt, A. E. (2017). Taxonomic and thematic semantic systems. *Psychological Bulletin, 143,* 499–520.

Mitchell, M. (2009). *Complexity: A guided tour.* Oxford, England: Oxford University Press.

Miyake, A., Just, M. A., & Carpenter, P. A. (1994). Working memory constraints on the resolution of lexical ambiguity: Maintaining multiple interpretations in neutral contexts. *Journal of Memory and Language, 33,* 175–202.

Miyatsu, T., Nguyan, K., & McDaniel, M. A. (2018). Five popular study strategies: Their pitfalls and optimal implementations. *Perspectives on Psychological Science, 13,* 390–407.

Montello, D. R. (2009). Cognitive geometry. In R. Kitchen & N. Thrift (Eds.), *International Encyclopedia of Human Geography* (Vol. 2, pp. 160–166). New York, NY: Oxford Elsevier Science.

Newell, A. (1973). You can't play 20 questions with nature and win: Projective comments on the papers of this symposium. In W. G. Chase (Ed.), *Visual information processing* (pp. 283–308). New York, NY: Academic Press.

Newell, A. (1990). *Unified theories of cognition.* Cambridge, MA: Harvard University Press.

Newell, A., & Simon, H. A. (1972). *Human problem solving.* Englewood Cliffs, NJ: Prentice-Hall.

Nirenburg, S. (2017). Cognitive systems: Toward human-level functionality. *AI Magazine, 38,* 34–42.

Norman, D. A. (1988). *The psychology of everyday things.* New York, NY: Basic Books.

Norman, D. A. (2013). *The design of everyday things* (Rev. exp. ed.). New York, NY: Basic Books.

Novack, M. A., Congdon, E. L., Hermani-Lopez, N., & Goldin-Meadow, S. (2014). From action to abstraction: Using the hands to learn math. *Psychological Science, 25,* 903–910.

Novack, M. A., & Goldin-Meadow, S. (2017). Gesture as representational action: A paper about function. *Psychonomic Bulletin & Review, 24,* 652–665.

Novick, L. R., & Hurley, S. M. (2001). To matrix, network, or hierarchy: That is the question. *Cognitive Psychology, 42,* 158–216.

Ohlsson, S. (2018). The dialectic between routine and creative cognition. In F. Vallee-Tourangeau (Ed.), *Insight: On the origins of new ideas* (pp. 8–27). London, England: Routledge.

Opendak, M., & Gould, E. (2015). Adult neurogenesis: A substrate for experience-dependent change. *Trends in Cognitive Sciences, 19*, 151–161.

Ortiz, C. L., Jr. (2016). Why we need a physically embodied Turing test and what it might look like. *AI Magazine, 37*, 55–62.

Paivio, A. (1969). Mental imagery in associative learning and memory. *Psychological Review, 76*, 241–263.

Paivio, A. (1986). *Mental representations: A dual coding approach.* New York, NY: Oxford University Press.

Pease, A. (2011). *Ontology: A practical guide.* Angwin, CA: Articulate Software.

[Delete] Pecher, D. (2013). Discourse comprehension. In D. Reisberg (Ed.), *The Oxford handbook of cognitive psychology* (pp. 668–681). New York: Oxford University Press.

Pennycook, G., Fugelsang, J. A., & Koehler, D. J. (2015). Everyday consequences of analytic thinking. *Current Directions in Psychological Science, 24*, 425–432.

Pereira, W. L. (1969). Central Library University of California at San Diego. *University of University of California, San Diego.* https://library.ucsd.edu/speccoll/DigitalArchives/z679_2u54w7_1969/z679_2_u54-w7-1969.pdf

Pezzulo, G., Barsalou, L. W., Cangelosi, A., Fischer, M. H., McRae, K., & Spivey, M. J. (2013). Computational grounded cognition: A new alliance between grounded cognition and computational modeling. *Frontiers in Psychology, 3*(612).

Poldrack, R. A., & Yarkoni, T. (2016). From brain maps to cognitive ontologies: Informatics and the search for mental structure. *Annual Review of Psychology, 67*, 587–612.

Radvansky, G. A. (2012). Across the event horizon. *Current Directions in Psychological Science, 21*, 269–272.

Rahwan, I., Cebrian, M., Obradovich, N., Bongard, J., Bonnefon, J.-F., Breazeal, C., . . . Wellman, M. (2019). Machine behavior. *Nature, 568*, 477–486.

Randel, J. M., Pugh, H. L., & Reed, S. K. (1996). Differences in expert and novice situation awareness in naturalistic decision making. *International Journal of Human-Computer Studies, 45*, 579–597.

Reder, L. M., & Anderson, J. R. (1980). Partial resolution of the paradox of interference: The role of integrating knowledge. *Cognitive Psychology, 12*, 447–472.

Reed, S. K. (1972). Pattern recognition and categorization. *Cognitive Psychology, 3*, 382–407.

Reed, S. K. (1974). Structural descriptions and the limitations of visual imagery. *Memory & Cognition, 2*, 329–336.

Reed, S. K. (2005). From research to practice and back: The Animation Tutor project. *Educational Psychology Review, 17*, 55–82.

Reed, S. K. (2010). *Thinking visually.* New York, NY: Taylor & Francis.

Reed, S. K. (2016a). The structure of ill-structured (and well-structured) problems revisited. *Educational Psychology Review, 28,* 691–716.

Reed, S. K. (2016b). A taxonomic analysis of abstraction. *Perspectives on Psychological Science, 11,* 817–837.

Reed, S. K. (2018). Combining physical, virtual, and mental actions and objects. *Educational Psychology Review, 30,* 1091–1113.

Reed, S. K. (2019a). Building bridges between AI and cognitive psychology. *AI Magazine, 40,* 17–28.

Reed, S. K. (2019b). Modeling visuospatial reasoning. *Spatial Cognition & Computation, 19,* 1–45.

Reed, S. K. (2020). Searching for the big pictures. *Perspectives on Psychological Science.* doi.org/10.1177/1745691619896255.

Reed, S. K., & Dumontier, M. (2019). Adding cognition to the Semanticscience Integrated Ontology. *Edelweiss: Psychiatry Open Access, 3,* 4–13.

Reed, S. K., & Evans, A. C. (1987). Learning functional relations: A theoretical and instructional analysis. *Journal of Experimental Psychology: General, 116,* 106–118.

Reed, S. K., & Pease, A. (2015). A framework for constructing cognition ontologies using WordNet, FrameNet, and SUMO. *Cognitive Systems Research, 33,* 122–144.

Reed, S. K., & Pease, A. (2017). Reasoning from imperfect knowledge. *Cognitive Systems Research, 41,* 56–72.

Reed, S. K., & Vallacher, R. R. (2020). A comparison of information processing and dynamical systems perspectives on problem solving. *Thinking & Reasoning, 26,* 254–290.

Reicher, G. M. (1969). Perceptual recognition as a function of the meaningfulness of stimulus material. *Journal of Experimental Psychology, 81,* 275–280.

Reidmiller, D. R., Avery, C. W., Easterling, D. R., Kunkel, K. E., Lewis, K. L. M., Maycock, T. K., & Stewart, B. C. (Eds.). (2018). *Impacts, risk, and adaptation in the United States: Fourth national climate assessment* (Vol. 2, Report in Brief). https://www.globalchange.gov/nca4

Richmond, L. L., & Zacks, J. M. (2017). Constructing experience: Event models from perception to action. *Trends in Cognitive Sciences, 21,* 962–980.

Rios, J. A., Ling, G., Pugh, R., Becker, D., & Becall, A. (2020). Identifying critical 21st-century skills for workplace success: a content analysis of job advertisements. *Educational Researcher, 49,* 80–89.

Rips, L. J., Shoben, E. J., & Smith, E. E. (1973). Semantic distance and the verification of semantic relations. *Journal of Verbal Leaning and Verbal Behavior, 12,* 1–20.

Rittle-Johnson, B., & Loehr, A. M. (2017). Eliciting explanations: Constraints on when self-explanation aids learning. *Psychonomic Bulletin & Review, 24,* 1501–1510.

Robson, D. (2019). *The intelligence trap: Why smart people make dumb mistakes*. New York, NY: W. W. Norton.

Rosch, E., & Mervis, C. B. (1975). Family resemblance: Studies in the internal structure of categories. *Cognitive Psychology, 7*, 573–605.

Rosch, E., Mervis, C. B., Gray, W. D., Johnsen, D. M., & Boyes-Braem, P. (1976). Basic objects in natural categories. *Cognitive Psychology, 8*, 382–440.

Rouet, J.-F., Britt, M. A., & Durik, A. M. (2017). RESOLV: Readers' representation of reading contexts and tasks. *Educational Psychologist, 52*, 200–215.

Sager, P. (2005). *Oxford & Cambridge: An uncommon history* (D. H. Wilson, Trans.). London, England: Thames & Hudson.

Schaffhausser, D. (2019, July 11). Survey: Higher ed is not the first choice for AI training. *Campus Technology*.

Schank, R., & Abelson, R. (1977). *Scripts, plans, goals and understanding: An inquiry into human knowledge structures*. Hillsdale, NJ: Erlbaum.

Scheffer, M., Carpenter, S. R., Lenton, T. M., Bascompte, J., Brock, W., Dakos, V., . . . Vandermeer, J. (2012). Anticipating critical transitions. *Science, 338*, 344–348.

Scherer, R., Siddiq, F., & Viveros, B. S. (2019). The cognitive benefits of learning computer programming: A meta-analysis of transfer effects. *Journal of Educational Psychology, 111*, 764–792.

Schwartz, D. L., & Black, J. B. (1996). Shuttling between depictive models and abstract rules: Induction and fallback. *Cognitive Science, 20*, 457–497.

Sejnowski, T. J. (2018). *The deep learning revolution*. Cambridge, MA: MIT Press.

Shepard, R. N. (1988). The imagination of the scientist. In K. Egan & D. Nadaner (Eds.), *Imagination and education* (pp. 153–185). New York, NY: Teacher's College Press.

Shtulman, A., & Valcarcel, J. (2012). Scientific knowledge suppresses but does not supplant earlier intuitions. *Cognition, 124*, 209–215.

Shute, V. J., Sun, C., & Asbell-Clarke, J. (2017). Demystifying computational thinking. *Educational Research Review, 22*, 142–158.

Silver, E. (1981). Recall of mathematical problem information: Solving related problems. *Journal for Research in Mathematics Education, 12*, 54–64.

Simon, H. A. (1973). The structure of ill-structured problems. *Artificial Intelligence, 4*, 181–201.

Simon, H. A., & Reed, S. K. (1976). Modeling strategy shifts in a problem-solving task. *Cognitive Psychology, 8*, 86–97.

Sloman, S. (2002). Two systems of reasoning. In T. Gilovich, D. Griffin, & D. Kahneman (Eds.), *Heuristics and biases: The psychology of intuitive judgment* (pp. 379–396). Cambridge, UK: Cambridge University Press.

Sneider, C., Stephenson, C., Schafer, B., & Flick, L. (2014). Computational thinking in high school science classrooms. *The Science Teacher, 81*, 53–59.

Soni, J., & Goodman, R. (2017). *A mind at play: How Claude Shannon invented the information age.* New York, NY: Simon & Schuster.

Spataro, R., Chella, A., Allison, B., Giadina, M., Sorbello, R., Tramonte, S., . . . La Bella, V. (2017). Reaching and grasping a glass of water by locked-in ALS patients through a BCI-controlled humanoid robot. *Frontiers in Human Neuroscience, 11*, 1–10.

Sridhar, A. N., Briggs, T. P., Kelly, J. D., & Nathan, S. (2017). Training in robotic surgery—An overview. *Current Urology Reports, 18*(58). doi:10.1007/ s11934-017-0710-y

Stanfield, R. A., & Zwaan, R. A. (2001). The effect of implied orientation derived from verbal context on picture recognition. *Psychological Science, 12*, 153–156.

Stanovich, K. E. (2018). Miserliness in human cognition: The intersection of detection, override and mindware. *Thinking & Reasoning, 24*, 423–444.

Stevens, A., & Coupe, H. P. (1978). Distortions in judged spatial distances. *Cognitive Psychology, 10*, 526–550.

Stewart, I. (2012). *In pursuit of the unknown: 17 equations that changed the world.* New York, NY: Basic Books.

Swinney, D. A. (1979). Lexical access during sentence comprehension: Reconsideration of some context effects. *Journal of Verbal Learning and Verbal Behavior, 18*, 645–659.

Swinney, D. A., & Hakes, D. T. (1976). Effects of prior context upon lexical access during sentence comprehension. *Journal of Verbal Learning and Verbal Behavior, 15*, 681–689.

Tenenbaum, J. B., Kemp, C., Griffiths, T. L., & Goodman, N. D. (2011). How to grow a mind: Statistics, structure, and abstraction. *Science, 331*, 1279–1285.

Thaler, R. H., & Sunstein, C. R. (2008). *Nudge: Improving decisions about health, wealth, and happiness.* New York, NY: Penguin Books.

Trabasso, T., & van den Broek, P. (1985). Causal thinking and the representation of narrative events. *Journal of Memory and Language, 24*, 612–630.

Triona, L. M., & Klahr, D. (2003). Point and click or grab and heft: Comparing the influence of physical and virtual instructional materials on elementary school students' ability to design experiments. *Cognition and Instruction, 21*, 149–173.

Tversky, B. (2005). Visuospatial reasoning. In K. J. Holyoak & R. G. Morrison (Eds.), *The Cambridge handbook of thinking and reasoning* (pp. 209–239). New York, NY: Cambridge University Press.

Twenge, J. (2017). *iGen: Why today's super-connected kids are growing up less rebellious, more tolerant, less happy—and completely unprepared for adulthood.* New York, NY: Atria Books.

Vallacher, R. R., Coleman, P. T., Nowak, A., & Bui-Wrzosinska, L. (2010). Rethinking intractable conflict: The perspective of dynamical systems. *American Psychologist, 65*, 262–278.

Vallacher, R. R., & Wegner, D. M. (1987). What do people think they're doing? Action identification and human behavior. *Psychological Review, 94*, 3–15.

Vallacher, R. R., & Wegner, D. M. (2012). Action identification theory. In P. A. M. Van Lange, A. W. Kruglanski, & E. T. Higgens (Eds.), *Handbook of theories of social psychology* (pp. 327–348). Thousand Oaks, CA: SAGE.

VandenBoss, G. R. (Ed.). (2006). *APA dictionary of psychology.* Washington, DC: American Psychological Association.

Vosniadou, S. (2013). Conceptual change in learning and instruction: The framework theory approach. In S. Vosniadou (Ed.), *International handbook of research on conceptual change* (2nd ed., pp. 11–30). New York, NY: Routledge.

Vosniadou, S., & Skopeliti, I. (2014). Conceptual change from the framework theory side of the fence. *Science & Education, 23*, 1427–1445.

Walker, E., Adams, A., Restrepo, M. A., Fialko, S., & Glenberg, A. M. (2017). When and how interacting with technology-enhanced storybooks helps dual language learners. *Translational issues in psychological science, 3*, 66–79.

Ward, N. G., & DeVault, D. (2016). Challenges in building highly interactive dialogue systems. *AI Magazine, 37*, 7–18.

Watson, J. B. (1924). *Behaviorism.* New York, NY: Norton.

Watts, D. J., & Strogatz, S. H. (1998). Collective dynamics of a "small world" networks. *Nature, 393*, 440–442.

Weir, K. (2018). Virtual reality expands its reach. *Monitor on Psychology, 49*(2), 52.

Weisman, K., & Markman, E. M. (2017). Theory-based explanation as intervention. *Psychonomic Bulletin & Review, 24*, 1555–1562.

Wilson, M. (2002). Six views of embodied cognition. *Psychonomic Bulletin & Review, 9*, 625–636.

Wright, S. (2020, January 15). Fires raise extinction threat in Australia. *The Wall Street Journal*, p. A18.

Yee, E., & Thompson-Schill, S. L. (2016). Putting concepts into context. *Psychonomic Bulletin & Review, 23*, 1015–1027.

Yoon, S. A., Go, S.-E., & Park, M. (2018). Teaching and learning about complex systems in K-12 science education: A review of empirical studies 1995–2015. *Review of Educational Research, 88*, 285–325.

Zane, J. P. (2019, February 2-3). Physics, biology, and economic inequality. *The Wall Street Journal*, p. A13.

Zemla, J. C., Sloman, S., Bechlivanidis, C., & Lagnado, D. A. (2017). Evaluating everyday explanations. *Psychonomic Bulletin & Review, 24*, 1488–1500.

Zimmer, B. (2019, February 2-3). An age cohort hits the end of the alphabet. *Wall Street Journal*, p. C2.

Index